FATHER RICK

Roamin' Catholic

Rick Prashaw

 FriesenPress

One Printers Way
Altona, MB, ROG OBO
Canada

www.friesenpress.com

ISBN
978-1-03-912616-9 (Hardcover)
978-1-03-912615-2 (Paperback)
978-1-03-912617-6 (eBook)

1. RELIGION, CHRISTIAN LIFE, PERSONAL MEMOIRS

Distributed to the trade by The Ingram Book Company

Praise for Father Rick, Roamin' Catholic

"Rick's book is a testimony of hope in its assertion that faith can sustain life's most tumultuous offerings. His writing is about the foundational belief that there is room for everyone's story, without judgement or exclusion; he's a light to be trusted leading us forward." - **Joan Grundy, Author**, "A Deepening Life"

"fast-paced, full of humour, irreverence, and deep humanity. Rick is large-hearted, drawn to the places of fracture in search of wholeness. He has learned and honed the capacity to hold so much together that could naturally pull us apart." - **Sister Margo Ritchie**, Congregational Leader, Sisters of St. Joseph of Canada

"Your writing invited me to keep reading, not polarized but your honest and sincere purpose to understand and appreciate the complexities of a system that allowed such trauma to take place in the lives of children and adolescents, the negative impact on the faithful and mistrust in the institution that publicly professed gospel values." - **Father Sam Restivo**, Congregation of the Resurrection, chaplain, counselor

"Rick's story is powerful, deeply personal and beautiful, full of insights that connect to our own stories. I related to his stories as one who grew up Roman Catholic. It's for all who struggle with the unquestioning faith many of us were taught, to the enduring call to service and empathy, as well as to the priesthood of all believers as well as non-believers." - **Reverend Éric Hébert-Daly**, United Church of Canada, former Federal Secretary, New Democratic Party of Canada

"Are there times in the hectic chaos of life that you stop and wonder what happened to your faith, your community and the Church that seems so determined to break your heart? If you don't have answers, don't worry. Rick Prashaw guides us through the troubles and on to hope, to a big God, our work for justice, beginning with real reconciliation with Indigenous People." - **Charlie Angus**, MP, Author, Musician

To Dad and Mom, grateful for a parents' love
that let us grow and go

Pat
keep the faith
Rick Prashaw
2022.

CONTENTS

Study them stories.
And enjoy this being washed
With a secret we sometimes know
And then not.

- Jalāl al-Dīn Rūmī, Sufi mystic

PREFACE

The questions started soon after the release of *Soar, Adam, Soar*, a memoir on my late son and its heart-stopping, roller-coaster love story as a dad.

"You were a priest?"

"Yes."

"Catholic priest?"

"Yes."

"You married?"

"Yes."

"You're proud of your trans son?"

"Very proud."

"Are you still Catholic?"

Erika Engels of the *Bay Today* (Ontario) news chain was the first journalist to ask that last question. I paused, heading towards a sermon when, instead, I replied.

"That's another book I'm writing."

On February 8, 2019, a week after the first book's release, I was a guest on Rita Celli's *Ontario Today* open line show on CBC Radio. I was anxious. Even though I had been a public figure that had preached for twelve years, I had since staffed three Members of Parliament where I hovered in the background, far from the microphones.

Unnerving me was what callers in the hinterlands might say to a former Catholic priest who loved his boy "to the moon and back, three times," the boy who, at birth, had been identified as a girl we named Rebecca Adam. Celli's introduction set the table for her listeners. "Father Rick Prashaw becomes proud father of Adam, his transgender son." Ken from Orillia, the second caller, catapulted me past my fears and straight into his hell. His "in the Bible" damnation of Adam and me concealed a "Godsend," however, as other callers doused those hell fires. I will tell that story and how I answered Ken.

Thank God!

Am I still Catholic?

One surprising place Adam has taken me to since his drowning in 2016 is being an organ donor advocate. Adam saved four lives because he had registered as a donor at sixteen and, vitally important, told us his wishes. I was interrupted when writing this memoir to answer a survey for an organ transplant network. They were keen to improve the ways they might communicate with a prospective donor family during the most difficult circumstances, i.e., the day(s) their loved one is to be pronounced dead. She guided me through that awful weekend at The Ottawa Hospital. When she was done, there were demographic questions.

"What religious denomination are you?"

"Do they have Roamin' Catholic?"

"Yes."

"Spell it."

"Pardon?"

"Spell 'Roamin'."

"R-o-m-a-n."

"No, not that one. I am Roamin' Catholic. R-o-a-m-i-n'."

"No, we don't have that one," she chuckled. She checked off *other*.

Roamin' Catholic.

We may be a legion, even before I count others who have outright quit the Roman Catholic Church. Ex-Catholics. Recovering or retired Catholics. There are cradle Catholics. Cafeteria Catholics. Lapsed Catholics. Wistful Catholics. There are Catholics who practice social distancing from Rome. There are cultural Catholics who might self-identify while rejecting parts of Rome's Catholicism. Let's not forget the good or devout Catholics. There are left and right-wing Catholics too.

I winced when a niece once introduced me to her friends as "her uncle who had been a priest, married, and divorced." Is that my epitaph? I better tell my own story. Ego and legacy first sat me down at the computer.

But why tell the story at all? On the surface, it is intriguing—Father Rick, a Catholic priest, marriage, a new vocation as a father to Adam, a cruel tragedy, and a permanent grief that has discovered a surprising, life-saving gratitude in the choices I could still make.

Dig deeper, and in the convoluted chapters of my life there is a story that endured, a faith in my God, the gods, in the divine energies, and, significantly, a faith in myself. Well, save for a million self-doubts! This is the tale of my crooked, straight journey to heaven's doors, of a faith remarkably intact yet so radically changed, a Roamin' more than Roman Catholic, a God and the heavens bigger than any catechism taught me. I am a believer still standing who finds this all astonishing.

In case eyes dull at the prospect of reading a faith memoir, know this. I have an unredeemed side that I take great pleasure in. Before ATM machines, I killed time in bank line-ups inside masterminding a foolproof, no guns, "Robin Hood" robbery. I once brought a case of beer to the pulpit. For marriage talks, I cued Leonard Cohen's "Dance Me to the End of Love." Wine might explain some wayward behaviour but, in truth, there is an unrepentant Rick too. I lived the God questions as much as the answers because, at times, the answers could be unsatisfying, or worse, so infuriating, begging further questions of faith.

For more than half a century, I journeyed through turbulent times in our world and the Catholic Church. I did so as a man, a believer, a priest, and then a parent. I thrived on the promising renewal experienced in the first few decades after the Second Vatican Council (1962–1965) profoundly changed the Catholic Church to thrust us into the modern world. Social justice. A preferential love for the poor and vulnerable. Vibrant faith communities, social hubs, living fresh this ancient love story between God and humanity. It was radical, and it was revolutionary.

I, and enough others, became disappointed with a conservative retrenchment that obscured this miracle.

Still, I have friends who continue to worship in this same Catholic Church. Other friends attend a Christmas or Easter service because of their faith or for their annual "insurance run." There are other friends who dismiss religion as a spiritual crutch, opium for the masses. They are all kin. From my childhood and ministry days, there has been a steep, steady decline in church attendance or religious affiliation. Congregations are greying. There is disenchantment with some teachings. Children raised without organized religion in secular times are less likely to be members now. Acknowledging all of that, millions of people in Canada still worship and pray. I keep them all in mind as I tell my story.

Most authors who write a book will wrestle with one's motives—why write this story, and why now? I wanted to tell my story because, well, it is my story, and it touches on questions of self-worth and meaning for others. That is the power of storytelling. A light shines in dark recesses and cobwebbed shadows of faith responses, some still lived, some relics from long ago, some stirring new concerns and questions.

Authors can be surprised where their story takes them. Indeed, *Father Rick, Roamin' Catholic* has surprised me as I sort out my creed today. I did not want back in the pulpit to preach or proselytize, bless or damn. Frankly, spewing damnation was never really me when I wore that black shirt and white collar. However, I did discover a *River of Life* beyond, but somehow and somewhat, still coupling my Catholic roots. There were visits to energy healers where Adam, after his death, visited me. Indigenous elders taught me. There is plenty of good news in bad times.

Readers can connect the dots of my faith story to their lives as their stories, their church or faith memories, brush up alongside mine. People are curious about the Catholic faith, and some are clueless on what it is really like being a Catholic priest. These tales from priesthood and my life as a journalist, non-government organization and then political staff, author, and Dad to Adam hook humour, irreverence, and "I can't believe that happened" moments, some inane and others eternal. In faithfulness to other pilgrims, I comment on disturbing issues these sixty years have uncovered: the scandal of clergy abuse; women's place, or lack of place, in many religions; the Roman Catholic Church's inexcusable, slow embrace of truth and reconciliation with Indigenous Peoples; and those gay, lesbian, transgender and other non-binary people hurt by a church bent on condemning who they are. I do not side with the church in these matters. For those personally violated by church teachings or officials, take care of yourselves as you read. Find refuge with loved ones when needed, knowing which stories might trigger painful memories.

"Freedom is what we do with what is done to us," Jean-Paul Sartre believed. There were moments after my son died when I wanted to join him. Life was unbearable. It was then I discovered genuine freedom. Thank God that, long ago, my dad had taught me that, in bad times, to choose life, to be not afraid.

Am I still a Catholic?

I savour that question. In our Facebook generation, those from priesthood days friend me again.

"Were you Father Rick?"

"It depends. Is that good or bad to confess?"

"Ha! You haven't changed!"

"Oh, but I have."

Inevitably, as a storyteller, I circled back again to tell those stories that had mattered to me, to family and friends, to parishioners, and others touched by the sacred or profane encounters that hinted at more. I find it worthy to ponder, more so than ever, as we reel and recover from the COVID-19 pandemic, shaken, quarantined, figuring out a "new normal" that might bring us nearer to salvation, nearer to our true selves. As God hung over the waters of Creation in the book of Genesis, COVID-19 hangs over my story I tell here, first to a niece and her twelve-year-old, bi-racial son on Good Friday in Toronto. The Catholic chasm between my Claire and I are a compass for what has happened in only two generations. Her Cruz is religiously following news on Black Lives Matter.

To see the face of the Creator. To dance with God and the gods, especially in the poorest and most marginalized on the edges of our communities. To choose love. This has always mattered to me.

> "The light crying out to be rediscovered is that every human
> being born into the world has the seed or the spark of the
> Divine within; it's what we do with that reality that matters."[1]
>
> - Tom Harpur, *Born Again*

1 Tom Harpur, *Born Again* (Toronto: Dundurn Press, 2017), 2.

PART ONE

Rick

CHAPTER 1

Pretty Woman

Early 1980s

She was an athletic, attractive woman. I had married her. But I forgot her name.

It was Tuesday night in North Bay, a typical "date night" with my good friend, Peter Moher.

Moher answered to Father Moher, Father Peter, Pete, to anyone really who appreciated his puns or latest *Far Side* cartoons he had clipped and fastidiously folded in his pants pocket. I did not need to read *Far Side*. Peter had the funniest to share when we next met.

Our Tuesday routine was Ten Commandments rock solid. On a day off, Peter drove from Sudbury to visit his parents, John and Rose Moher. My part of the bargain was to finish a weekday evening Mass at the Pro-Cathedral of the Assumption where I was an associate pastor. We wanted to be in our seats at the Capitol Theatre for a 9:00 p.m. movie.

Cheap $2.00 Tuesday night movies, a half-price blessing on a modest priestly salary. We wore civvies, no clerical shirt nor collar beaming an SOS light for any poor, lonely, lost souls. We vowed to be back on duty tomorrow. A movie, extra-large buttered popcorn, jumbo-size soda—this friendship, which started in high school and was going on fifteen years now—washed away stressful salvation blues from ministry. If Peter had his way, we would watch a horror flick. I would slump behind the large popcorn to duck half of Freddy Krueger's murders.

It was not the movie we remembered this night. It was the pretty woman. As we settled in our seats, I spotted her first. I was good at that! Long-blond hair down her back, probably in her late twenties, she was in the aisle to the right, hesitating, two rows ahead of us. She entered that row and sat in front of three older women directly in front of us. In my head, I heard the voice of Father Jim Hickey, the wry Ottawa Valley native. He would have described the three women as the "blue rinse crowd," members of the Catholic Women's League (CWL), or "Critical Women's League," as Jim affectionately called them.

Now, Peter noticed the pretty woman.

"I know that woman," I said. "I married her. I can't remember her name."

It was the last few words spoken in my already hearing-impaired, loud whisper that caught the attention of the CWL. One already had her head half-turned to catch sight of this wretched man who had forgotten his bride's name. Father Moher delivered my head on their platter with this coup-de-grâce comeback.

"Rick, you've married so many women. You can't possibly remember all their names."

Now, three CWL heads were spinning, Exorcist-like. Peter's kind of movie! They had no idea we were officiants, not husbands. Thankfully, the lights dimmed, curtains rose, and damnation was paused.

Who knows what movie we watched? All I remember was the pretty woman, the CWL trio, and how, no doubt, they left the theatre to talk about the creepy fellow behind them who had married so many women he could not remember all their names.

I am that man.

CHAPTER 2

Highway Jesus

Summer of 2005

On the car radio, I listen to Gordon Lightfoot singing "Carefree Highway".
I sing along as I drive through the spectacular, signature rock cuts of the
Canadian Shield in this northeast part of Ontario. I am a northerner. North
Bay and Sudbury roots frame my life; northerners boast that we're NOT
from Toronto.

This blue-sky day stretches as far as the eye can see. A cloudless, celestial
canopy. The shimmering blue-green lakes bless the ride too. The black flies
have peaked in the bush, meaning the moose are less likely to be seeking
refuge on the highway.

My five Prashaw siblings, our twenty-three nephews and nieces and their
families, are scattered across the continent now but the north has not left us.
The rugged rock cuts nurtured a bigness of character, an earthiness, a resilient
spirit. In North Bay, I grew up five minutes from Lake Nipissing and Trout
Lake, both within city limits, pickerel and pike flopping on piers and off fish
lines. Feet in the sand or water. Camping, cottages, soulful loons, the four
distinct seasons. Hot sun and refreshing lakes squeezed into the precious but
too short, summer interlude between the bookend, long winters.

I am driving now past the hello and good-bye signs for the City of Greater
Sudbury, Northern Ontario's biggest city whose boundaries captured more
rock and shrubs than people. A "rye on the rocks" regreening program

hiring students to throw grass seeds on the bleak, moonscape terrain had the old-timers up in arms. Finnish and Eastern European immigrant miners loved those rocks—money in the bank. Long ago, when I was a summer cub reporter at the *North Bay Nugget,* the newspaper had printed extra copies of one edition to ship to Sudbury, teasing our neighbours with the headline, "ASTRONAUTS LAND IN SUDBURY!"; the Apollo 16 and 17 mission astronauts had come to Sudbury to practice a moon walk there. True story!

I am heading to Sault Ste. Marie and constituency work with my old friend and new boss, Tony Martin. We have been friends since the late 1970s when he was hired as a pioneering lay pastoral staff in Elliot Lake. Martin had hired me as his legislative assistant after his victory in the 2004 federal election. Martin had already been Sault Ste. Marie's provincial member for thirteen years, work he began when he bucked his proud father Mick Martin's Irish Catholic warning on his running for the Ontario New Democratic Party, "Jesus, Mary, and Joseph, son, you're always backing a loser!"

It was an idyllic drive until I saw the billboard.

"If you loved Jesus, you'd be in church this Sunday."

Man, how "to shit on my Shreddies," to quote another friend, John Medina. It was a billboard from a highway evangelical church, yet it snared my Catholic guilt. I would talk back to that billboard for the next three hours driving to Sault Ste. Marie.

I did love God, and yet, I was no longer in church most Sundays. I had left the priesthood fourteen years earlier. I rhymed off family and friends who likewise had a faith not wedded explicitly to church attendance—most of them still believing, while not finding the Sunday services speaking to day-to-day lives. It was no longer the daily and weekend Mass habits from those priest years from 1980 to 1991, certainly not the earlier "Sunday, go to Mass" era in my parents' home.

"If you loved Jesus . . ."

I spotted theological fault lines as deep as the rock underneath Highway 17. Clearly, there were people not in church who loved their God. And, from ministry, I knew others who might be in church for a myriad of reasons, insurance runs and all. The billboard needed a good edit. Former parishioners popped into my mind. Their confessions, hopes, struggles, failures, and lamentations.

"If my teenager and I hadn't fought Sunday morning, I might be in church today."

"If my husband hadn't left me."

"If I hadn't lost my job this week."

"If the church let me go to Communion."

"If they welcomed my gay son."

"If God ever answered my prayers."

"If the priest hadn't done what he did."

"If the priest stopped lecturing and damning us." (obviously not Father Rick.)

Shouldn't those life bites have drawn the faithful to church and down on their knees? Life is more complicated than that. In fact, they were not in church. I chose not to "should" on them. Holy Mother Church could do a good enough job "shoulding" on us, no?

So, back to my billboard edits.

"I love Jesus, and if the kids stopped fighting, and we could make ends meet, beat this illness, be hired for that job, make my church inclusive, stop hating gays, practice what we preach, and explain all the suffering that is happening in the world, I MIGHT be in church this Sunday."

That was an improvement, a billboard that might even bump church attendance. There was still a problem. All those words made the billboard large, wordy, expensive, and impossible to read while speeding by. And, for the drivers determined to read my billboard, the odds were two to one that, not "carefree driving", they would cross the centerline, collide head-on with a tractor-trailer. Dead, they would meet God and get the definitive word on church as a prerequisite for heaven.

No, I needed a simpler, truer edit. The billboard had salvation backwards!

"If you knew how much God loved you, you would be in church this Sunday."

This love story, which I had never tired of telling parishioners, began with God loving us. One Sunday, I had shared an excerpt from *Parable of Community* by Brother Roger Schütz, popularly known as Brother Roger. He had founded the Taizé, France, ecumenical community where I had landed one day in the throes of a vocation crisis.

"That is the meaning of your life: to be loved forever, loved to all eternity, so that you, in turn, will dare to give your life," Brother Roger wrote. "Without love, what is the point of living?"[2]

I arrived in Sault Ste. Marie. I had a new billboard message.

"If you knew how much God loved you, you would be in church this Sunday. Maybe!"

As a priest and preacher, I had invited people to have a life exceeding all their hopes. I believed God, the Creator, loved us first. Life is our response.

Still, as with all bewildering, seductive love stories, there has been enough mystery, misery, maybes, and mess along the way to cloud the blue skies. "Highway Jesus" threw up a detour or two for me to take. I needed to revisit where all this Jesus talk had started.

2 Brother Roger of Taizé, *Parables of Community* (London: Mowbray London & Oxford, 1984), 49.

CHAPTER 3

My First Vocation, "The Bad News"

2021, Looking Back

As a young boy, and even into my teens and early twenties, I never imagined I would be a Roman Catholic priest. Not once.

Like Saul in the New Testament, it took a Damascus Road conversion in a Seattle rectory while visiting a first cousin priest to shatter my life's plans. The Damascus description captured more a radical career change from a journalist to a priest than to any literal persecuting of Christians like Saul was up to before becoming the apostle, Paul. My "conversion" occurred in 1975 when I was living in Crescent Beach near White Rock, B.C., close to the Canada-U.S. border. Crescent Beach was this sunny, left coast hamlet with many hippies, artists, and U.S. draft dodgers. I commuted the half-hour drive to work in the newsroom at the *Vancouver Sun*. There were a few speeding tickets on those late-night drives home. I was not behaving that badly but, ahem, it was the seventies—long hair, rock and roll, parties, beer, occasional weed, and a kiss or two.

Given my Prashaw family's strong Catholic DNA, one might suspect I had pondered a vocation to the priesthood sooner. My parents, Dick and Gert Prashaw, had marched their six kids to mass every Sunday. By the time I hit my mid-teens, I had learned that ejaculation, a short, devout prayer, was equally a loaded Catholic homonym. Most of the Prashaw kids have since dropped or tweaked the childish sounding "y" or "ie," endings to our names. Instead of Marty, Ricky, Margie, Judy, Johnny, and Patty, we now were Marty, Rick, Margie, Jude, Jon and Pati. Marty and Margie, the oldest boy and girl, must have had their "shit together", sensing no need for their names to grow up.

Four of us—Marty, Jude, Pati, and I—had red hair, in truth carrot orange, topping hundreds of freckles on our faces and arms. Brown-haired Margie seemed to come to us from the heavens. We teased our blond-haired brother, Jon, that we had found him one morning at our door. I cringed when older women tousled my curly carrot hair. Well, not every woman. In Grade 3, I had a crush on Miss Sinisac at St. Martin's School in London. Dad must have noticed because, picking her up in his station wagon once after Mass, he told her about my unrequited love. I died in the back seat. And Miss Daly, at St. Alexander's School in North Bay. I'd be okay if she tousled my hair.

Were we all large families, birth control be damned? Marty was born in 1948. I showed up in 1951, followed by births every two years through the 1950s. Mother never caught a rest. For a long time, we thought we were six kids. However, Mom, besides several miscarriages and before Marty, had a baby in 1947. Danny lived one day. Did she hold her angel? I wonder if anyone ministered to her for her loss. I wonder if Danny has shortened his name. One of the reasons I believe there is a heaven is to meet my oldest brother and, of course, reunite with Adam. I talk to Danny from time to time.

So, Danny was the oldest of the Prashaws, all born in London, soon to raise a little hell in North Bay. It was not dull growing up with three sisters and two brothers. There was always someone to play or read with and corral enough players for Monopoly or Clue.

Now, half a century later, the wicked years 2020 and 2021 snared my diaspora family. No longer able to meet regularly, we're surrounded by social bubbles, flattening the curve, social distancing, masks, and Zoom.

Good God!

After a madcap car ride home from a shortened writing sabbatical in Mexico, the COVID-19 pandemic had me in isolation with a niece, Claire, who is my goddaughter, and her twelve-year-old son, Cruz, in their Toronto home across from High Park. I had first done a solo isolation in Picton, ON. because I had sub-let my apartment in Ottawa for several months. No other doors of siblings opened either as they each faced their own specific COVID-19 isolation conundrums.

How could it be that, in less than two generations, this niece from Marty's good Catholic family can sit on the couch beside me, listen to those family faith stories, and not remember?

"When is it Catholics put that black mark on the forehead?" Claire asks.

"What's so special about the time right now, 3:00 p.m. on Good Friday?"

Growing up, Claire had gone to Sunday Mass and Catholic schools. My gorgeous great-nephew Cruz though, is not baptized. He attends a public school. Indeed, among my extraordinary two dozen nephews, nieces, and their partners, I do not know of one who is in church regularly. Most of their kids are not baptized. Only a few go to Catholic schools. There are a few peers who tell of similar habits in their families. Of course, not going to church, not being into a religion, is not the same thing as not being spiritual or not believing. My nephews and nieces can thrive on their good works in communities, good conversation, and figuring out what it means to be a good human and live an ethical life. One of the most consoling messages I received after Adam died came from a nephew, Joshua Klar, who wrote, "As you may know, Uncle Rick, I am not a religious man, but I do have faith, faith in the existence of the soul. When someone passes, the soul must find a place to go, some person that individual touched, changed, or loved. I am confident that Adam's beautiful soul has entered into the love all around you."

Still, listening to Claire's questions, what a different world it is between my priest years and now with my niece. Uncle Rick, the priest who had married in 1992, beats down ancient, haunting voices.

No, you are not going to hell if you don't go to church.

Yes, the children are alright.

I have changed too!

"By the way, beautiful Claire, in case you have performed a Catholic cleanse, it's Ash Wednesday when Catholics and Christians might have the black mark on their foreheads. This begins the forty-day penitential Lenten period leading to the Easter Tridium celebration of Jesus forgiving our sins and saving us. Tradition has Jesus dying on the cross at 3:00 p.m. today, Good Friday. All stores and businesses closed back then. We were forbidden to eat those chocolate Easter eggs you are stuffing in your mouth."

I reached over for one of her cream-filled eggs.

"Claire, 'forty' is a symbolic number for Jews and Christians alike, with the Israelites wandering in the desert for forty years, Jesus fasting in the desert forty days and forty nights, and forty being the days between His resurrection and ascension into heaven. He'd be desert-proof cool with our COVID-19 isolation and social distancing. No doubt, Jesus would wear a mask."

Rick with Claire Prashaw, his niece and goddaughter, and son, Adam.

Cruz is half-listening. He is playing video games and looks over at the mention of ashes, desert, and talk of a resurrection. He has his own superheroes. Cruz's father lives in Honduras, swim trunks and deep-sea diving his happy place.

On this Good Friday, I like it here on this couch, munching Easter eggs with Claire and Cruz. Overall, the Coronavirus isolation has been difficult but manageable, if you permit my grumbling on the two-year-and-counting *Groundhog Day* movie set that we all tumbled on. And don't get me started on the *Monty Python* sideshow of masks fogging glasses, sabotaging hearing, and snaring hearing aids. Still, even as an extrovert, I've often relished time alone. Spiritual retreats were quiet respites in otherwise busy, hectic priest years.

Cruz Prashaw and Rick at Extra Butter Coffee Toronto, for Soar, Adam, Soar reading.

"Claire and Cruz, let me tell you my crooked, straight journey, the stories from childhood, seminary, priesthood, marriage and the part you, Cruz, know the best, father to Adam, your special cousin. Yes, I am astonished that I count myself still a believer, albeit more Roamin' than Roman Catholic, enjoying the love story of God and us lived in community. I am fond of the Greek word for community, '*koinonia*' (koi-no-nia). Solid word."

Cruz is back on his iPad.

"Claire, let me unwrap this love story, my figuring out the troublesome parts of suffering, evil, and the breaking of hearts."

"Tell me your story, Uncle Rick," Claire smiled.

"Our story, Claire."

Richard Arnold Prashaw was born in 1914 in Berlin, Ontario, now Kitchener-Waterloo. The name, Prashaw, is traced back only five generations to Québec where a St. Lawrence riverboat captain named Francois Prégent (Prégeant)—his surname meaning, "John who lives in the meadow"—emigrated with a wife to northern New York state. The Yanks stumbled over the French name, Prégent became Prashaw. Joachim George Prashaw Sr., born Oct 11, 1831, in the United States and baptized at St. Jean, L'île-Perrot near Montréal, had listed as his parents, Francois Prégent and Adelaide Montpetit dit Potvin. That Canadian-American pollination would dominate our family tree for the next two hundred years. There would be cross-border marriages of my dad's parents, mom's three sisters, dad's sister, and now two of my own sisters.

Until my twenties, I never really appreciated this man, my father, his curious story, the wonder of him surviving at all. Dad, his sister, Dorothy, and a half-brother, Harry, had spent a part of their childhood at St. Agatha's Orphanage near Kitchener while their parents, Cecil and Ethel, barnstormed North America.in a vaudeville troupe owned by Ethel's father, Harry Lindley. Bill, Dad's youngest sibling, traveled on the tour with his mom. Orphanage records reported one six-year stay; shorter drop-offs were never recorded. Harry Lindley was the stage name for Harry Woodall, my father's mother's father who had quit a seminary in Ireland to emigrate to the United States, serving briefly in the Confederate Army, and then launch a forty-year travelling theatre company.

"Claire, Dad would have been at that orphanage at four years of age in 1918 as the Spanish Flu spread, eventually killing fifty million people in the world."

"Oh my God, poppy as a little boy, the poor soul," Claire sighed.

"Claire, Dad's generation had a pandemic, the Roaring Twenties, prohibition, the Great Depression, and two world wars by the time he was thirty."

"I should stop complaining," Claire sighed.

Dad's parents split up quite young and, other than as a little boy, he would only meet his dad once more at the Chicago World Fair when, at nineteen, his mom had put him on a train in Buffalo. That father-son reunion did not go well. Dick Prashaw served as a "D-Day Dodger" on the miserable Italian front in World War II. Lady Astor in England was the source for that odd "dodger" phrase, teasing the Canadian soldiers NOT on the beaches of Normandy even though they had been fighting and dying in Italy for two years. Lady Astor claimed she was joking. Bad joke!

Dick Prashaw's fiancé, Gertie Beaton, was a favourite for Dad's Perth Regiment platoon as she shipped him the rejects from her chocolate bar assembly line job at McCormick's candy factory. Dad's Fighting Perths called her the "Molly-O Kid," a reference to a popular chocolate bar.

Gertie Beaton had this stoic Cape Breton Gaelic DNA. Her staunch faith, fun, and common sense were rooted in her ancestors, directly in her father, John Alexander Beaton, who in a typical migration looking for work, had landed in Boston before coming to London, Ontario, to work at Silverwood Dairy. He married Emily Fallon. Gertie Beaton and her three sisters, Margaret, Beatrice, and Florence, and a brother, Alexander, were born in London. Growing up, we gravitated easily to the better-known maternal Beaton family history. Mom's strength of character, her independence, fidelity to prayer, a good game of cards, and parties were all traced to Cape Breton. Once married, she stayed home to raise us, even though, as a single girl, she had worked at McCormick's and then for a dentist. Smart lady. Make the sweets, and then get paid again as her second boss filled cavities.

At the funeral of Sister Sarah Ann Beaton in 1989, a sister of Mom's dad who had lived to 101, Rev. John Barry eulogized Sarah's "go with the flow" determination through the century of turbulence both in the world and in the church. He paid tribute to the Beaton ingenuity, industriousness, and devotion to Celtic language, music, and arts. As a Congregation of Notre Dame sister, Sarah, the legendary matriarch of the Beaton clan, had taught half a century before continuing to teach Gaelic in retirement. Father Barry's final words in his homily for Sister Sarah were, Fois sìorraidh gu robh ga h-anam, "May her soul rest in eternal peace."

"Go with the flow" was Mom's gospel too. No matter the cards life dealt, she was game if she could count on daily Mass with a heaping side plate of golf, Toronto Blue Jays games, and a good, stiff drink.

We claimed the Beaton name proudly. Jon is Jon Beaton Prashaw. Jude's son is Alec Beaton Connor. My middle name is Alexander; a name passed down through generations of Beatons that traced back to Scotland in the sixteenth century, where they lived on the Isle of Skye before moving to the mainland in Lochaber. The Beatons were a kin of professional physicians that practiced medicine in the classical Gaelic tradition from the Middle Ages to the Early Modern Era.

"The *Outlander* Netflix series mentions the medical Beatons as charmers," Claire chuckled.

"Yes, Claire, herbs, Forget-Me-Not mouse-ear plants, potions. Charmers, indeed, our ancestors!"

"Jamie Fraser can transport me back a few centuries to my ancestors and charm me with his Gaelic and kilt anytime," Claire smiled.

"There'll be no time travel, my dear. Calm down, and back to our story!"

London memories are few as we moved north after Grade 4. There was a life-size poster of the *Lone Ranger* in my bedroom, my masked superhero with his silver bullets fighting the bad guys. And a night so rare when I saw my mother cry. I was eight years old. Mom had been talking to Dad on the phone. During the call, she let the wall phone hang, walked over to the kitchen table, opened a map of the Province of Ontario, traced her finger from London all the way up to North Bay, and cried. Dad had announced we were pulling up stakes for a grand adventure in the northern wilds. His decision, for all of us, to accept a move as a General Foods salesman. She shed more tears after the call while sipping tea and staring at the map. She was leaving the one city where she had ever lived. She could not fathom yet how the north would be THE special gift from the gods, what lie ahead of us as northerners—on the streets, in the woods, and part of a new church, diocese, and a prophetic bishop.

"Cruz, when I was your age, there was a parade of visiting priests to our North Bay home who were friends of my parents."

Among them, a suave Bernard Pappin who became a bishop; a smart, sunny Dennis Murphy; and Peter Fehrenbach, a jovial religious order priest with the Congregation of the Resurrection, a teaching order at my then all-boys Scollard Hall High School. Priests at the altar who had come for supper were not as shrouded in mystery as they might be for other Catholics. Dad poured them drinks and teased them mercilessly.

Other than a handful of detentions and stupidity, school and mine, I have few bad, early Catholic memories.

"Claire, considering the news on clergy abuse, this leaves me grateful yet perplexed, pondering what I escaped. How do I thank God for watching over me without that begging another question, 'God, why did you not protect THEM too? Were they being punished?' My answer has always been an unequivocal no. I find it odd though when people crawl out of a bus or plane crash to shout, 'Hallelujah,' to their God, standing a few feet from dozens of fatalities."

What about them, God?

The Theo-idiocy continues. On Facebook, a friend shared someone's faith pandemic post that left him shaking his head. "Some of us will walk out of this pandemic like Shadrach, Meshach and Abednego, untouched. Giving God all the praise. Hallelujah!"

"Those are weird names," Cruz frowned.

"Here's another weird name, Cruz. Nebuchadnezzar. He was the Babylon king in the Bible who threw those three cool dudes into a furnace before God saved them." (Dan 3: 16-28)

Oddly, as for influences on becoming a priest, I have no recollection of any strong vocation pitch from my parents either.

"Cruz, are you there?

"These are my parents, your grandpa's parents. There were stories from earlier generations where a Catholic family, often with several children, was expected to offer a son, usually the firstborn, to the church. Hearing of that custom, dark, Old Testament images haunted me, like the prophet, Abraham, taking out his knife to obediently sacrifice his son, Isaac.

"Jesus, Mary, and Joseph, spare me! Take Marty. He IS the firstborn!"

"Leave my father alone!" Claire shouted.

While our parents were friends of priests, their eyes were wide open about a few "bad apples."

"Claire, Mom told Margie how a young curate at St. Martin's Parish called her to the rectory one night. When she entered, there he was, at the top of a staircase, stark naked. He invited her to come up. Gertie Beaton instead pirouetted one hundred eighty degrees and was out the door in a flash, racing to the safety of her dad's home."

John Beaton liked to play cards, drink Scotch, and speak Gaelic with a retired Bishop Alexander MacDonald, a fellow Cape Bretoner and regular visitor. Mom would be furious when, every single time her dad and the bishop finished a story or joke, they would switch to Gaelic for the punchline. John Beaton was fond of priests. He had been the best church bell ringer in Mabou, Cape Breton, taught by priests to keep the exact rhythm. Gertie told her Pa about the naked priest inviting her upstairs. With Pa's episcopal grapevine nearby, I suspect the young curate did not stay long at St. Martin's. Sadly, we were to discover later that a priest's problems travelled with him.

"Brutal," Claire said.

Dad's exposure to priests and religious sisters came first at St. Agatha's Orphanage. Dad never spoke a word about those days; his sister, Dorothy, told Jude the German nuns were strict. So, while Dad and Mom passed on their faith, prayers, and respect for most priests, I never heard any not-so-subtle commercial for the priesthood. No, my dad's lifelong sermon was simple, powerful, and at the end of pre-Internet letters he wrote us when we were away later at university.

Choose life.

Be not afraid.

This was his gospel. As I grew older, I appreciated how, no doubt, he needed to say those lines first to himself. He had to be scared in that orphanage, then surviving grim Depression years, and in the trenches in Italy. One day, I would corral Dad's "choose life," "be not afraid," inspiration when love vanished, and a son died.

Surprisingly too, neither any parish nor school priest wooed a vocation out of me. Or, if they did, it did not matter. I was oblivious to any calling because, as early as twelve, I knew exactly what I was going to be when I grew up.

"I was your age, Cruz."

Sitting on my bundle of *North Bay Nugget* newspapers to deliver, I cut the rope and inhaled the heavenly incense of a freshly printed newspaper. I smudged the newsprint on my fingers. Newspapers, now that was my religion. I read most of the first page of the *Nugget* before delivering the afternoon newspaper to customers.

MAN LANDS ON MOON.

BOBBY KENNEDY ASSASSINATED.

TRUDEAU CAMPAIGNS IN NORTH BAY.

The whole wide world was at my fingertips long before I discovered the Internet. Years later, as a young curate, long-ago customers and now parishioners had forgiven their cute carrier for reading THEIR paper before they did! One customer, tall John Doyle, told me that I assured him it was important I read the newspaper first to know the product I was selling. He shook his head. He told me how adept I was at collection time, rummaging in vain for the change that was due him until he waved his hand in exasperation—his change now my tip. I knew where the money was. I left that pocket to the end of my search.

I winked at Cruz.

Yes, I wanted to be a journalist. Or, in those days, the term was reporter. I imagined myself as a foreign correspondent in Washington or Moscow. Or I could file stories on this jet-setting, flamboyant Pierre Elliot Trudeau captivating a swooning Canada. Soon there would be a Major League Baseball team in Montréal. I would be a sports reporter. They paid you to watch baseball! There was not a shred of doubt why this God of my parents had put me on this Earth.

I dodged Career Days, I hung out with Father Fehrenbach, working on the next edition of the school's *Examiner* newspaper. I talked the principal, Rev. Jean-Leon Shanks, into a morning newscast with announcements and sports segment, which I delivered over the school PA. As the show morphed into interviews with a football coach or theatre director, as buddies showered gratitude for my broadcast shortening first period, Shanks had had enough. One day, he unceremoniously flipped the PA off in mid-sentence and sent me back to the classroom. My *Morningside* show was axed.

"Claire, I empathize with fired media celebrities!"

"Bahahaha."

The Prashaws played the card game, canasta, in the rummy card family—seven-card suits, melding, freezing the deck; our version was cutthroat canasta. Mom's competitive gene passed on in spades to each of us and to several grandchildren. Cheating, talking across the table, eye talk, anything to win. As a boy, I drew up draws for all-day ping pong tournaments on our basement table. Winning was good. A consolation prize was impaling a sibling on the oil furnace: a series of innocent volleys moved the unsuspecting victim closer and closer, and then I'd smash the ball at the furnace. I could count on my siblings' DNA to crash the furnace. I never considered how I would tell my parents I had won but injured Pati.

Boyhood and early teen years were filled with endless street hockey games and skating on Lake Nipissing as we put the hockey nets a quarter mile apart. It was our time of innocence. Mom's roast beef, butter tarts, fudge, Chelsea buns, graham wafer butterscotch pies, and peanut butter and jam school lunches for six children that fed our childhood. As Margie says, "of our family's earth, Mom was the salt."

Does anything in life ever match the magic of a child's imagination?

My next question, God. Why do we lose this imagination? What happened along the way? God, you know I have other questions I will ask. And, by the way, I will question your answers too.

"Claire, my generation likes to eulogize the safety we felt playing as kids all day outside: no Internet, no cellphones, no locked doors, on our bikes from dawn to dusk, not wanting to trade anything for a time when, 'people respected one another,' and 'we had love.' Up to a point, it was true. Today's hindsight is a reality check—for most of us, it was living in a sphere of middle-class whiteness that had its share of racist jokes, locker room misogyny, and blatant discrimination against Indigenous Peoples. Indeed, not everyone was respected, not everyone felt the love. Dad called them 'the good old bad days'."

By the time all six kids appeared, Dad was full-bore the larger-than-life Dick Prashaw clown, Patch Adams in technicolour, as he entertained everyone with his jokes and masks—ringleader for his circus.

"Cruz, Poppy was such a joker," Claire said. "He'd wear Grandma's dress. He had this clock where a cuckoo popped out and squirted us with water. He walked an imaginary dog on a leash."

Dad called my friends by name, his names, of course, either "Bub" or "Doughhead." Countless times, I stood beside him as he talked animatedly with another adult. He slapped them on the back and then turned to whisper, "Who the hell was that?"

His parents' vaudeville lurked deep inside him. I had perfected my eye-roll while enduring his performances, preferring to meet friends anywhere other than my house. As Dad mastered selling Maxwell House coffee, Tang sugar-laced orange juice, and Sugar Crisp—no, the Canada Food Guide to healthy eating was not out yet—he switched sales to a home basement office. After classes, Scollard Hall friends piled into his company station wagon for five minutes of craziness, a perfect detox from the Catholic school.

I had not taken any psychology courses yet to understand how Dad's humour masked a sadness from earlier years. He did not talk about his feelings. My family, back then, did not talk much about feelings either. I detected Dad's feelings best when he took his belt off and chased me through the house, my life spared by a desperate dive underneath my bed, curled up in the corner. His dire threats about "a lickin" were enough.

Dick and Gert Prashaw, Dad and Mom.

I did not grasp the love that bound us tight. Dad and Mom's love glue for the zoo we found ourselves in. It may have felt like a "cuckoo's nest," this religiosity of my childhood. It was anything but dysfunctional. We as kids could be visible. We felt safe. We dwelled in a place that helped us forge our own identities. Dad was this good husband and good father steeped in traditional family life. It was obvious that my parents loved each other. We seldom heard those words spoken. Mom lived in his shadow, and I guess we did too, although, remarkably, their love produced six, strong, independent, and self-confident children.

As a boy, I threw a red, white, and blue rubber ball against the back of the house for hours, sometimes hitting the concrete foundation or the forest green siding. Depending on the pitch location, the ball bounced off in one of several directions. In my imaginary game, I played the pitcher, hitter, and fielders. Those games went on for hours with my Boston Red Sox always beating the damn Yankees. (Montréal Expos and Toronto Blue Jays were not yet franchises). I broadcast the games out loud, imitating the legendary Detroit Tigers' play-by-play announcer, Ernie Harwell.

"Yastrzemski lines a ball past a diving Bobby Richardson at Fenway. That will score another run. The ball is heading all the way to the Green Monster!

Mickey Mantle throws the ball in, and Yaz has a stand-up double! Yaz's third hit of the afternoon. Boston leads New York 4-0."

Thump.

Thump.

Thump, against the back wall, the imprint of the rubber ball on the green siding.

My poor parents.

Broadcasting the games.

Our poor neighbours.

On one side of our house was the Coward family. All I remember of the father, Ross, was his immaculately kept lawn. By the hours, he cut, raked, and manicured every single blade of grass. Mr. Coward must be in a Lawn and Gardens' Hall of Fame. My sole interest in his lawn was to retrieve countless baseballs that landed there. Mr. Coward did not want my balls on his lawn. Mr. Coward did not want me on his lawn. This would not end well. After many warnings, Mr. Coward confiscated all my balls. I decided it was time to grow some myself.

I winked again at Cruz.

A friend and I made signs, "Give Us Back Our Balls" and "Don't be Mean to Kids." We marched in front of Mr. Coward's house, making sure to stay off his lawn. It was not long before Dad learned of the protest, came out and brought us inside quickly, taking our signs. He was not mad. The adults must have talked because my sport balls were returned. I had an early lesson in solidarity forever on the picket line.

Mr. Coward had a pretty daughter older than me. A boy started courting her. Mike Harris, a good-looking young man, a talented golfer, and destined for Page One stories of his own two decades later. Yes, the future Premier of Ontario. Unlike Mr. Coward, Harris threw my football back. We played catch. He was a nice guy. I didn't know it then, but it was the first instalment on an important life lesson in recognizing a bit of humanity in a fella who would be on the extreme other end of my political spectrum. One day, I would be back on the picket lines with teachers, social workers, and poverty advocates to denounce the Harris government's draconian cuts to Ontario's vulnerable. Cynical politics by leaders recruited a generation of voters alienated from the obligations to the common good. The vulnerable became the right wing's scapegoats.

Dudley George, dead in 1995. Anthony O'Brien "Dudley" George, a member of Stony Point First Nation, was shot by an Ontario Provincial Police (OPP) officer.[3] The Ojibway band had occupied land at Ipperwash Provincial Park taken from them in World War II. A former Ontario Attorney General testified in the inquiry that Harris told him he wanted "the fucking Indians out of the park," a profanity Harris denied saying. However, a judge concluded Harris uttered those words and ruled that the Harris and federal governments, along with the OPP, shared responsibility for the events that led in George's death.

Kimberly Rogers, dead in 2001. She took her life, eight months pregnant, while she was under house arrest in Sudbury for a disputed welfare fraud conviction during the Harris' government crackdown against low-income individuals who needed government assistance.[4] Countless others, nameless and faceless to most, were victims of those cuts.

In politics, it proved increasingly difficult not to demonize opponents while still delivering the emphatic denunciation of their nasty policies. I drifted to a social gospel that inspired politicians like Tommy Douglas, a Baptist minister, first a premier of Saskatchewan, and then leader of the federal New Democratic Party.

By seventeen, in the Trudeau-Robert Stanfield election in 1968, I planted a then hideous looking, Halloween black and orange New Democratic Party (NDP) sign between Dad's blue Progressive Conservative sign and Mom's red

---

3 Kelly Wang, "25 Years Later: Remembering the Ipperwash Crisis and Dudley George," *Global News*, Toronto, June 4, 2021, https://globalnews.ca/news/7318404/ ipperwash-crisis-dudley-george-25-years.

4 David Galvin, "Remembering Kimberly Rogers," Hamilton Spectator, Aug. 16, 2018, https://www.hamiltonnews.com/ opinion-story/8843112-remembering-kimberly-rogers.

Liberal sign. A *Nugget* photographer took a picture of the Prashaw front lawn sign wars. The photo with the caption, 'A House Divided,' made page one.

"The NDP had not yet discovered the softer orange in the Pantone Bible of colours," Claire commented. Claire had worked five years for NDP leader Jack Layton in his Toronto-Danforth constituency office.

Indeed, the Prashaws were a typical family growing up then, a crazy clan where one honed survival skills on how not to be voted off our island. We have grown close in adult years, but I did not always sense that closeness as a kid even though we were together enough, acting out the assigned or assumed roles in the family play. What sticks out for me from childhood was our epic fights, with me in the centre of the ring.

Cruz was back listening. The Vaillancourts were our neighbours on the other side of our house.

"Once, Cruz, God only knows what little Ricky, me, was up to. My normally mild-mannered brother, Marty, your grandpa, chased me out of the house. This may have happened after he drew a Berlin Wall line halfway across our shared basement bedroom floor. He was annoyed at my messy side. Marty wanted me dead that day. Marty chased me into the refuge of the Vaillancourt home that had front and back doors on the sides of the house. The Vaillancourts were at their dining room table eating; their supper entertainment was two Prashaw boys barging in without knocking, bolting Donovan Bailey-like from door to door."

"Uncle Rick, I am glad my dad didn't catch you. And he still has a clean bedroom," Claire laughed.

Another time, with my parents away on a Caribbean holiday, Jon chased me into a bathroom. I swung the door closed and locked it. Safe, I probably said something foolish. The next thing I remember was Dad's golf putter smashing through the cheap wooden door, Jon's Jack Nicholson *Shining* look telling me I was about to die. Quickly though, we turned our attention to the hole in the door. We dabbed putty and stain in a pathetic repair job. Yes, Dad did notice the patch, but chose rather to pour Manhattan cocktails instead, not wanting to ruin the last relaxing feeling of their splendid, adult vacation away from their children.

"Uncle Rick, your brothers chased you a lot," Cruz smiled.

Gert Prashaw did what moms did day and night, cooking the meals, making lunches for school, endless vacuuming and cleaning up on the heels of six messy kids. Gert navigated the shoals of those *Leave it to Beaver* Ward and June Cleaver years, the husband lord of the manor. While clearly in Dad's shadow, she cleverly figured out how to live her own life—golf, bridge, parish ladies' guild—while also heading next door at night to a neighbour, Mrs. Beattie, now in the Vaillancourts' home. Somehow, Mom brokered real power behind Dad's throne, accomplished with no evidence of liquor bottles stashed in the laundry room. Mrs. Beattie did the pouring next door. As Beatons had done for generations, Mom went with the flow. The worst, hellish mom days came in "snow day" storms, when she was stuck inside with the six of us until she despaired and threw us outside in the blizzards.

"Moms know the feeling in the pandemic, believe me," Claire said. "Remember after that out-of-control first presidential debate between Donald Trump and Joe Biden, someone on Twitter said that any mom home with kids in the pandemic could have been a better moderator and shut the president up."

Certain of my career path, I attended Carleton University in Ottawa for a four-year School of Journalism Honours degree. Good years. I lived, or should I say, partied in the *Animal House* on the fifth floor of Glengarry Residence, the lads pursuing university degrees and night courses like getting drunk and getting laid. One night, my buddies carried me home from a night of drinking across the river in Hull, Québec, where the legal age was eighteen. They lit votive candles, discussed funeral arrangements, and who coveted which of my LP albums. They lit those candles because, apparently, I was already outed as a practicing Catholic, even in this first foray away from home. I had joined the Catholic Newman Club for Sunday liturgies, followed by meals. I trekked the *La Montée* pilgrimage to the Oka monastery in Québec. Hiking. Singing. Prayers. Life conversations. And girls! It had not dawned on me yet that my parents' faith was slowly becoming mine.

At school, I wrote for the *Charlatan* newspaper and did the colour commentary for Radio Carleton's CKCU broadcasts of Carleton Ravens' hockey games. Dad was upset when I announced at the end of my third year at

Carleton that I was taking a year off to travel in Europe with a friend, Allan Bartley. I guess this was my gap year. Dad, a Grade 9 Depression dropout, urged me to get my degree first and then travel. He was convinced I would never go back to university; Dad's doubt doubled down on my stubbornness to prove him wrong.

There were five glorious summers of newspaper jobs—two summers at the *Nugget* and three at the *Toronto Star's* premier internship program. My first bylines. My vocation was signed, sealed, and delivered.

At the end of my third summer at the *Toronto Star*, Jim Proudfoot, the sports editor, sat me down. Chomping on a cigar, he offered me a full-time job covering car racing and winter skiing. I am not sure why I turned the offer down. Life has a plan of its own. Instead, I applied to two newspapers, the *Telegram* in St. John's, Newfoundland on the east coast, and the *Vancouver Sun* out west. I must have wanted out of Toronto. I may have had an inkling on the Maple Leafs hockey team not winning another Stanley Cup!

I threw a third wink at Cruz. A few months ago, he had worn his Maple Leafs' jersey and I, my Ottawa Senators jersey, at an Extra Butter Coffee book signing on Toronto's Roncesvalles Ave.

"Your Sens suck," Cruz shouted. "The Leafs are winning the Cup!"

The *Sun's* offer came first. Its newsroom in the Pacific Press Building was my first, full-time newspaper job, although newspapers and I had been joined at the hip, forever it seemed. That first year there was the typical reporter initiation: filing stories on city hall, school boards, the police beat. I then had a gem assignment to join the Victoria, B.C., Legislative Bureau to cover the strange, surreal, socialist first term of NDP Premier Dave Barrett's government.

All was going swimmingly well until that visit to my priest cousin in Seattle.

When journalist friends heard of my decision to leave newspapers for the seminary, they joked that I was going from the "bad news" to the "good news." It would take two decades to confirm what I intuitively sensed. There was considerable good in journalism's bad news. And there was some bad news in the "good news" of faith and religion. I would relate easily to Protestant theologian Karl Barth who read the Bible and newspapers every day.

To appreciate that conversion in Seattle, I should start with the first seminary I attended, what it was like living inside the Roman Catholic universe of the Prashaws. Roman and Roamin' Catholics know the place well.

CHAPTER 4

Jesus, Mary, Joseph, and AlPaMa

1960–1975

A thousand miles' journey indeed has its first steps. The marriage of the Prashaws to the Holy Roman Catholic Church was a match hanging precariously between heaven and hell, cooked in a *Cuckoo's Nest* laboratory.

Holy water, ashes on the forehead, grace before meals, meatless Fridays, the rosary, and making signs of the cross that appeared to be poor attempts at dousing a fire burning on our shirts. All done religiously, so we would not burn in hell. For the sign of the cross, we traced on our upper body the cross where Jesus was crucified: touching the forehead first, down to the lower chest or stomach, over to the left shoulder, and across to the right shoulder. You did this while reciting the prayer, "In the name of the Father, and of the Son, and of the Holy Spirit." The Holy Spirit was a makeover on the Holy Ghost. Eastern Rite Catholics and Orthodox Christians touch the right

Christmas 1967: We gathered around "Mother Margaret Mary." Front row, left to right: Pati, Margie, Jon; back row, left to right: Rick, Marty, Jude.

shoulder first and then the left shoulder, a practice the Latin-rite Catholic Church did until the sixteenth century. Back then, churches were reforming, breaking up, and choosing different devotions and beliefs.

"Cruz, do you remember what your name means in Spanish?"

"The cross," Cruz replied, not looking up as he destroyed another incoming missile.

"He was named Cruz after his Honduras grandmother's maiden name," Claire added.

"Cross your heart and hope to die" became a solemn oath to swear growing up. John Vianney, one holy person in the church—we called them saints—said a good sign of the cross could make hell tremble. Sadly, my speed dial version was not scaring Satan at all!

"Cruz, believe me, there were no dinosaurs in my childhood—the 1960s and even into the 1970s."

"Ha, Uncle Rick, Brontosaurus and Raptors were your Jurassic pets," Cruz laughed.

"Cruz, wait till I destroy you again tonight in our WWF pillow fight."

"Uncle Rick, you have never ever won once against me."

It was all so God-smacking normal, the norm for Catholic families. If it was not your childhood, it was your parents' or grandparents' universe. If you were a Protestant with Catholic friends, you know these stories. I have been hooked on faith's love story, personal and community, the hard mission to chase after love, justice, peace, and inclusion. Help one another. Be kind. Be true to ourselves. God's mercy was oxygen to live another day. For the longest time, faith was exclusively this Roman Catholicism that became an integral part of who we were. God could seem distant at times, prayers unanswered too, but the faith was still there. My faith has puzzled me enough days while opening doors to ponder life, death, and where we go from here.

What's it all about, Alfie?

I bow to the Prashaws' altar.

In my adult years, fighting hearing-impaired loss, I went to an audiologist who, it turns out, was Irish Catholic. On his graph, when he identified a loss so severe that it looked like a stock market crash—and knowing my northern roots—he asked if I had ever been in a mining accident. A dramatic hearing drop, trouble with high-pitch *p, f, t, s* consonants starting so many words, suggested that an accident had damaged my hearing.

"No, a loud Catholic family," was my best guess.

The audiologist laughed. He had a club membership.

"My God, we are a loud family," Claire concurred.

A "loud Catholic family" where we never let anyone finish a sentence. Our story was better! We were laboratory rats to be injected with a catechism, votive candles, prayers, rituals, incense, and a road map to heaven. Benediction, the Corpus Christi, Holy Name, and the Crowning of Mary processions. Who doesn't love a parade to show off our team colours? Thank God, this was in North Bay and not Belfast, where Catholics and Protestants might toss rotten tomatoes, eggs, and missiles at each other. We had those nine First Fridays each month in honour of the Sacred Heart of Jesus to confess, receive Communion, and pray for a happy death, done so we can check off a sure plenary indulgence, a "get out of hell" pass. Hell mattered!

One Christmas, I gave Dad the radio recording tapes of the great American orator, Archbishop Fulton J. Sheen. I regretted that gift as he played them loud and often from his bedroom.

It was all the authentic piety of the day, inspiring a belief in God and religious worship. Being Catholic then providentially meant a faith anchored in what the dramatic Second Vatican Council did to our universal Holy Roman Catholic Church. Like taking Queen Victoria to be outfitted on 5th Avenue! I would better appreciate this Council's importance later but, even as a boy, it was impressive to take in the breath-taking changes. English and other vernacular languages replaced the Latin, priests and altars turned around to face us, the option of Communion in the hand, handshakes between people for the kiss of peace, a veritable Vatican vertigo spinning us forward. For my entire faith journey and priestly ministry, I was a child of the Second Vatican Council.

"We went to Mass on Sundays. It was called Mass, not Eucharist back then. Or was it, 'uterus,' as Debbie Rosenthal, a Jewish friend of Pati's, swore she heard a dozen times while attending my priestly ordination?"

"Bahahaha. I am never going to hear the word, Eucharist, again," Claire laughed.

"So that I do not go to hell, Claire, I should add that this same Eucharist, the sacrament of sacraments, would feed my spiritual hunger for a long, long time."

The Mass, then always on Sunday mornings, not the post-Vatican Council Saturday night or later Sunday night Mass that counted as fulfilling the Holy Day obligation.

After supper, we knelt in the living room to pray the rosary, racing through the five decades which stood for a collection of prayers—five series of one Our Father, ten Hail Marys, and a Glory Be prayer. Repetition was so Catholic. The soothing sound that the prayers hummed. If Dad recited those prayers fast, I could switch to breakneck speed when I heard the street hockey game start. Dad's ominous stare slowed me down. I planted myself at the end of the kids' rosary row farthest from Dad, partly in self-defence, a buffer from pending doom.

"Cruz, it was the devil, no, who possessed me to make faces at the sibling leading the decade of the rosary?"

I felt that I won when they laughed. Then, I knew I had lost, as Dad cuffed the kid laughing, and me.

How did he know?

In punishing the culprits, Dad's arm miraculously grew as we prayed "the beads," the term older Catholics called the rosary. Only later did it dawn on us who this "AlPaMa" was who we had been praying for every night in the third decade of the rosary. I was clueless, thinking it was Latin or some Andes mules. No, as Margie later deciphered it, AlPaMa was our nightly remembrance of three dead members of Mom's family. A younger brother, Alec Beaton, a Montréal police officer who had died quite young in an off-duty car accident leaving his wife, Anne, twenty-five, a widow with three young children. We then remembered mom's Pa and Ma, both deceased. AlPaMa! There were no prayers for dad's Pa. And his mom was still alive.

God could figure it out better than us kids.

"Cruz, you might see Muslim men and women in High Park walking with their prayer beads in their hands. In Islam, prayer beads are referred to as Misbaha (Arabic: مسبحة mas'baha), Tasbih or Sibha and contain ninety-nine normal-sized beads, corresponding to the ninety-nine names or descriptions of God in Islam and two smaller or mini beads separating every thirty-three beads.[5] They use them to keep count of prayers as well."

Priests encouraged our praying. "The family who prays together, stays together," they taught. The Prashaws also fought when we prayed.

We learned our catechism at Catholic schools. The stories of saints inspired us. St. Francis, a lover of the poor and animals, was an early favourite of mine. A nun might whack the back of our heads when we slouched while kneeling. Marty endured a rap on the knuckles for writing with his left hand. Lefties were deemed "children of the devil;" in classical Latin, the word *left* is "sinister." Still, all in all, it was not a bad thing to be taught one's life had meaning, a purpose. Being good mattered. Life was about treating one another well.

"Claire, I asked Facebook friends to share childhood Catholic memories. Different generations chimed in with variations on a familiar Catholic script:"

> **Sharon Oliver, Sudbury, ON:** I once gave my parents a huge scare when I didn't return from school one day when I was in Grade 1. I was eventually found at around 9:00 p.m. that night by Father Salini as he was checking the church. I was sitting in the front pew in front of a statue of Our Lady, waiting for her to talk to me like she talked to Bernadette of Lourdes. Or was it the children of Fatima? They were all such a big part of my life! I figured that if she spoke to them, why not me as well!

---

5 Diane Morgan, *Essential Islam: A Comprehensive Guide to Belief and Practice,* (Oxford, England: Praeger/ABC-CLIO, 2010), 10.

Heidi Berrang, Collingwood, ON: Kneeling on those gym floors will be forever ingrained in my mind (and knees)! We also had a priest that could tell if someone was chewing gum, and he stopped the school Mass and said, "I will not continue until the person gets rid of their gum." Since no one was going to admit it, we'd all be sitting or kneeling on the gum floor for ages while he stood waiting, lol!

Gina Goss, Morro Bay, CA: The Latin Mass, my dad being the charming usher at the 11:00 a.m. Sunday mass, the smell of incense burning along with real candles glowing off the faces of saints, choir singing on the holy days. Lining up for the confessional, nervous. Donuts after mass. First Communion with [a] white dress and veil, smiling. Not chewing the host with it stuck to the roof of my mouth. My parents [being] judged by the church after their divorce in the 1960s.

Colleen Humbert, Digby, NS: We took out the centre of Oreo cookies and 'played' Communion. Oh, my goodness, we are probably going to go to hell! :)

Deborah Byrnes, Ottawa, ON: When I was twelve, I was disallowed from being an altar boy. That pissed me off. When I was fourteen at confession, I told the priest I was having great difficulty with the virgin birth. He told me I was not praying hard enough, to go on out [and] do the Stations of the Cross and five rosaries every day and to come back in a week. That was my last confession.

Mickey Naccarato, Sault Ste. Marie, ON: My brother was an altar boy, and we practiced mass at home. Flatten white bread slices to make hosts and go through the whole ritual. Too funny that we were trying to help him be the best altar boy! There was no wine! Lol!

Linda Leinan, Ottawa, ON: My father, being of Scandinavian extraction, and my mother, being of Polish extraction, were deemed to be a 'mixed marriage.' My father agreed, as per the pretty rigid Catholic rule, to let the children (all six of us) be raised Catholic. I always admired my parents for the harmony in which they each practiced their respective denominations, although I realized that it was my father who had to be the flexible one. As our rural community was replete with Norwegians, my father at least did not feel alone in his faith practice. And the kids in our family were even invited sometimes to participate in his church's Christmas concerts. Of course, when my parents got engaged, my stubborn Polish grandfather was opposed to the idea of his daughter marrying outside of the Catholic faith, and he did not even go to the wedding. Fortunately, he warmed up to my father with time, as my father was a good man.

Sara Krynitzki, Toronto, ON: I remember my grandmother taking me and my sister to the Catholic church during the week (she was Catholic, but we were not) where we needed to be quiet and sit with her in the pew and light a candle each time we went for my dad, her son, who passed away.

Rosemary Klein, Winchester, England: Always keep your knees together, ladies; they are best friends. Sister Rosemary Carroll, R.I.P.

Katy Kidd Wright, a friend who described herself as a "non-RC heathen raising RC kids going to Catholic schools" confirmed that ashes on foreheads was still in vogue. "The modern curriculum even has a robotics lesson in Grade 2 where my eldest learned to mechanize Mary and Joseph's walk to Bethlehem."

In my school days, we wrote JMJ on the top of scribbler pages for a Holy Family Jesus, Mary, and Joseph blessing. Other times, we wrote BVM for the Blessed Virgin Mary. It was an alphabet acronym heaven. Whenever Dad felt no one was listening to him, he spoke to the Blessed Virgin Mary statue on the living room mantle. They talked a lot.

We feared the confession line. English-speaking lads might search for a Polish or a hard-of-hearing priest to miss catching our list of sins—swearing, stealing, fighting, and, of course, impure thoughts. Protestant buddies caught a big break confessing directly to their God! We were taught an examination of conscience to review one's day over and against the Ten Commandments of God or the precepts of the church. This review was not a bad idea. Heady, though, for a school kid who had not robbed a bank nor kissed a girl yet.

Nevertheless, to this day, I practice a simpler examination of conscience most nights, identifying on the pillow one blessing and one struggle from the day.

Once, in confession, a priest stopped me when, in reciting the Act of Contrition prayer to express one's sorrow, I said I was "hardly" sorry for my sins. He told me the word was "heartily." "Oh my God, I am heartily sorry."

Was my imperfect act of contrition another sin?

Protestant friends might tag along to church.

"Cruz, your Nona, Maggie, recounted how in Collingwood they took the neighbour's kid to Mass."

"She called Mass the show," Maggie said. "She came home—she was probably five or six years old—and told her mom, 'I don't know why they shove Jesus in that tiny metal box up on the altar. That was mean.'"

That "metal box" was the tabernacle where the consecrated hosts, God we believed, were stored.

"Cruz, Catholics adapted the older Hebrew notion of the tabernacle, which was a tent for God's earthly dwelling place."

For some Québec French-speaking folks exorcising their oppressive Catholic upbringing—being told how to vote, who to love, the number of babies to have—*tabernak* became a top-shelf, sacrilegious swear word. There was other religious-inspired swear words: *Hosti*, the communion wafer, *calice* or *colis*, for chalice. Quebecers could excel in Catholic cursing.

There were hints of how different it might be for a girl in the Catholic Church. Religious sisters and other women friends would one day become my teachers on this gender schizophrenia. Nuns told girls they better leave room for the Holy Spirit when they danced with a boy. If you had trouble measuring the Holy Spirit, girls heard the instruction to leave room for a telephone book, presumably a Toronto or Montréal-size phone book. Good God, telephone books have all but disappeared. Is it any wonder the sexual revolution happened?

"Bahahaha," chortled Claire. "Telephone books and rock and roll."

Marty and Margie were destined to marry two O'Connor siblings, Maggie and Jerry. Living at that O'Connor home in Strathroy. ON, was an adventure.

"My sister, Rosie, was sick of the same old sins all the time," Maggie remembers. "So, at age eleven, she read a pamphlet at the back of the church on adultery and then went into the confessional to confess she had committed adultery three times. The priest said, 'How old are you?'"

The family in 2001 at Mom's funeral. Left to right: Marty, Rick, Margie, Jude, Jon, and Pati.

Like the media, I report here on what makes news. If it bleeds, it leads. We bled. Still, like the kid digging through the manure pile, certain there was a horse underneath, the stories remind me that as a Catholic, I learned how to pray, share, practice the Golden Rule, say sorry, and discover the good in being good. There was a purpose to living. Dad and Mom's mission was to pass the faith on to their children and to lead us into heaven. I do not mock any of that. Mom and Dad walked their faith with us; they treated all people with the same dignity, reminding us that differences were more fascinating than threatening, that vulnerable individuals had difficult lives not of their own choosing, that they were every bit as good as we were. I learned a lot tagging along with Dad as he delivered North Bay Santa Fund hampers each Christmas. He joked with the adults and teased the kids. There was never any pity nor condescension. Mom and Dad taught us to celebrate the seasons of our lives. It was the best school I ever attended.

It anchored me in a safe harbour for the Roman and Roamin' years ahead.

Unimaginable to this teen was what lay ahead. Holier, older folk kneeling before me for divine absolution from God's representative. The joy of looking in lovers' eyes as I witnessed their vows. Pouring holy water on a baby's forehead as faith was passed from generation to generation. And sitting quietly in a hospital room for a death vigil of a loved family member after I had anointed them with holy oil, witness to a soulful, intimately strange passage to the unknown.

For the most part, many Catholics sharing those stories thought those times were positive. Until, for some, they weren't.

CHAPTER 5

Why Did God Make Me?

There is a question in the old *Baltimore Catechism* from when I was a young child at St. Martin's School.

Why did God make me?

"Claire, fifty years later, like my generation of Catholics, I rhyme off the answer."

"God made me to know him, love him, and serve him in this world, and be happy with him forever in the next."

Unfortunately, I memorized that answer for all the wrong reasons. One day, a nun branded those words on my soul and on my hand, whacking me with a black strap for not knowing the answer. Twice, on the same day!

"Was it Grade 2? Cruz, I was seven or eight years old."

Mercifully, I have forgotten the nun's name. Standing over me with her flowing black robes, veil, sleeves, and starched white bib, Sister Saint Something or Other cast a dark, ominous shadow like the total eclipse of the sun. She had called on me to tell classmates why God made us. I was virtually clueless then on God and religion, although I was starstruck in St. Martin's Church daydreaming at the speckled, gold frescoes, dreamy clouds, an archangel's sword crushing a serpent, cherubs, the church's life-sized statues, and burning candles. Still, religion homework could not compete with the blue sky outside, a girl's curls, and sticking a tongue out at a friend.

Sister Saint Something or Other was determined to have us worthy to receive First Communion by year's end. She ordered me to the front of the classroom, admonished all to learn their catechism, and told me to put out my hand. Down came the leather strap. *Whack!* It stung. I fought back tears. Back in my seat, Sister Saint Something or Other asked me the same question again.

I had a strong hunch God had not put me here to be strapped by this nun. Nonetheless, if she did tell me the right answer after the first strap, I forgot. Round two. I was at the front of the classroom with my hand out. There was no holding back the tears this time. Did she think my memory was in that hand?

No matter how common the strap was then, it was cruel. I am glad I forgot her name. I was unaware then how some who vowed a chaste life might have demons lurking inside. I honestly hope she discovered with the rest of us the loving God introduced in the new catechism, a Catholic seismic eruption from a fear-and-paranoid schema with its shadows of hell, sins, and purgatory delivered in Hollywood-casted cold, dimly lit churches. There would be better times ahead, religious sisters who, as hospital chaplains, spiritual directors, and youth ministers, put away the straps and recognized the good news of a Creator breathing a Spirit God into us.

CHAPTER 6

Bishop Alex and "The Pro"

1960s–1970s

When the Prashaws arrived in North Bay in 1960, both the world and the Roman Catholic Church were changing dramatically.

John Fitzgerald Kennedy, a boyish, charismatic Massachusetts senator, had defeated Richard Nixon to become the United States' first Catholic president. Joe Biden is their second Catholic president.

"Claire, one of the great lines ever spoken by a spouse was Jackie Kennedy wondering what all the fuss was about her husband's religion because he is such a bad Catholic."

"Hahaha. A good-looking, wealthy Irish Catholic politician," Claire winked. "What could possibly go wrong?"

Kennedy's presidency lurched into crisis mode. An inept Bay of Pigs Cuba invasion. The Vietnam War. A Cold War with Russia. Sister Geralda, principal at St. Alexander's School, interrupted studies on Nov. 22, 1963, to lead us in prayers for a dead President Kennedy, a Lee Harvey Oswald bullet shattering Camelot.

The Cold War boosted North Bay's fame beyond pickerel fishing and being close to Callander's Dionne Quintuplets' home. The Canadian-built CF-100 jets and their crews' training centre came to the "Gateway to the North" city. So too did NORAD, the North American Air Radar Defence, twinned with the American headquarters in Colorado.

"Cruz, it was like one of your video games for real, an air defence system buried deep in a hillside along Trout Lake four miles from our home. Hundreds passed through the steel doors to work in 'The Hole.' Those missiles stored horizontally could be raised through an opening for launching. Prime Minister John Diefenbaker's minority Conservative government would be defeated after deciding against Kennedy's request to put nuclear warheads on the missiles."

"If there's war with Russia, we have one of the world's leading opportunities of getting blown off the map," one resident quipped to a *Maclean's* magazine writer.[6]

It was the Baby Boomer generation, people making babies, making money, and getting ahead, "full employment" decades. A Gallup poll reported a strong majority of Canadians attended a religious service each week.[7]

My universe was smaller and safer—St. Alexander's and playing for Kinette Playground baseball and hockey teams with Dad my baseball coach. When we moved, Dad had called Sister Geralda to tell her he had "six Indians" to enroll. She was clueless on the joker on the line. He meant no disrespect using a word now viewed as derogatory except in proper historical or legal context. He figured his teasing was colour blind. However, I would need another generation to school myself on how, in fact, language does matter, "who we call what," and how others hear our words far differently than we intended. I thought I was smarter than Dad, but I would make mistakes as well. One day, much later in staff work for Members of Parliament, I learned never to say, "our Aboriginal Peoples." I had used the phrase in a householder draft for MP Rachel Blaney, intending a positive affiliation. Indeed, Aboriginal Peoples were not mine, yours, nor Canada's. They were here first. I was the settler. As a child, I had that poster of *The Lone Ranger*, Hollywood

6 Don Delaplante, "How North Bay Got Rid of Its Inferiority Complex," *Maclean's Magazine*, Aug. 15, 1954, https://archive.macleans.ca/article/1954/8/15/how-north-bay-got-rid-of-its-inferiority-complex.

7 Rick Hiemstra and Karen Stiller, "Religious affiliation and attendance in Canada," *In Trust*, Centre for Theological Schools, New Year 2016, https://intrust.org/Magazine/Issues/New-Year-2016/Religious-affiliation-and-attendance-in-Canada.

casting his companion, Tonto, as a half-breed "Native American" who spoke dumbass, pidgin English for the TV series. Tonto in Spanish means "stupid." The character was a racist stereotype.

I joined the altar boys at our new parish in North Bay, the Pro-Cathedral of the Assumption, proudly wearing the pleated starched white surplice and black soutane. We wore red soutanes for special liturgies, mastering how to lift the chains on the thurible, a metal censer in which incense was burned. Angelic may be overstating how I looked, given my perpetual untied shoelaces and chocolate stains on my face.

"They're still untied, Uncle Rick," Claire chided. "You're going to kill yourself one day!"

Dad joined the Holy Name Club. He became an usher. By handshake, joke, or flirting, no one passed Dick Prashaw unscathed. My parents were THE influencers for growing my faith. They believed. They prayed. They immersed their children in the liturgical and social life of a faith community. It was all real. They were not perfect by any means. Their infrequent spats hung ominously in the air for a day or two. Dad yelled. Mom withdrew. I'd join Mom in a silent protest. Dad seemed to forget quicker than I did. Nevertheless, my parents were flesh and blood for grasping acts of mercy, charity, and justice. Believing, praying, choosing a faith are their influences. Then, until the teen years, there was no sense of this being forced on us. Well, except for the broccoli Mom commanded us to eat because there were starving children in China.

"They can have mine!"

"Hahaha," Claire laughed. "I tell Cruz he better eat the food on his plate because it's expensive. I work hard to spend money on groceries and, yes, there are kids starving all over the world."

"Does he eat the food?"

"Yes, Cruz is a good kid."

"Our dog, Kelly, ate my vegetables."

Faith was like the air we breathed, there, hanging around. As others did, I would discern what of this childhood faith was a keeper and what to discard.

In the lower sacristy, I enjoyed the mass piling on of Father Brian McKee, the legendary curate. Here was a new superhero. Big and rugged, he would skip down the flight of stairs, scream a server's name, and threw that boy in the air, signalling our turn to jump on Father Brian. McKee had been pursuing a professional football career as a lineman in the Canadian Football League when a call to the priesthood tackled him. McKee had found studies hard, exacerbated by St. Augustine Seminary's strict discipline smothering his independent, northern spirit. With a promising vocation in jeopardy, a new bishop, Alexander Carter, intervened. Carter designated his cottage as a temporary seminary to pull McKee north to complete his studies. McKee, ordained, became a driving force for a soup kitchen, and then an impressive Catholic charities initiative. Churches then delivered social programs that governments took over later. McKee, in a later Sudbury assignment, would throw a used refrigerator on his back to bring to a striking miner. On a Friday night, he drove his pickup truck through neighbourhoods to deliver a six-pack case of beer to the forlorn miner he spotted sitting on a porch, barely surviving on a meagre strike pay.

"Claire, I will get to the 'bad apples.' There were plenty of good priests like McKee. I spotted their generosity, faith, passion, and ideals." I am reading pandemic news that already over two-hundred sixty-five priests alone have died in Italy, some elderly for sure, many though from ministering in harm's way to the sick and the dying.[8]

McKee travelled to Toronto to play hockey with other priests whom he persuaded to perform in North Bay at a charity fundraiser. The event birthed the Flying Fathers as the media dubbed them. McKee, Father Les Costello, and the Flying Fathers filled arenas, scoring salvation with nuns on skates and cream pies in opponents' faces. If an opponent was talented, they'd stop the game to "ordain" him a priest and flip him a Flying Fathers' jersey. They raised millions of dollars for charities, delighting believers and heathens alike.

---

8 Reguly, Eric. "No sanctuary: COVID-19 threatens Italy's elderly nuns and priests in cramped quarters," *Globe and Mail*, March 10, 2021, https://www.theglobeandmail. com/world/article-no-sanctuary-covid-19-threatens-italys-elderly-nuns-and-priests-in.

At one altar boy meeting, McKee told us, "Look, guys, if you forget everything else, don't forget that if you fart, you have to sit in your own pew."

After I left the priesthood to marry, Suzanne and I visited McKee's Festival of Lights live nativity scene with sheep and goats along the shores of Ramsey Lake. McKee was at the entrance. He took our donation and chatted briefly. Minutes later, as we parked our car, he was back at the window. He muttered something about our needing help now; he stuffed two bills in my hand, more money than our donation. Now I was that miner on the porch. McKee took. He gave. He loved.

I may never throw a fridge on my back, but McKee was a good, early billboard for the priesthood. And, yes, Claire, he stopped celebrating Mass to tie my shoelaces. Twenty years later, in my early curate years, I started an altar boys football league, an inspiration from McKee's rough housing. However, this sacristy mayhem would cease abruptly as other priests announced the imminent arrival of Bishop Carter from the rectory.

Oh My God!

As a young boy raised on *The Lone Ranger,* this was an impressive scene. Carter wore his bright fuchsia cassock, a large silver cross dangling around his neck, the episcopal skullcap, the zucchetto on his head, and no shyness in extending his hand with a large amethyst ring. Cue the trumpets and the Vatican Swiss Guard!

Mark Balfe, a friend and fellow priest, would fill me in later on that episcopal ring. Two jewellers in Montréal had wanted to honour their friend with a suitable ring as he left a metropolis for "the boonies" in northern Canada. He did seem genuinely mortified whenever an elderly person knelt to kiss his ring, but make no mistake, from those princely arrivals, he enjoyed the perks of his office, extending his hand for a submissive, symbolic kiss.

We addressed the bishops as "Your Excellency," archbishops "Your Grace," and cardinals like Carter's brother, Emmett, in Toronto, "Your Eminence." The pope was "Your Holiness." It would be during a papal visit to Canada in 1984 and again in Rome in 1987 when I said, "Your Holiness" directly to Pope John Paul II.

"Cruz, Margie, your great aunt, bristled at the bowing, scraping, and saying 'your grace' to any bishop. Grace, she discovered, was in nature, Mother Earth, the divine feminine, in children, birds, and all living creatures. There was an abundance of blessings not requiring any religious institution or clergy. She spoke of being a second-class citizen in the church. She told me she was "sick and tired" of being "sick and tired." As a woman in the church. Her Gods and Goddesses were increasingly at cross purposes with a religion that could leave many women invisible and devalued. In fact, while there were other influencers in my faith journey—priests, religious sisters, teachers, and a handful of wise spiritual directors—Margie, in a singular, graceful way, swayed my spiritual path. I stopped at her watering holes that immersed me in reading scripture, attending lively charismatic renewal meetings with singing and praise, studying social justice, and feminist spirituality.

That all came later. As a kid though in North Bay, the single rival to my parents' spiritual influence was Carter and that limestone building of the Pro-Cathedral. Carter was born in 1909, five years before my dad. Carter served as Sault bishop from 1958 to his retirement in 1985.

The bishop should have resided in Sault Ste. Marie, 350 miles further west. Carter came to North Bay instead, to a Pro-Cathedral, and this happened because of a decision Father Joseph Scollard had made in 1904 when he was named the first bishop of a new Diocese of Sault Ste. Marie. At the time, Scollard was overseeing the construction of an impressive church called St. Mary's of the Lake. Wanting to finish its building and remain closer via train to Toronto and Ottawa, Scollard stayed put. St. Mary's became the Pro-Cathedral of the Assumption, the word "Pro" in Latin meaning "standing for" or "in the place of."

We called our church "The Pro." This parish family would be my faith home for twenty-five years.

Carter was pastor, teacher, and somewhat friend to the degree any bishop might be. But do not dare read before he did *The Globe and Mail* which was folded on the dining room table beside his chair. I committed that unpardonable sin only once as a young priest. Carter's death stare was on a par with Adam's thrown my way whenever I mixed up new pronouns for my son.

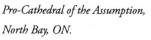

Pro-Cathedral of the Assumption, North Bay, ON.

Bishop Alexander Carter, Diocese of Sault Ste. Marie, ON, 1957-1985.

Father Brian McKee in his Catholic Charities "office" truck.

Interior of Pro-Cathedral of the Assumption before and soon after Vatican II changes.

In our family's first years at "The Pro," we had a front-row seat to what was happening to this Holy Roman Catholic Church. Carter was in Rome with two thousand bishops from around the world attending the extraordinary Second Vatican Council Pope John XXIII had announced in 1959, stunning a seemingly immutable church. There were four sessions, each lasting several months, held over three years. The bishops gathered to reflect on and renew the church's mandate. Carter returned home to share his excitement on what was happening, to announce that we were the people of God, light to the world and that we had this God-given mission in the real world.

"The joys and the hopes, the griefs and the anxieties of the men and women of this age, are the joys and the hopes, the griefs and the anxieties of the followers of Christ. Indeed, nothing genuinely human fails to raise an echo in their hearts. . . ."[9]

Magnificent! I would gladly memorize those words from the Council's *Pastoral Constitution on The Church in the Modern World* easier than the "Why God made me" answer in the *Baltimore Catechism*.

"Claire, one cannot overstate the importance of this council. Imagine a government today introducing at once extreme taxes for the rich, a universal basic income, strict climate change goals, equity in pay for women, a fair voting electoral system, and more."

Radical reform, to that extent, hit the Catholic Church. This was a revolution, an *aggiornamento*, that Italian word for a "bringing up to date." A staid, Latin rite, a universal church growing irrelevant to many in a modern world, was launched on a remarkable makeover, ready or not.

Mass in English was only the beginning of the reforms. Priests who once wore mystical Middle Age vestments on high altars turned to face us, wearing simpler albs and stoles. Gone were those pulpits with winding staircases to heaven, replaced by simpler lecterns closer to the faithful. Gone too was the communion rail separating clergy and laity. Hollywood still likes to portray the dark confessional as the norm despite for decades there being bright,

---

9 Vatican 11 Documents, *Joy and Hope, A Pastoral Constitution on the Church in the Modern World*, December 7, 1965, https://www.vatican.va/archive/hist_councils/ ii_vatican_council/documents/vat-ii_const_19651207_gaudium-et-spes_en.html.

larger rooms of reconciliation as penitents chose either to kneel behind a screen inside the room or walk around to sit across from the priest. The fear-based catechism was rewritten to teach a "Come to the Father" loving God. There was still no "Come to the Mother" catechism.

Dig deeper, and there were blueprints for understanding that we, the people, were the church, far more so than The Pro's limestone. Flowing from our baptism was this universal call to holiness. Our mission was to share this good news to the world, to do justice, with special attention to the poor. I liked what I was hearing. My parents embraced the changes. To his usher and greeter roles, Dad became a reader, Minister of Communion, and parish councillor. Some women read or gave Communion and became parish councillors. Still, this was a predominantly male world.

Carter had this habit of wrapping one arm around the lectern, leaning towards the congregation as he preached. What he was sharing seemed important. We felt important. Carter held back little, enthused by the renewal and yet aware of opposition ahead. Change can be difficult. We may all be the church, but not all Curia and clergy had plans to share their power any time soon. Some Catholics preferred their religion exclusively other-worldly. Some preferred Latin and other traditions that had defined Catholics all their lives. I was gagging on the incense, pleased at a "more worldly" church.

In North Bay, churches opened a home for unwed mothers and a clothing store for the poor. Carter established a mission link with a diocese of Gualan in Guatemala, diocesan priests becoming missionaries. Carter began a popular New Year's levee, cocktail parties, really, for people from different religions to mix socially. The drinks loosened tongues. My happy father arrived home from these levees, smiling and heading early to bed. There were interfaith prayer services and an earth-shattering exchange of pulpits with Protestant clergy. Some Catholics applauded. A few covered their ears. I was learning no one church had a monopoly on God.

Encouraged by two priests, Chester Warenda and Don Orendorff, Carter initiated a permanent diaconate for men. The married deacons preached, officiated at weddings, and worked at soup kitchens, matrimonial tribunals, and jails. Carter created a novel Diocesan Order of Women (DOW) to train leaders. It was his legitimate effort within the constraints of church law to implement a new and vital role for women. In doing so, he reached back to an early church served by deacons and deaconesses. Mandated women might offer sacramental programs, marriage courses, serve in liturgies, and other pastoral care. In reply to a woman asking about women deacons again, Carter said, "that participation of the restoration of the diaconate would also bear out the wish of the Council that women take their proper place as first-class members and with full equity."[10] Within a decade, there were one hundred permanent deacons and sixty DOW ministers. However, Carter's successors folded the DOW women ministers into a new Diocesan Order of Service that included men. As conservative theology resurfaced, the entire ministry program was shelved even though those already ordained or mandated still serve. Enough other bishops resisted Carter's progressive ideas.

With First Nations reserves throughout the north, Carter began handling the "native parishes"[1] as they were called then independently from French and English diocesan sectors. He supported the establishment of a spiritual centre the Jesuits opened at Anderson Lake near Manitoulin Island. Carter called for married Indigenous deacons because celibacy was foreign to their culture. A married Indigenous deacon would be respected in his community. Carter made this demand in vain for his entire time as bishop. In his memoir, Carter repeated comments he had made at the pre-Vatican Council International Commission on the Laity. He shared his frustration at how slow the church was in dealing with priest-less parishes. "We are afraid, scared stiff in fact, of the laity and we do not want to allow them, in any way, shape or form, to share in any creative action in the church. They are there to listen and to obey. This will not do."[11]

"This will not do, Claire."

"Wasn't this reform supposed to happen everywhere in the church?"

"Yes, and no. The English language, interior architecture, and catechism changes were happening in most dioceses. It was left to individual bishops to apply the Council's provisions, and some did so only partially or minimally."

---

10 Alexander Carter, *A Canadian Bishop's Memoirs* (Crystal Falls, ON: Tomiko Publications, 1994) 235-237.

11 Ibid., Carter, 167.

I need to say here, though, that there were other files on the bishop's desk that I would not hear about for almost half a century.

"Claire, we will get to them."

I counted my blessings for living this early Vatican II era in the north. As high school students, we hung on every word of Carter's homily at a school Mass, knowing what was coming, his signature announcement that school was done for the day. Once, we gasped when he finished speaking without saying anything. He walked five feet away from the pulpit, turned, grinned mischievously, and returned to ask us if he had forgotten something. We cheered lustily. The teachers might have cheered the loudest.

At sixteen, I joined forty-five altar boys who travelled with Father Raymond Van Berkel and Scollard Hall teacher, Jim Mallory, to Expo 67 in Montréal for the World Fair, which proved to be a high point of Canada's Centennial celebrations.

These are good memories. My faith had a home while I was still chasing normal.

CHAPTER 7

Playboy Magazine

My Uncle Bill Stotesbury was my favourite uncle even before I discovered his pile of *Playboy* magazines in the bathroom of his home in North Bay. Bill and his wife, Dorothy, Dad's older sister, operated a cottage tourist business on Lake Nipissing. Bill and Dorothy were first cousins as their moms were sisters. They had been forbidden to marry in the Catholic Church, but hey, love is love, and a wise priest once blessed them in a sacristy.

Uncle Bill Stotesbury, sailor, cigars, Manhattans, and stories.

Their cottages were a kids' mecca. Bill's howling basset hounds—Ralph, Brutus, and Leslie—chased us forever around the cottages.

Late afternoons, after 5:00 p.m., Bill smoked his cigar with a Manhattan drink in his hand. Of course, those happy hour(s), often with my parents, capped the hard work of cleaning the cottages, servicing the rental boats, and acting as a fishing guide. As a young boy, I stood eye to eye with the fish being fileted, their scales raining down on me.

Bill was a character. Imagine a roguish, swashbuckling pirate. Epic in our childhoods was his ever-changing story on how he lost his index trigger finger. Cue the *Jaws* music.

Bill, an American, had joined the U.S. Navy in WWII. He fought in the South Pacific on the USS *Renshaw,* a PT boat, the PT standing for the fast patrol torpedo boats, the kind President Kennedy served on. Bill told Ben, Marty's youngest and one of his great-nephews, how he had lost his fingertip, which he said happened after a torpedo hit the boat, ripping a hole in its side. Bill recounted how he put his arm through the gaping hole to save the boat when a shark bit his finger off. This might have been Ben's first encounter with fake news or BS news, also known as Bill Stotesbury storytelling. Bill had learned a thing or two as the son and grandson of the vaudeville actors in the Prashaw-Stotesbury-Harry Lindley ancestry.

Brian, Margie's son, heard that, yes, Bill's heroism saved the ship, but it was the torpedo that had blown the finger tip off. Brian needed a few years to reflect on how Bill managed to emerge unscathed from the torpedo, except for the lost end of a digit. A third version was told to his brother, Brendan: Bill with other seamen had lifted an engine to a dock when a cable broke, and the engine crushed his finger.

We went with the *Jaws* and torpedo story.

Bill took a pass on church religion when a priest told him that his basset hounds were not going to heaven. Later, as a young priest, I reassured Bill that his basset hounds were indeed now in heaven and that the odds were good for him too. I prayed for the soul of the mistaken priest. Bill's obituary in 2005 noted, "he believed in the Great Spirit, and lived by the Native American credo, take only what you need."

I discovered those *Playboys* as a young teenager. Bill had them piled beside the toilet in his bathroom, the current issue on top. I spent a great deal of time going to the bathroom at Bill's house then, unrivalled until my senior years. There came the day I wanted my own *Playboy.* I was sixteen.

How do I do this? I was small for my age. I could not fake being an adult. I did not know any delinquents. So, I did the next best thing. I stole a *Playboy* magazine from McKerrow Pharmacy at the Hillside Plaza on Jane Street in North Bay. McKerrow's was on my walk home from school.

Bless me, Father, for I have sinned!

This capital offence, not to mention "grave sin of lust," might damn me to the hottest room in hell for reasons not immediately evident. That I stole a *Playboy*, even in my adolescent Catholic morality, was the least of my problems.

"Claire, I am glad Cruz is upstairs on the phone with his friends. Among my groaning list of questions to ask the omniscient and omnipotent God someday when we meet up, 'What possibly possessed you to give adolescent teens those raging hormones at that early age?' Their interest in sex, climaxing early when it's erotic, illicit, and so everything. Is this your chaos theory, God? Why not at twenty-five, as some parents pined for their teens, not, of course, that age for themselves? Were you having a bad day? Divine comedy? Revenge for Adam and Eve eating the apple?"

"Uncle Rick, the *Playboy* story, please," pleaded Claire.

Right. Wilf McKerrow owned McKerrow Pharmacy. His family lived four doors down from my house in Pinewood neighbourhood.

Jesus, kid.

They were our neighbours, for God's sake. So, while one might be distracted by the skin magazine I took, my real crime was stealing from my neighbour. Worse, Wilf, and his wife, were my parents' friends. The adrenalin rush from the snatch and grab of Hugh Heffner's *Playboy* quickly descended to the hellfire script of being caught. I imagined Dad marching me to the McKerrows for the confession, conviction, and sentencing before the public hanging at noon on the street for all to witness. Teach the children well, they would say.

I have no defence. It did not matter that, in those years, *Playboy* had only the semi-nudes that left something to a boy's imagination. I was clueless about the pornography industry. It was peeking at a tempting adulthood, the vice of sex with women dancing in my head and other body parts. And, no, I did not want to read those great *Playboy* articles.

No, stealing from Wilf, our neighbour and parents' friend, was the crime of the century and the real violation of God's Ten Commandments. From a good Catholic upbringing, I figured I had broken three of God's biggies.

Thou shall not steal. The Seventh Commandment, for sure.

I broke Commandments Four and Ten too!

Honour thy father and thy mother. Ouch!

Thou shall not covet your neighbour's goods.

Three strikes. I was damned. No friend had dared me. There was no plan, no accomplice, no getaway bike. I had entered the pharmacy after school, cased the joint, waited for Wilf to turn his back to fill a prescription, grabbed the *Playboy*, and stuffed it down the front of my yellow gold Scollard shirt.

Did stuffing a *Playboy* down a Catholic uniform break another commandment?

I beat it for the exit. There were no sirens nor barcodes in those days. I ran all the way home, half scared and half excited. I went downstairs to my bedroom, flipping through the *Playboy*, feeling I had taken a time machine to adulthood. I was impressed.

What was I to do with the stolen goods? I stashed the *Playboy* in our pullout couch in the basement recreation room. It stayed there for three weeks, with more pull-outs, so to speak, for a fleeting moment of pleasure.

I swear I must have wanted to get caught; Catholic guilt had now ruined the fun. At the time, I was Wilf's *Nugget* newspaper carrier. I had to face my victim once a week to collect money. My restorative justice work was decades away, so it never crossed my mind to wave the collection the next few times, a surreptitiously quid-pro-quo settling of accounts. No, I took Wilf's money, eyes downcast, a shuffling of feet, and a quick goodbye.

About three weeks later, I threw the *Playboy* out. Uncle Bill's magazines were at his cottages.

Wilf, I am hardly sorry!

Heartily!

CHAPTER 8

God is Calling Me

1975

Beware the white lie!

At least, the white lie wrecking life's plans I had carved in stone. I told such a lie to my night editor at the *Vancouver Sun* one spring day. I suspect my patient God slipped through this slight crack to choreograph my call to the priesthood.

A year into coming west to be a reporter, I was on the night shift along with other young journalists like Rod Mickleburgh and Vaughn Palmer, who were both destined for successful careers in the newsroom. Life was good. The west coast was paradise. For a recent Journalism school graduate, it was heavenly. I could not be happier!

After my move west, I had met a maternal cousin, Tony Formby. I did not know this west coast family that shared Mom's Cape Breton ancestry. Tony's and my maternal grandparents were siblings, making us second cousins. Formby called asking if I was interested in joining him in a drive to Seattle the next day for an appointment he had with our mutual cousin, Father Barry Ashwell. Barry was my first cousin, the son of Mom's sister, Marg. He was another cousin I did not know well.

Formby needed to talk to Ashwell about his upcoming wedding and fill out the paperwork; he wanted company for the two-hour drive. I was scheduled to work that next day but the lure of Seattle, a day with cousins, a meal together, tempted me. So, I picked up the phone and told my editor I was not feeling well.

Simple, no?

All went smoothly until we walked into Barry's office. Once the small talk ended, I made a move for the door, knowing the cousins had their wedding business to conduct. Barry blocked the exit. He said he might as well "kill two birds with one stone," that, down the road, I might come there for my own marriage preparation. I should know what the church expected. So, Barry poured me a scotch on the rocks and motioned me to a chair in the corner.

As my cousins spoke, God stormed into the room. In a flash, it became overwhelmingly crystal clear that I was here on this Earth to do what Barry was doing in this room in ministry, to be a priest. A voice. A clear Mount Sinai thunderbolt.

God, this was not why I had come to Seattle! It was only a white lie!

Most vocation calls I know develop slowly, more naturally over many years. There are no words to do justice to what happened there. I did not hear trumpets nor any thunderclap, but the effect was as if I had. Eyes, heart, and soul were opened. Ripped open. They were on paperwork while I, for the first time, was sensing the divine energy in the room, a God inviting me to serve as a priest. Words do not come easy. So clear, so certain were the feelings that stirred inside; this instantaneous calling would overcome rocky times ahead. No matter the later trials, temptations, and vocation crisis, I never once doubted the veracity of what happened in that Seattle rectory.

God wanted me to be a priest. A call so powerful it erased forever a newspaper career planned for over fifteen years.

Oh my God!

Shit.

"Claire, I had no steady girlfriend, yet I liked girls. Cruz, the only 'Father' title I wanted was being a real-life father to my kids."

God wanted me to be a priest. No kids of my own?

I was a journalist bent on a long career. And yet, in a matter of minutes, my life had a new purpose. It was this falling in love, seeing the girl or the guy who instantly entraps you, smitten with that one look. But Jesus, this girl was no one I had imagined—this God of mine, this Holy Mother Church. For the rest of the appointment, I did not hear a single word of what they were saying. I do recall God vividly revealing my vocation. My head and heart were spinning!

Of course, I did what any red-blooded, young Canadian lad might do. I ran in the opposite direction. The prophet, Jonah, would become my special Old Testament hero—thinking God was nuts to ask him to preach to a pagan Nineveh, he had headed far away before, as the allegory recounts, a whale swallowed him. Full denial on this vocation for now. There would be no immediate divulging to either Barry, or Tony on the way home, what had happened in that office. We went out for a meal, and then Tony and I returned to Canada. This was my secret.

Was it the scotch speaking? One drink. I don't think so.

Back across the border, I steered clear of whales and burrowed myself deeper into the newsroom, my first love. I forcibly ignored what had happened. I partied. Still, bit by bit, in the days and weeks to come, the call seeped into my thoughts. I started attending daily Mass at Star of the Sea Church in White Rock. I began reading a Bible in earnest. I prayed more than I had.

And, of course, the call being so dramatic, God could wait a bit longer. I sank myself into writing news stories and drinking with buddies. Weeks later, I summonsed up the courage one morning after Mass to speak with the Star of the Sea pastor. He appeared non-plussed with my front-page news. And he had peculiar questions too.

Did I want to be a religious priest? Weren't they all? He was referring to religious orders, living in a community instead of in a diocese, men who took additional vows of poverty, chastity, and obedience. I had known Congregation of the Resurrection priests at Scollard Hall.

And where did I want to study for the priesthood, at a seminary in the west or in Ontario? That might determine which diocese I serve. Daily Mass, talks, and prayer convinced me that life was unalterably changing. And, as shocking as it all was, the calling was undeniably anchored deep in a lifelong RC family life steeped in prayers, good priests who were guests for supper, priests I had met who, as friends of my parents, had an authentic side—their sports teams, humour, some who liked their scotch. It was not so mysterious, not a jumping off the cliff, not yet at least.

Eventually, I broke the news to my night editor, Bruce Smillie. He was known as Mr. Nightside. Later, Palmer would write an obituary where he characterized Smillie perfectly. "At a time when people were still throwing typewriters and screaming at each other in the newsroom in those days. It wasn't exactly the pinnacle of kinder, gentler human-resources relations, Smillie succeeded in herding a motley collection of young, aspiring journalists."[12]

Smillie was a devout Catholic, father of seven kids. He was delighted with my news. We had good talks before I left.

I wrote Bishop Carter. As magnificent as those Rockies and Pacific Ocean were, I chose to begin studies for priesthood for my home diocese. I called my parents. My father and mother were delighted, although I suspect it was my father who did a fist pump after our call, he the closet priest, his parish a second home. My parents, Marty, and Jude drove to the west coast for a vacation. Mom and Dad returned home through Canada with my worldly belongings in their trailer. Meanwhile, Marty, Jude, and I headed back to London via a holiday odyssey through the United States.

God wanted me to be a priest, notwithstanding the white lies, straps, family fights, *Playboy* magazines, the parties, and all.

God knows best, right?[13]

---

12 John Mackie, "They Called Him Mr. Nightside: Former Vancouver Sun Editor, Bruce Smillie, passes away," *Vancouver Sun*, Jan. 17, 2018, https://vancouversun.com/news/local-news/they-called-him-mr-nightside.

13 Barry Ashwell would face several allegations of abusing boys. A victims' organization notes the Archdiocese of Seattle settled numerous claims in the millions of dollars. Ashwell denied all abuse. There appear to be no criminal charges against him. The diocese defrocked him. Before any of this broke, I would see my cousin again at Sister Sarah Ann Beaton's one hundredth birthday when Barry and I co-celebrated wearing the Beaton tartan. I comment on clergy abuse in Chapter 31.

CHAPTER 9

Road Trip to St. Peter's Seminary

If ever I needed a map to frame my crooked, straight journey to heaven's doors, it was this road trip. We headed south to California, east to Las Vegas, Texas, New Orleans, north to Chicago, and then over to the Windsor-Detroit border. A final, hellacious hurrah before God snared me at the seminary.

Three moments of "faith" grounded the trip.

Jude's Prayer

We were to meet Mom's cousins in Riverside, California, near Los Angeles. After that visit, my bright yellow Pontiac Astre, "no guts, no glory," conked out on a California freeway. With the hood up and the three of us staring incomprehensibly at the engine, Jude vowed to stop drinking if God jump-started the car. This was a peculiar piety that, thank God, I never embraced.

VA-ROOM!

Jesus!

The roar of the four-cylinder engine was deafening. Marty and I threw a shocked look at Jude, who solemnly returned to the back seat. Astonishingly, she kept her sombre, sobriety vow for the entire trip, sliding into what her brothers remember as a crabby, cantankerous teetotaler. As a true Prashaw, Jude remembers it differently. At a Vegas Wayne Newton show, when Jude declined her three drinks that came with the ticket, I kicked her under the table and told the waiter to bring HER two Black Russians (my drink) and a scotch (for Marty) to add to our own three drinks.

Dad's Dad

I had asked Dad if he would be okay if the three of us visited Plano, Texas, where we had learned his father lived, a respectable judge no less. Dad said we could do what we want and, revealing more, he asked us to take a picture.

In Plano, without any real plan, we found Cecil J. Prashaw's name in the phone book. We flipped a coin to see who called this grandfather we never knew. I lost. I dialled the number.

"(Deep breath) Mr. Prashaw, my name is Rick Prashaw. I am travelling through the United States with my brother, Marty, and sister, Jude. My dad is Dick Prashaw, your son, I believe. You are our grandfather."

BOOM! Silence. I repeated my exact words a second time, explaining who we were and how we hoped to see him. Again, silence.

What the hell!

Did he fear his inheritance to his Texas family vanishing? His second wife had

died, but their daughter and her family lived in the area. Finally, mustering a smidgen of Texas hospitality, he welcomed us and again asked me to repeat who I was. Man, was this some deep suppression of his fathering three kids when he was seventeen, nineteen, and twenty-three, the second my dad, while their vaudeville troupe toured Canada and the United States? He corrected us that he was a

The 70s—long hair and rock-n-roll

"Pray-shaw," not Pra-shaw. This was the American pronunciation. He did say we could drop by.

When he opened the door, we were dumbfounded. There stood my dad, twenty years older. Cecil was a spitting image—same size, face, nose, a crewcut with grey hair. This is the face I am becoming. People say I look so much like my dad. My grandfather too!

Cecil was hospitable. On his office wall were dozens of plaques and awards for a career as a judge, work in the community, and work for the Republican Party. He was curious about our trip and our lives. He graciously bought us a meal. However, he never once asked about his son, our father. Now that I had met my grandfather, could I hate him too? Did Dad even hate his father? We never knew Dad's true feelings.

We were subjected to his Republican, Texas, and conservative rant on young people—their long hair, politics, and aimlessness.

God help any young offender in his courtroom!

My long, west coast hair had not yet been shorn.

"Fucking unbelievable," I muttered to myself.

Sir, can we talk about your youth?

I swear blood was trickling from my lips. I shot a side eyeroll at my brother. Marty gave me a "shut up, Rick" look. I reluctantly decided to behave.

We took the picture and left town. Cecil died three years later. That fall, the next time I visited North Bay, I handed Dad the photo. He looked at his dad and said nothing. I do not know what he did with that picture. The feelings, pain, and disdain, if any, must have bunkered deep into a vault.

"Claire and Cruz, another reason I believe in heaven is to sort out life's relationships unfinished or broken. I wonder how Dad and Cecil are doing. I want to believe they are talking."

Chicago Exit

The road trip zigzagged on to jazz clubs in New Orleans, then to Cousin Mary Anne White and Bob Nelms home, and a barber in Tulsa. His shears produced a Bible Belt crew cut. Cecil would have approved. With Jude still not drinking, it was getting miserable in the car. On a Chicago turnpike, Marty and I had enough. We pulled over and suggested Jude get out. Jude had this stubborn streak. So did we. She obliged, and we took off for Canada. About a half-hour later, Marty and I started thinking about how our parents might react to the news that we had ditched their daughter on a Chicago freeway. We went back to retrieve her. She had not moved.

"Poor Jude. Abandoned by her brothers." Claire said. "I'll get her version of this trip when the borders open up again."

I had no clue yet how influential Chicago would be in my faith journey ahead. It would become a watering hole for yearly conferences as a priest. It would be where, one day, I sealed my love for a lady.

This road trip was over. I was ready for the adventure of studies for the Catholic priesthood.

CHAPTER 10

Seminary, Celibacy, and Sex

1975-1980

That September, I arrived at St. Peter's Seminary. I returned to my birthplace, London, the Forest City, home to insurance companies and the University of Western Ontario (UWO), a place and people more conservative than the north. London is where I had spent the first nine years of my life. I did not look up Sister Saint Something or Other.

I was twenty-four years old.

It was the best of times with only vague hints of the dark shadows dancing in this English gothic building. The seminary adjacent to Kings College and near the UWO main campus looked Medieval European—English monastic arches, fortress wooden centre doors, a St. Thomas Chapel with a majestic nave, its Corinthian columns, and a spacious sanctuary. I settled in to pursue studies on God, the Bible, theology and, as it turned out, me!

God wanted me here, dramatic call and all. I answered that call. Now there would be further formation, a definitive answer whether I wanted to be a priest. Did the seminary want me to be a priest? What about this call to celibacy? My teen years had been more being chased than chaste.

The transition was surprisingly easy. Once I aligned the calling to my Prashaw and Roman Catholic upbringing, the suit fit, made to measure as it were. As I was only one year from Carleton, it was easy hitting the books again. I did a make-up philosophy year before beginning four years of theology—classes in dogma, scripture, church history, sacraments, liturgy, pastoral ministries, homiletics, among others.

I learned the philosophical proofs for the existence of God as First Cause Uncaused, First Mover Unmoved. Go back in time, and the philosophers found a way to deify the origins of the universe. Even a case could be made that a Divine Being generated the chaos some credit for how we landed here. First chaos uncaused!

"Claire, frankly, those classroom proofs belonged in a parlour with cigars and brandy. It was mildly engaging. On the other hand, there was Woody Allen's excellent idea of becoming a believer by God making a large deposit in a Swiss bank in Allen's name."

"Bahahaha. A million dollars would crush all my doubts," Claire exclaimed.

"Seriously, Claire, First Mover Unmoved did not move me as much as experiencing a God who is Love."

Indeed, rational, logical thinking could only take me so far. There were other beliefs to ponder, like this breath-taking claim that we who are but a tiny blip on the scale of the cosmos would be considered important enough to warrant a word or two from God. In a Christian tradition, to attest to a God in the flesh, Jesus, a God so desiring intimacy with us that he would become one with us and die for us on the cross. Now, that is quite the leap in faith. I didn't pretend, nor need then, to have God all figured out. My faith was beyond petri dishes or microscopes conducting experiments on whether God existed. My studies here would help me own what Dick Prashaw and Gert Beaton believed, even if not continuing all their dated devotions or rituals. I believed in a God who made heaven and earth. I believed this God's love was bigger than any sins. I believed in Jesus' resurrection and ours, that there would be life after death, somewhere, somehow. I believed in grace, which for me, was another word for love. And that grace wins in the end. As a cradle Catholic, my faith seeped through a long flow of Eucharists, confessions, sacraments, priests, nuns, popes, saints and prayers. I could bow to mystery and impenetrable truths like the three-in-one Trinity God, the quirky details on the virgin birth, or a bodily resurrection, and everlasting life, wherever, whatever. This took me beyond the mind, but not yet to anything I deemed stupid or utterly illogical. I was slowly coming to a comfortable place, acknowledging that there was a God, and I wasn't it. This last revelation—that I was not God—seemed obvious and yet would be vital later in priest years caught up in debates on who was worthy, and not, to receive Communion.

I breezed through a recitation of the Creed, not yet stumbling over the reference to God as only a Father, or this exclusive membership and salvation in a Holy Roman Catholic Church. Frankly, all arguments for God were to be road tested one day as I listened to tragedy after tragedy from parishioners asking why bad things happened to good people. The suffering of good people merited discussion, but strangely then, and now, it was not a dealbreaker for my own profession of faith. It helped to witness to a God in Jesus who redeemed the suffering by his own suffering. One day, that thorny issue would become personal in Adam's tragedy. I have lived that question on suffering more than ever answer it. I still ask it. I suspect I will ask it until the day I die.

There were favourite teachers like Joan Lenardon, a classy scholar with impeccable diction, breathing life into the history of the church. I took notes on the gnostic gospels discovered with the Dead Sea Scrolls that captured other words of Jesus that never made it into the Bible; the early centuries with married clergy; the slow evolution from the band of disciples Jesus left to the formal organization and institution of a Catholic Church centuries later. I relished a social justice class taught by Father Mike Ryan, its themes on justice, peace, and liberation as constitutive parts of the gospel. It did not seem to be a favourite course for many seminarians.

I had not been in a dorm since my second year at Carleton. This was not the fifth floor of Glengarry! There were no women on the floors, obviously, save for the rare Open House Sundays to welcome family and guests. There was no alcohol on the floor, although we drank at pubs and at the fall retreats at cottages as we befriended one another. In those days, the seminary was full, with about one hundred seminarians living on three floors above the main floor. We were divided into seven alphabetical groups, each with its own spiritual director, a tv lounge, and a common phone cubicle. I was on the top floor in Group F, F Troop. An affable Father Jack Flaherty lived with us as our spiritual director. I met with him about once a month or whenever the need surfaced. He was my confessor, the person on faculty to bless a recommendation to be ordained.

Personally, it was the best of times—new friends from across the country, passable dormitory food; we students sat by ourselves while faculty had their own table. Like Carleton, my personality drew me to different tables and conversations. I settled in comfortably with those I subconsciously branded as "normal", i.e., not incessantly quoting scripture or engaged in pope talk over the pizza. I found a good routine in the classes, spiritual lectures, and the rhythms of daily prayer, the praying of the *Divine Office of the Church* or *Liturgy of the Hours*—psalms, scriptures, hymns—at different times of the day. We celebrated Eucharist in the afternoon. I was grateful for hockey on Thursdays, a tennis court in the back, and squash games to book at the UWO gym.

Classes were either right at St. Peter's or, better, at Kings College or Brescia College across the UWO campus where, again, thank you, God, there would be young women. Squash games with my favourite female opponent and those classes away from the seminary served as a vaccine against this dominant male, clerical world I had joined. Had I clicked my heels in Vancouver and ended in Kansas?

"Claire, it all appeared normal then. Telling it now, I shake my head."

"Not my normal ever," Claire winked.

For Sunday liturgy, we invited guests to attend Eucharist and a special brunch. Interestingly, the guys invited mostly women friends. I had not grasped the seriousness of this gender inequity. The rector, Fr. J.J. Carrigan, sure had. Carrigan resembled one of those Mt. Rushmore presidents who had come down from the mountain and into St. Peter's Seminary as the rector. We referred to him as "The J." His chiselled, Lincolnesque, granite face and ramrod posture suited the office he held. As a former World War II chaplain, he fit effortlessly into the divine chain of command from God to pope to bishop to rector to our motley crew of enlisted men needing to be whipped into shape. Beyond his severe look, I spotted an Irish farmer's face lined with gentleness. In the sanctuary of his office, he smoked cigars. Yes, I had a soft spot for Carrigan even though we were destined to cross swords.

At one spiritual lecture, the rector addressed the disproportionate female-male ratio at Sunday Mass.

"Gentlemen, last week at Sunday Eucharist, there were eighty-six guests and all but four of them women," he said, his finger characteristically rubbing inside his collar. "Now, don't get me wrong. I was not counting (muffled laughter). It's worth thinking about why we would have so many women at Sunday Mass."

I whispered to a friend beside me, "Who in hell had invited the four guys?"

At one Sunday liturgy, my sister, Pati, nineteen then, was a visitor. Casting her eyes on dozens of guys prepping for a chaste, celibate life, a few she described as "hot" caught her eye.

"God, what a waste!" she exclaimed.

"You go, Pati! My thoughts exactly," Claire shouted.

Thursdays after hockey, the theology students settled into spiritual lectures before Mass. Sex and celibacy were talked about a lot, mostly in a circumvent Catholic kind of way. We were told to avoid "the danger of the second look at a woman." Father Pat Cavanagh, a wonderful man from Thessalon in my diocese, explained that, as celibates, we might be on thin ice if we looked at a girl a second time. The danger of breaking a fast is looking at the menu for too long.

Jesus.

I raised my hand.

"Father, is it all right to keep looking at her the first time?"

The guys laughed. Father Pat now knew I was from Northern Ontario.

I was not hearing any talk about looking at a guy even once. Still, there was code for that lecture too. We were admonished not to have any "particular friend" in the seminary; I struggled to imagine what that extraterrestrial creature might look like. They were concerned about exclusivity, meaning that, when we only spent time with certain persons or groups, as in one guy, then we were not open to minister to all God's people.

Really?

This was not anything remotely human as far as I could make out. The real fear, I suspect, is what two guys might do, "exclusively." In visits to a seminarian's room, it was advised we leave the door open. I was far from naïve entering the seminary at twenty-four, the Carleton years and newsrooms under, or was it, below my belt. Still, I was astonished that at least half the seminarians had no real-life or work experiences, arriving directly from high school to junior seminaries to St. Peter's. It might be a place for noble higher learning and contemplating life-long commitments, but there was no inoculating us from nature or hormones. Thankfully, castration had been abolished in the Middle Ages.

I ignored some counsel. My "particular friend" was Ray Renaud from Windsor. We closed our doors for long talks into the night, legitimate intimacies of a deep friendship, humour, sports, and, best of all, visits to Renaud's family on Jefferson Ave. in Windsor on free weekends once a month. There, I revelled in a welcomed, normal respite; Ray's ten brothers and sisters living their special calling to test seminarians with their flirting, swearing, dirty jokes, and all-around mischief. Apparently, I passed their trial by ordeal with flying colours. The Renaud's blessed my readiness for ordination. The seminary, not so fast. I loved Ray. He would die from cancer while a priest, before he was fifty years old.

I was noticing the round-about way sex was addressed. Of course, the seminary was not unique in this regard. I never had a sex talk from Dad other than his vague references to respect girls. On a visit home from Carleton once, Dad had overheard me in a bedroom singing this refrain from a racy song his fellow soldiers likely sang in Italy.

Roll me over in the clover, roll me over, lay me down and do it again.[14]

Dad knocked on the door, asked me what I was singing, and laughed. Mom, who cleaned my sheets, sat on the end of my bed one night to talk about sex. I regret cutting her off, my embarrassment ending a better sex education than I had learned in *Playboys* and locker rooms.

14 Anthony Hopkins, *Songs from the Front & Rear: Canadian Servicemen's Songs of the Second World War* (Edmonton: Hurtig, 1979).

"Particular friendship" appeared to be a mistrust and fear of sexuality. Sex was the "elephant in the room" all the years in the seminary. Slowly, I stumbled on a darker side to this holy place. At the back of the seminary, a well-known window was left open if you happened to be out late at night past a 11:00 p.m. curfew. That might happen on occasion, a pub visit, or late-night pizza and walk. We could unlock the side door, but that meant walking directly by Carrigan's apartment. So, this one night, unlike other jumps from the window to the floor, I landed squarely on two guys locked in a passionate, feverish embrace. They moaned, swore, and stood up in the darkness while I darted to my room, not keen to know their identities for when I looked across the chapel tomorrow at morning prayer.

Apparently, God was calling gay men to serve as well. That was fine with me. I assumed they, too, were assessing their potential to live a celibate life as a Catholic priest. The seminary could be a "figuring out" place. Formation went well beyond celibacy. Spiritual directors assessed maturity, grace, intellectual and spirituality strengths, holiness, and temperament. I remember an ink spot test. I wish there had been more tests on love, compassion, and kindness than this apparent fixation on sexual temptation. In fairness, my seminary years were long ago, and I have heard of additional spiritual and human formation programs in seminaries. May they err on the side of love, justice, and compassion.

As smart as I thought I was, as good as my course marks were, I had life lessons to learn. There were unknown prejudices, ignorance, fears, and biases to recognize and change. I had typical, clueless stereotypes and caricatures on gay guys, suspecting mostly effeminate appearances, high pitch voices, an unmanly walk, would out them. Who knew I was playing hockey with gay men on Thursdays? I was naïve and apparently content to be so. At Scollard Hall high school, I had walked every day to classes with a good friend, deep in conversation, that type of adolescent friendship where we talked about everything and solved all the world's problems. Except, it turns out we didn't talk about everything. Michael was also gay. I didn't know. We would talk about everything decades later when I visited Michael Saya-Moore and his husband in Vancouver.

After ordination, I became aware of the number of gay men as priests, in some dioceses and cities, even a gay subculture; one substantial American study in 2000 estimated about fifty-eight percent of priests were homosexual, with even higher percentages among younger priests.[15] From those years at St. Peter's, I appreciated how the seminary might not be the safest or healthiest place for a gay man to be who he was, or openly explore his vocation. One might rather memorize the answers that kept him in the seminary. Again, the Catholic Church was not the only institution wary of any real exploration of a recruit's vulnerabilities, addictions, and troubled pasts. *Don't ask, don't tell* were commandments elsewhere.

No sir, no medical issues.

No, sir, there's no one in my family with depression. I am in perfect condition.

Want to be kicked out? Talk about your sessions with a therapist. There are stories I've heard from friends in the military or police.

"Custody of the eyes" was another spiritual lecture. "Eyes forward, men!" This ran counter to my emerging Original Blessing inclination to praise the Creator for beauty in all its shapes and forms, women included.

God, are you certain you called me? Was my Seattle calling a wrong number? I may subconsciously have been looking for a faculty invitation to leave. None ever came. Carrigan warned us not to kiss a woman full on the lips.

Seriously?

Throughout my five years at St. Peter's, I craved normal. That meant regular escapes to my sister, Margie, and her husband, Jerry O'Connor, living on Hill St. in London South with Colin and Kevin, the first two of six children. I had chosen St. Peter's over seminaries in Toronto and Ottawa partly because of my sister. Bishop Carter agreed this was a wise consideration. Over the years, as the seminary drove me crazy from time to time, a visit with the O'Connors was good medicine. Food, family talk, wrestling, and pillow fights with their boys. It was a habit I would continue as a young priest. Head to families, many with children, play on the floor or in the backyard with them. A feast

---

15 Donald Cozzens, *The Changing Face of the Priesthood* (Collegeville, MN: The Liturgical Press, 2000), 83-91.

for an arid, childless celibate life. It worked for sixteen years in the seminary and priesthood. Pour me another scotch.

Margie and Jerry belonged to a Christian community founded by Father Marcel Gervais who was director of Divine Word Centre. Gervais, an Old Testament scholar, taught a splendid biblical studies course. I was inspired to hear the command of the prophet, Micah, to "do justice, and to love kindness, and to walk humbly with your God (Mic: 6-8)." Scripture was inspired and to be taken seriously, but not literally. There is a cultural, literary, and historical context to consider for Christians, an Old Testament to be reinterpreted by Jesus' words. Those lessons would prove valuable later as Adam's dad when we faced down Bible-quoting damnation. At Divine Word, I inhaled public lectures that breathed life into Father Ryan's social justice course. Peruvian theologian Gustavo Gutiérrez[16] shared a powerful liberation theology founded on a God who heard the cry of the poor. Father Carroll Stuhlmueller, a Passionist priest and Scripture scholar from Catholic Theological Union (Chicago), translated inspired, ancient words to the streets and real lives. He may have been the first priest I heard call for ordaining women. Bob Fox, a priest, spoke on his ministry on the streets of Harlem. Topping off St. Peter's studies, I was immersing myself in a faith that demanded authentic action and witness, with solidarity to all suffering.

Margie's community was a seminarian oasis for community liturgies and St. Mary's Church pub nights.

I established a permanent study desk near the back of the library. Margie had taken theology courses as a laywoman here, pausing her library studies to toss jujubes at a cute boy who was studiously buried in his books. Yes, Jerry O'Connor, a lay student, and her future husband. Jujubes, specifically Canadian sour jujubes, are a longstanding communion in the Prashaw-O'Connor family.

I grew in my faith. I returned to the practice of confession or the Sacrament of Reconciliation as it was now called. Long ago, as young boys, we had lined up nervously on Saturday mornings to confess our sins. It was now an adult

---

16 Gustavo Gutiérrez, *A Theology of Liberation: History, Politics, Salvation* (Ossining, NY: Orbis Books, 1988, first published in 1971).

experience, face-to-face conversations that broke out of the childhood list of sins to exploring God's blessings and our struggles to live the gospel and this celibate life. I relied on God's mercy. It was liberating, new adult lessons in healing and being loved.

Carter visited us occasionally, and we hoped that he would take his seminarians out for supper. He usually obliged. Carter seemed a favourite among the visiting bishops as the students appreciated his progressive views on clergy, laity, and social justice. Soon enough, a drift to a conservative church shifted the scales dramatically to orthodoxy, judgment, and a growing intolerance.

On one visit, Carter patched up an apparent crisis I was embroiled in but had hardly noticed. Early in my second year, I had joined a joint faculty-student council that oversaw regular activities and rules. This advisory body was not democratic. We were seminarians, not voting priests yet. Remember, Carrigan enjoyed the direct hotline to God. At one council meeting, we discussed whether alcohol should be allowed in our group fridges. We were adults and, with alcohol in church rectories after ordination, might it not be better to identify a problem now? I volunteered to research the issue. I mailed surveys to the bishops. They had quite the investment in their seminarians.

The first clue that this may not have been my brightest idea came when only one of about forty bishops returned their survey. Yes, Sault Ste. Marie's Carter, not his brother, the cardinal. My Bishop Carter approved of alcohol in the seminary. What I did not know was that other bishops had contacted Carrigan directly on their views on alcohol and their alarm at this upstart seminarian's survey. Apparently, I needed a refresher course on the hierarchy. Carrigan summonsed me. He mentioned the survey, the bishops' calls, their annoyance, and how this was one of his more embarrassing moments as a rector.

Really? Surely, life as a rector cannot be that dull!

I was dismissed. The subcommittee was disbanded. There would be no alcohol in our fridges.

On Carter's next visit, he had no time to join us for dinner and instead left us money to dine. As he circled the group of his six seminarians, he left me for last. Turning his back on the others, he said:

"How's it going, Rick?"

"Good, bishop. I am enjoying my studies."

"Great. By the way, if you ever are tempted to write a bishop again, write me."

He was grinning. That night, in my examination of conscience, I gave thanks for studying for the Diocese of Sault Ste. Marie. We had a *je ne sais quoi* joy, passion, and independent streak as northerners.

There were hints of troubling times ahead. News would spread about a seminarian suddenly gone. There was seldom any official explanation, more whispered conversations filled in the reasons—a sexual incident, a touching by a seminarian of another, reported to a spiritual director. There were at least three seminarians I lived with on that fourth floor who later, as priests, were jailed for abuse with young children or women. I cannot say that I would have picked them out of a line-up. And that scares me. How could I not have known? Was I blind? Were they biding their time, giving the "don't ask, don't tell" answers that might keep them there? Did priesthood change them?

"Claire, we will get to that chapter."

While I dwell on celibacy and my rudimentary sex or gender perceptions, in truth, it was in the late 1970s, and I was still in my "times of innocence." My daily calendar was filled with studies, prayers, friends, and sports. I knew God wanted me here. I did not dwell too long on how I was going to live this celibate life. There was plenty to give thanks for, a confirmed vocation, a growing faith, a strong knowledge base, and five splendid years with my London Prashaw-O'Connor family. I cherished new meditation practices, jumping into gospel scenes and stories Jesus told, countless hours of silence in the majestic beauty of the chapel, the sunlight streaming through the blue and yellow glass, my spending time with the Lord, lost in my thoughts, the knowing, liking and, yes, loving this God of mine, of ours. As useful as formula prayers might be, I preferred praying like I was talking informally to God as a friend, conversation punctuated by listening and silence. There was an abundant good happening. I had learned a great deal about myself, about different personalities and spiritual types that explained how I viewed others and the world. All in all, I liked what I saw.

Summers as a seminarian were part of the formation. In 1975, I dropped six bolts into engine blocks on the assembly line of a Windsor Ford car plant. Apparently, a machine fastens twenty bolts at once now. The money was good. More important, I confirmed this was not what I wanted to do for the rest of my life, that may have been the seminary's true goals for those jobs. I learned valuable life lessons though on blue collar workers, unions, fair wages, and safe working places. And it's good to know who is in the pews suffering through your homilies.

A second summer, I was a chaplain assistant at the Cecil Facer Youth Centre in Sudbury—teaching religion, preaching, and hanging out with young people in trouble with the law. I liked them. It felt like I was looking in the mirror as I ministered to them.

I spent six weeks improving my poor French at a UWO immersion program in Trois Pistoles, Québec. I smile, recalling Carter's answer to my question on the best way to learn French.

"Rick, the second-best way to learn French is a course," he said. "The best way you cannot do."

Damn, a summer fling with a French girlfriend would so improve my accent!

"Bien sûr, oncle Rick!" Claire laughed.

The ordination to the temporary diaconate was a quiet affair in a chapel up north. For this final year in formation, I was assigned to Father Don MacLellan in my home parish at the Pro-Cathedral. As a deacon, I could baptize, officiate at weddings, and preach. I recruited my father and others to supervise an altar boys' trip to Toronto to a Blue Jays game and the Canadian National Exhibition. There was the Challenge Summer Youth program's *Jesus Christ Superstar* production, acting as the cast's spiritual advisor, left fielder for their baseball games, dance chaperone, and fetching lumber with the stage crew.

In January 1980, I returned to the seminary for four final months. This was getting real.

PART TWO

Father Rick

CHAPTER 11

Ordination

May 9, 1980

As I lay prostrate on the carpet of a packed Pro-Cathedral, two-thousand years of Catholic tradition washed over me. The choir led the congregation in the singing of the Litany of the Saints.

"Holy Mary, Mother of God, pray for us.

"Saint Peter, pray for us.

"Saint Paul, pray for us.

"All you holy men and women, pray for us."

On and on it went, majestically through a roll call of about fifty saints.

St. Francis, help me be a simple parish priest.

It was during the litany that Pati's nursing friend, Debbie Rosenthal, "Eucharist-uterus" Debbie, wanted to rush the altar to revive me, certain I had fainted when I hit the carpet.

St. Peter was the first Bishop of Rome and, as Roman Catholics believed, a direct apostolic line to Bishop Carter. Carter imposed his hands on my head to bring me over from a deacon to priest. Dozens of priests then imposed their hands to welcome me into this mysterious club. According to Catholic teaching, I had been granted powers to change bread and wine into the Body and Blood of Christ, absolve sinners in God's name, anoint the seriously ill or dying, witness marriages, and more.

Solemn matters to most Catholics. "Hocus pocus" to some others, the magical derivative of the Latin, *Hoc est corpus*, the "This is my Body" phrase priests pronounced at the Eucharist. Everything changed at that moment. And, please, God, not too much.

"Claire and Cruz, I was now Father Rick. Still, it mattered I do my best to remain Rick."

This Catholic celibate conundrum—on the one hand, submission, "dying to self," as St. Paul extolled in his Epistles (1 Cor. 15:31), yet, on the other hand, this incarnational God declaring flesh and blood mattered. To be myself, and loyal to the church, a man of the church and yet my own man. My enduring struggle.

At twenty-eight, I sensed a profound joy to arrive at this moment, grateful for perseverance, a dedication to my faith, and a passion for building and serving in strong, inclusive communities.

As the celebration ended, Carter returned to the pulpit for a mischievous announcement on my first assignment. In those days, when there were still a significant number of vocations, it was a given I would be assigned as an associate pastor in a larger parish in Sudbury, Sault Ste. Marie, or here in North Bay.

"I suppose you want to know where Father Rick will be a priest. You had him eight months as a deacon, and there are parishes in need of a young priest. There is an argument that a priest should not be in his home parish, familiarity, and all. Father Rick bears a close watch, though, so he will be your new associate pastor."

Ahem, a close watch indeed!

The people stood to applaud. I grinned at my parents. I had kept the secret. What a grace it was that I could go home for a quick visit or a meal, a place where I could be Rick, not Father Rick. On this night, I could not imagine the final four ovations coming at farewell liturgies eleven years later.

"Nor I suspect, Claire, could the bishop and faithful imagine a radically different church in barely two generations where parishes and dioceses were now closing or being amalgamated, with half the priests coming from India and Africa to plug shortages. The supreme irony—a missionary church needing missionaries themselves."

Father Rick Prashaw, May 9, 1980

"This is 1980? I was there. I was one-year-old."

In the parish hall, family, clergy, friends, and parishioners enjoyed a meal and roasting of the newly minted priest. An ordination dinner is like a wedding supper, minus the clinking of glasses and kisses.

Oh, well.

In his remarks, Dad wisecracked that he had known of my vocation since I was a young boy in London. He held up a framed poster of me as a boy in pyjamas playing priest. For vestments, I had tucked a towel into my pyjama top. The tabernacle was an upside-down wastebasket covered with linen. A Pope Pius XII parents' wedding blessing sat on my altar. Most important, the *Lone Ranger*, my childhood patron saint, looked down upon me, gun drawn.

Who could know then that, in the final years of ministry, the *Lone Ranger* would become an apt metaphor for my celibate priesthood? On ordination night, though, granted those priestly powers, I was raring to save every soul, defend my church, and convert the entire world. On my ordination card was my motto, "All my words for The Word."

I unpacked a dark oak wooden chalice, a family gift, wood my choice over gold. I was conscious of this singular blessing to serve in my home parish where my parents worshipped. Yes, it would mean a perpetual humbling from my father. Anytime I went to the pulpit to preach, he caught my eye before fiddling with his hearing aids. Was he turning them up, down, or off? He only grinned when I asked him. I was not the only cleric my father kept humble. As usher, he asked Carter at the back of the church if he was preaching and, hearing an affirmative, told him this was good because Dad needed a nap after being out late last night. Carter laughed his way to the altar.

The Challenge Youth Group did a mock musical. There were references to my Blue Jays, beer, and fun. They were on to me. Familiarity, indeed. In a split second that night, I had crossed over to this unique life as a Roman Catholic priest.

God, help me please.

CHAPTER 12

Ministry, The Early Years

1980–1984

As a young priest serving in a large, flourishing parish, there was plenty to do. Daily Mass, hear confessions, preside at liturgies each weekend, preach every third weekend. I took my turn with city priests to carry the beeper that summonsed me anytime day or night to a sick call at St. Joseph or Civic Hospital. There were schools to visit. As the new kid on the block, I officiated at weddings for about fifty couples each year.

"Yes, Claire, all those women I married!"

"HA. Soooooooo many women. Good one," Claire laughed.

For the Marriage Preparation weekend talks, I did play Leonard Cohen's "Dance Me to the End of Love" for an out-of-the-box priest take on the passion and physicality of this divine love immersed in the love of husband and wife.

My first gift as a priest was this assignment joining Father Don MacLellan's pastoral team. Tom O'Connor was the other associate pastor and Bonnie Chesser, a Sisters of St. Joseph, helped with music, liturgy, and catechetics.

I thrived on Don's pastoral approach, his genuine love of people, schooled in a Falconbridge, Ontario mining family's intolerance to pretentiousness or false gods. Don spoke of what it meant for us to be a church, our being a community, "Jesus assembled, where, when I am present, I am noticed, and, when I am absent, I am missed."

Father Don MacLellan, Rick's first pastor. A smile, love, and a "wee dram".

Occasionally, Don's temper surfaced when people confused gospel or parish priorities. A women's guild member complained about the noisy youth in the hall, missing the miracle they were there at all. His face turned beet red listening to a janitor upset by the people of God messing his clean church. Don seethed when the parish council focused solely on the furnace or debt rather than feeding the poor.

A favourite Don MacLellan memory was any gathering at his cottage. His shirt was off, a glass of scotch cupped in his hand, and his sunny smile kissing life. The image was another Brian McKee vocation billboard.

As priests, we could be busy morning to night. I headed to Mother St. Bride School to teach religion or, as a grateful Marie Carmichael told me, give her a smoke break. The teachers sometimes stayed to enjoy this young priest sparring with their budding agnostics. Kids in Grade 7 still had their hands in the air waving madly to answer. Then, with puberty on the doorstep, the hands went down, and the walls went up. They were already skeptical about the Immaculate Conception.

Strangely, the Pro had become a magnet for teens to hang out at, largely because of Challenge. That popular summer theatre program had been cooked up by Sister Cathy Williamson and Greg Humbert in 1973 when he was a seminarian. Father Al McMillan and Gerry Sallie helped stage the first plays. Challenge attracted mostly Catholics and some Protestant youth in the parish hall every night for practices for the end of summer, polished productions of *Sound of Music, Fiddler on the Roof,* and *West Side Story, etc.* Saturday night was the youth Mass, packed, many incredibly "wanting" instead of "having" to attend—guitars, choir, youth serving as readers, ushers, Ministers of Communion, my chance to relate their songs, their teen idols to a gospel. A brief caging of hormones at play for summer and longer romances. "Meet at the Pro" was Act One for teens' Saturday night: movies, dances, and permission to sleep in Sunday morning having gone to Mass already. A Protestant mother telephoned me once to confirm her daughter was indeed at this Catholic Church every night as she swore she was.

1981 Summer Challenge production of "The Wiz."

"Father Rick, I never thought I'd be calling a Catholic priest complaining about a daughter spending all her time at church," she laughed. It was all a mystery to that mom until she and others attended the heart-stopping, sellout performances by Marti Southcott, the brilliant, uber-talented director and her cast, orchestra, and company, one-hundred-plus, at summer's end.

"Claire, it's hard to find the right words to describe a faith community where teens wanted to go to church and where they thrived."

"I don't know that church," Claire sighed. "We might occasionally go when we are back home on holidays to see old friends. Grandparents like to show off their grandchildren."

"Yes, Claire, many now worship Sundays at running clubs and Costco."

"If Mom asks me to go now, I ask, what, did the Catholics get a female pastor?"

"Your poor parents!"

After I married, news that I had been a Catholic priest woke up even jaded listeners.

"What was that like being a priest? What do you miss?"

Beyond a repartee of jokes—no diapers, no Father's Day ties, no teenage angst—I might have surprised them with my answer. If the listener seemed sincere, I recalled the early mornings in the church before I unlocked the doors. I opened the windows. The fresh air splashed on my face. In the precious silence, I sat in the empty church near the front side tabernacle. Before the day became too crazy, I prayed for the people on my groaning prayer list, those ill, parents of stillborn babies, those without work or hopes dashed in loveless marriages. I'd enjoy the silence, a moment to wed my energy to the energies of nature, my tiny hectare to a universal church.

Preaching was a favourite priestly passion. God's radical grace, God's Original Blessing, the priest as a wounded healer, that we who gathered around the Eucharistic table were starving sinners, not the virtuous chosen. Each time I kissed the altar to begin the Eucharist, I faced my own unworthiness. Like others, I could swear, drink, and judge. I wanted that kiss to be with God, not the devil.

Within weeks of ordination, on the feast of St. Peter and St. Paul, I preached on the work cut out for ourselves as believers.

"Being Catholic is not a 'get into heaven pass.' You know those cards we carry, 'I am a Catholic. In case of an accident, please call a priest.' With our notion of church at times, that may as well read: 'I am a Catholic. Admit to heaven at moment of death.' No! Membership is no guarantee of salvation. Instead of seeing the church as something alive, a force at work, we look on it as merely a shelter, a place of refuge from the world, a spiritual hotel."

It was the philosopher Søren Kierkegaard's insight into "becoming Christian," rather than "being Christian." I saw no need to pronounce who was superior and inferior, worthy or sinner. To dare preach, I had to speak from the heart, first to myself. If my homily did not disturb me, it surely snoozed parishioners. A powerful sermon demanded praying the readings, searching current news for teachable moments, landing on the ambiguities that God's words suggested, that most of us were struggling to live.

If those stories did not engage listeners at parties, I told them of a visit to Leo and Jeannine Moreau's family. Leo was that immaculate custodian at The Pro. At their supper table packed with young people, a born-again boyfriend grilled me on the Catholic faith. I ducked his inquisition, commenting, "Hey! I'm a priest. I'm in it for the money." They laughed.

I was prudent not to ruin supper by repeating McKee's observation that a few, insufferable "born-agains" he knew were born twice too often.

I tried broadening people's understanding of spirituality beyond the Sunday service. Other religions knew this membership challenge. Faith meant inviting people to consider choices about this loving God who wanted a genuine, ongoing relationship. Discipleship jumped past a churchy-institutional attendance to embrace work, sports stadiums, and even marriage beds.

I guess I was full of beans. When all else failed, I told another story or joke.

Those early years at The Pro were exhilarating. I moved into my "suite." It came with old spartan furniture and yet was my own apartment, a "move-on-up" from the single, solitary seminary room to now a living room and desk, a separate bedroom with a queen-size bed all for myself, and a private bath. I learned to tolerate, barely, the nightly fly-by bats in residence. Their occasional, mid-day dining room cruise was more disconcerting, like huge, creepy jet planes with a 747 wingspan!

I was initiated into the daily routine of living with my new family, Bishop Carter, and several priests. The long ornate, oak dining room table which sat sixteen usually had four to six priests huddled near the middle. Carter, or the rector, rang a bell to summons a high school girl that had been hired to help Henriette Potvin, the cook who had started at The Pro when she was sixteen.

"Seriously. A bell?" Claire shook her head.

Ding-a-ling!

Carter had come north from Westmount in Montréal, with a peculiar mix of clergy privilege, social gospel, and working-class doctrine.

"Dinner was at 6:00 p.m.," recalled Maryanne Garvey (Doyle) on her Facebook post. "Priests came in to start the pickle tray and, when they were ready, they RANG A DINNER BELL! That was our signal to bring in dinner without talking and clear away the first course. The next BELL was to clear the dinner plates and bring in dessert and coffee. When they left, it was time to go in and clean up."

From training at the Prashaw supper table, I made faces at the girls serving. The rectory girls were memorable for more than the infernal bell. Girls in my male, clerical galaxy! They worked till 9:00 p.m., making lunches for the homeless who rang the doorbell. If Tom and I were eating by ourselves, we might grab plates to dine in the kitchen with whoever was working. Their stories on families, early boyfriends, and school were a precious lifeline beyond those cold stone walls. In between evening appointments, I jumped on a kitchen counter for gossip with the students and laughing at this Catholic cathedral cosmos.

The other priests—the camaraderie, the chatter, the jokes—were like the seminary. God had a sense of humour in whom he called to the priesthood.

Ha, she called me!

We were a motley crew of different personalities and gifts. Some of the cufflinks crowd, and me, forever in blue jeans. Some priests gambled on the ponies or headed to the golf course on days off. Scotch was the favourite drink, mine too from even pre-seminary days. With MacLellan, it was a working man's Ballantine scotch, not any single malt.

There were legendary characters. Jim Hickey was that "Critical Women's League" priest who initiated me into the roller-coaster rhythms of a manic-depressive disorder. There were weeks of his intense, private suffering as we dropped dining trays outside his bedroom. He was a lost soul. Then, he emerged from his lair, soaring, full throttle, his manic inhaling life and anyone at the supper table. Do I dread the manic more than the depression? It was impossible to muzzle Hickey or identify a clear sentence in his run-on monologue. When Hickey was on, his wicked humour kept us all in place.

One night, in rare candour, Carter mentioned how lonely it could be as a bishop.

"I know it's kind of a cliché. It can be lonely at the top."

Hickey was having none of that.

"Hell, bishop, it may be lonely at the top, but it's lonely at the bottom too. If I had my way, I'd rather be lonely at the top!"

Carter laughed the loudest.

Father John Caswell was another gem with his impish smirk and twinkle in his eyes. I admired his communications ministry with Roseanne Lyons as he launched Cath-Com Productions, delivering its *Mass for Shut-Ins* for twenty-seven years along with his other media work. Caswell was a priest for fifty-six years, a walking miracle for thirty-eight of them after his diagnosis of esophagus cancer. In visiting the Precious Blood Sisters monastery in North Bay, he pretended not to recognize the nuns as they had recently dropped their living behind cloistered screens.

"Oh, Father John, you know me," a sister sighed. Caswell then put his two clasped hands together in front of the sister's face, imitating the thatched wooden grill through which everyone had viewed the sisters for years.

"Oh, Sister Alfreda, it's you!"

They laughed.

Hanging at the back of the church or outside in good weather offered relaxed opportunities to joke with people and forge community. Julie Hewitt, married to Cecil Hewitt, a former North Bay mayor, found me after mass to praise my sermon and prophesy I would be a bishop one day.

"I thought you liked me," I quipped. "Julie, for that blasphemy, your penance is to do a good deed!"

She laughed. I was serious. I yearned to be a simple parish priest. I loved this job.

There are dozens of stories.

CHAPTER 13

The Boat People

1980

The heart-wrenching news flooded our television screens. Millions of Vietnamese refugees fleeing conquerors, the killing fields, thrown into rickety boats in a stormy, pirate-infested sea. Hundreds drowned, the rest plucked to languish in refugee camps in Malaysia and Hong Kong as the world reeled from this latest humanitarian crisis.

The refugees became known as the "Boat People." Hundreds of faith communities answered the call to help the Canadian government resettle those refugees. Priests, rabbis, ministers, Mennonite Central Committee, and their faithful responded as Canada settled more than 110,000 refugees in the next five years, per capita the most of any western country.[17] What began in a spirit of charity slipped into justice ministry.

In his book on Carter and the *Diocese of Sault Ste. Marie*, Graeme Mount chronicled the Pro-Cathedral's response:[18]

---

17 CBC News, "When Canadians came together to help Vietnamese refugees," CBC News, May 12, 2017, https://www.cbc.ca/2017/canadathestoryofus/ when-canadians-came-together-to-help-vietnamese-refugees-1.4110755.

18 Graeme Mount, *The History of the Diocese of Sault Ste. Marie* (Sudbury: Laurentian University, 2013), 41.

"Five years later, as Communist forces completed their occupation of South Vietnam and political dissidents fled, parishioners sponsored six refugee families. The Rev. Rick Prashaw was the organizer, and his father was chair of the committee which raised funds to pay the rent, provided furniture, and introduced the new arrivals to the wonders of shopping in a supermarket. Parishioners helped the families find jobs, doctors, dentists, OHIP cards, and schools for the children. Two of the involved parishioners, Ida Bagno and Velma Bonany, recall that none of the families was Roman Catholic. Mrs. Bonany also remembers a family with two young girls and a baby. Despite adequate furnishings in their apartment, all five members slept in one bed. After all their experiences, they could comfort each other that way. In short order, all the Vietnamese families adapted readily to life in this country and moved to larger Canadian cities."

We scrambled to find homes, clothing, everything really, as they had fled their homeland with nothing but the clothes on their backs. The congregation responded with money, other donations, and prayers while fifty parishioners stepped forward to form groups to work closely with our anticipated families. We educated ourselves on Vietnam, the conflict and culture. However, it was mostly the organized chaos of readying to welcome our new friends. We discovered a large vacant house behind the rectory. It needed renovations, fresh coats of paint, furniture. There was no shortage of volunteers. This scene was happening in communities across Canada.

It was a bone-chilling, cold wintry day when the first family arrived. We bundled them up in the donated snow jackets and toques. The children squealed at the sight of snow until the cold had them burrowing deep into the parkas the parents wore. The adults felt the cold anxiety of protecting their families, fish out of water, people literally hoisted out of the sea, foreigners in a foreign land that had strange languages and customs.

Our neighbours flooded the bathroom until they figured out the shower curtain. Closing their front door to return to the rectory, I would look up at a dark night sky and ponder how abjectly lost I would have been had a national crisis coughed me up on their shores in Vietnam.

"I was a stranger, and you made me welcome." (Matt. 25:35)

"Claire and Cruz, that I worked side by side with my parents was such a blessing. Over the next few years, those families did leave North Bay for Toronto."

I lost touch with Tran, Minh, Linn, Huang, and other refugees. I think of them from time to time; this forever love story.

"Cruz, Canada has had waves of migrations like the boat people over many generations. They are strangers until they become our friends, threats to jobs until we notice how hardworking they are, and how they want what most people want in life, a new place to call home, to fit in, open their own businesses and take care of themselves. Your family roots are in Honduras with your dad and in Scotland, Ireland, and France with the Prashaw and O'Connor families on your Mom's side. We all come from away, except for the Indigenous Peoples."

CHAPTER 14

God is United Church!

I am on this "A Bit of the Bay Nostalgia, History and Retro " Facebook Group that Jeff Fournier launched for North Bay folk still there or living elsewhere. It has eighteen thousand members. Any post on the legendary DeMarco's Confectionary Store across the street from The Pro guaranteed hundreds of comments.

Joe Fazzari, a high school buddy, called Demarco's his second home, as did many others. Oldtimers nicknamed the store, "The Temple."

"Frank DeMarco made the best, real Tin Roofs on the planet," Fazzari recalled. "Many do not know the difference between a soda, malt, float, and milk shake. Frank put a fine fizz on the soda as the last stage. The soda machine was so old they could not buy the parts to repair it, so he had to replace it with a new soda dispenser without the fine fizz feature. I never had another chocolate soda after they replaced the old unit."

At DeMarco's, we scooped up hot dogs, shakes, and penny candy, listened to the jukebox, and played pinball, all under the loving watch of Tony, Joan, Frank, Connie, and Lisa Demarco.

Demarco's was a natural extension of The Pro both physically and socially. Priests better not mess with parishioner's religious rituals, i.e., breakfast or coffee right after weekday morning Mass. Catholics had a schedule to keep. I was on the clock.

One Monday, I walked past Demarco's and on to St. Andrew United Church led by their young, gifted minister, Jim Sinclair. He and I had already connected at ecumenical gatherings. We shared a passion for social justice. Sinclair would one day be elected General Secretary for The United Church of Canada. As I passed one side of St. Andrew's, I heard a voice.

"Rick. Rick!"

It was Sinclair calling. I could not see him. On my day off, I was game for fun. I was on the church side lawn. I now spotted Jim's silhouette in the stained-glass window.

"Rick!"

"OH MY GOD," I shouted, arms outstretched to the heavens. "GOD IS UNITED CHURCH!"

Jim grabbed a window ledge to halt his crashing to the ground.

That was the end of it, or so we thought. Unknown to each other, we began sermons the next Sunday with the Monday "God is United" story. We found that out afterwards, as members of both congregations retold the story at Demarco's.

"Of course, Cruz, I believe God has many names and is found in many places of worship, United, Anglican, Catholic, Baptist, Presbyterian, Pentecostal, Jewish, Muslim, Hindu, Buddhist, Sikh, Indigenous, and dozens more!"

This Roman Catholic priest was learning about this big God I could not pretend to contain, this God of different religions, names, and stories.

CHAPTER 15

"Damn You, God!"

For the first four years as associate pastor, I lived up on the top, third floor of the rectory attached to the back of the church—the "penthouse," with Tom O'Connor, yes, the bats, and a handy, small chapel for meditation. The bats inspired me to close my suite's two doors before lights out. A few still found their way in for low nocturnal flyovers. I slipped beneath the covers.

But it was another strange sound I heard this one night as I lay in bed.

A voice, a loud voice, colourful cursing words, were coming from the chapel. That had to be my pastor, Don MacLellan. He was not happy. And while I could not make out all his words, I did hear a damnation of God. He had grown up in that mining family, salt of the earth, I heard. Salty, too, this night.

Don was pissed off about something. It was a prayer, indeed praying, the likes of which I had never heard before. I heard the rest of the story at breakfast the next morning.

"You and God talk last night?" I asked.

"God, you didn't hear that?"

"Hard not to! I never knew I could pray that way."

"Well, sometimes God needs a shove."

This son of a Cape Breton miner stretched my faith world.

Don's visit to the chapel had come after returning from the hospital. Alarmed friends, parishioners, had called as the woman, pregnant and near her due time, was rushed to hospital, bleeding, and at risk of losing the child. This emergency happened about a year to the day their first baby had died. Then, they had returned home to the freshly painted baby room, the empty bassinet. They were cast into the hell of the Bereaved Parents Club, a club I could not yet imagine joining. Black holes. Shut tight windows on a summer night.

Father Don had grieved, counselled, and loved the couple back to life through the jagged debris of their mourning. It appeared another baby's death was imminent.

Damn you, God!

Once he finished praying with the couple, Don beat a path home to the rectory and chapel to give God an earful. Don railed against the heavens. He was livid. It was good Old Testament Job and Jonah, "shake your fist" at the deities. He noted the first baby's death; all this couple had been through. He implored God not to let this happen again. I was counting a half-dozen "damn you, God" invocations. As it turned out, this couple did give birth to a healthy, beautiful child. God had heard Don's prayer. I sure had!

It was a prayer that I would resort to in a hospital room decades later, holding my dying son's hand. There would be new "damn you" prayers, different answers that night. I do anguish with believers on why bad stalks good people of faith.

CHAPTER 16

Chicago!

1981

In our first year, Don took Tom, Bonnie, and I to Chicago for the Gathering, a Midwest liturgical conference. We were big news there, being the Canadians who are there as an entire pastoral team, in Lent, because their bishop was filling in for them back home.

Hearing this, progressive American Catholics wanted a swap, Carter for their conservative bishops. There appeared to be a few. No, thank you! It was my first visit back to Chicago since ditching Jude on a freeway.

Most years, I would return to the Gathering as a priest with other lay staff coming from different Sault diocese parishes. It was inspiring and influential to hear ways to forge a priestly identity within a collaborative ministry with lay people built on individuals' gifts, an emerging storytelling preaching school, and a down-to-earth liturgy rich in rituals and symbols. We brought home ground-breaking pastoral and liturgical ideas. A November Book of Life for a month-long remembrance of all who had died, lay funeral teams, a catechumenate for adults to be initiated in the faith, and smart, contemporary ways to retell the gospel stories. John Shea inspired us to make the Jesus stories our own rather than to tell them straight. Father Bill Bausch from New Jersey taught how to build ministry with talented and equal lay ministers. Bausch retold this story of how a woman Eucharistic minister wrote a letter to a Catholic newspaper on how she felt when she saw people leave her Communion line to receive the host from a priest.

"I wonder what you are thinking as you crossed over to Father's line to avoid receiving Communion from me. That I was unworthy to bear the Body of Christ to you? I readily admit that. The priest from whom you receive the eucharist is also unworthy. Both of us have been made acceptable through the saving grace of him you refuse to accept from my hands . . .If Christ was born of a woman, is it not fitting for a woman to be eucharistic Christ-bearers? Personally, my hands feel blessed. They have been trained to nurse the sick. They have prepared at least 30,000 meals and changed almost as many diapers. They have spent hours folded in prayer and in teaching others to pray."[19]

We imported Bausch's custom of having a Saturday night team supper after Mass in our living room as we took turns to cook and choose guests. We invited couples or someone flying solo, single or divorced, often left out of the parish social life. We could have talked all night, but we had an early Sunday Mass.

One Chicago trip, as we drove, Father Peter Moher blessed Lake Michigan to deal with any future holy water shortage. I was not about to report him to the Vatican as I had blessed the kitchen tap of an inconvenient woman parishioner incessantly demanding I bring her more holy water.

"Uncle Rick, you've seen the COVID-19 Catholic meme?" Claire asked. "All I needed leaving the house in 2019 was my keys, purse, phone, and water. Now, in 2020, it's that and a face mask, latex gloves, hand sanitizer, holy water, wooden stake, and full body armour."

"Hahaha."

In Chicago, Don dispensed us from Lenten discipline, noting a little-known canon law exempting visitors to the United States. We took his word, choosing not to look it up. It being before the Internet, I seized the important social convener role.

"What a surprise, Uncle Rick," Claire winked.

---

19 William J. Bausch, *Take Heart, Father* (Mystic, CT: Twenty-Third Publications, 1986), 14-15.

Each year, as we approached Chicago, I requested a pit stop to buy the *Sun-Times* newspaper to create a short menu of possible theatre or sports events to attend on our one free evening. One year, we laughed aloud at the play, *Do Black Patent Leather Shoes Really Reflect Up?* a riotous return to Catholic childhoods like the Prashaws' *Cuckoo's Nest*. Girls should not wear black patent shoes because, well, they did reflect up. We made it to a Chicago Black Hawks' game. Don, a "meat and potatoes guy" like my father, believed God had ordained supper to be no later than 6:00 p.m. Don's frown betrayed a migraine headache when we sat down to eat around 7:30 p.m. Mercifully, we discovered Lawry's The Prime Rib Restaurant, a steakhouse in a mansion in the Golden Mile. Don forgave us our trespasses when he savoured the first mouthful of the chef's medium rare prime rib cuts; his headache was gone, and his smile back. I liked the cut of the roast beef. I bet I was not the only clergy noticing the low cut of the black cocktail dresses of the stunning waitresses.

"Claire, I forgot 'custody of the eyes.'"

"Bahahahahaha!"

CHAPTER 17

Edwina Gately, Women in Prostitution, and a Big God

In *Soar, Adam, Soar*, I recounted how my son, still named Rebecca Adam, "played church" as a kid. This IS a Catholic thing! After bowing and genuflecting, he delivered this sermon:

"God is big. Very big. God is bigger than me or Dad or Mom or anybody. God is bigger than our house or our street. God is bigger than Russell [our hometown]. God is bigger than the sky. God is very big. Amen."

Edwina Gately, the British-born theologian, poet, and storyteller, would have applauded my biblically named (Rebekah) Adam, this seizing of power, this celebrant for the Eucharist, recognizing at such a young age this big Creator and Spirit God that Gately fondly proclaimed.

At the Gathering that first year, Gately was on stage telling her story of a contemplative life mixed with living on the streets of Chicago with the homeless, "winos," addicted, and women engaged in prostitution. She had founded Genesis House, a house of hospitality and nurturing for those women. I looked over at Don grinning, instantly smitten.

It was in Africa, Gately explained, immersed in the hospitality, generosity, and expanse of the African people, where she loved this big God diffused in us and the cosmos.

"One of the questions most frequently asked of me is: 'Why are you still a member of the Roman Catholic Church? Why are you still working full-time in the church? Where has her motivation and passion come from?' Not from musty books, she says, and not from hard theology. It has come from my experience of God, something over which I have not had much control. . . ."[20]

Exactly!

This would be my own lifelong landing place, this experience of God over which I had little control. There was mystery, miracles, and emotions along-side doctrine. I could not not believe!

Gately retold the evangelist Luke's "woman who was a sinner" anointing story found in all four gospels. We knew the story, or did we? Gately, prim, proper, British accent, and all, fleshed out Jesus' love for those "bad" women. Hurt by customers, they would know true love whenever it might finally show up.

The woman took her alabaster jar of perfume and, at Jesus' feet, weeping, anointed him. Bystanders are scandalized, including the apostle, Peter. Does this prophet not know who she is? She has a name in this town. In fact, Jesus knows her story and her history. And, with Peter his foil, he said, "Then turning toward the woman, he said to Simon, 'Do you see this woman? I entered your house; you gave me no water for my feet, but she has bathed my feet with her tears and dried them with her hair. You gave me no kiss, but from the time I came in, she has not stopped kissing my feet. You did not anoint my head with oil, but she has anointed my feet with ointment. Therefore, I tell you, her sins, which were many, have been forgiven; hence she has shown great love. But the one to whom little is forgiven, loves little.' Then he said to her, 'Your sins are forgiven.'" (Luke 7:44-48)

Peter had only seen her deeds, not the woman. Jesus' gaze went deeper. Gately was not done. She then nailed the staggering, scandalous scope of Jesus' love. Of course, Jesus knew exactly how this woman could afford to buy the expensive oil to anoint his feet. Her tricks. Her customers. Her great love expressed in her anointing Jesus, her tears, had redeemed all. Those around him, the church leaders, needed a pointed reminder of the breathtaking scope of God's love.

"That is beautiful. Perfect," Claire smiled.

---

20 Dear, John. "Edwina Gateley's Big God," *National Catholic Reporter*, Sept. 15, 2009, https://www.ncronline.org/blogs/road-peace/edwina-gateleys-big-god.

Scripture stories dazzled me. As a pastor, it was a never-ending challenge to help move people from that "little love" to "great love," through a gospel story that blew up any sense that we gathered around the altar were the holy ones, the saved, the "us" and not "them" beyond our walls. I, as their pastor, was a sinner welcoming other sinners. There were Catholics and people in other faiths who happily judged who was in and out, saved, or damned. It did not jive with Jesus' teaching. Holiness was never a calling to war against those not believing what we believed.

Put down those stones.

We try to use God as props, but who can contain God? The God we put away in our pockets or tabernacles escapes. Our God is "very BIG!"

There were other Chicago lessons on community. John Shea shared what, for me, is the only credible interpretation of Jesus' miracle of the loaves and fishes. It is a parable on how to love in a community. Do we really know the Gospel of John story (John 6:1-15), or, worse, do we know it too well? Crowds estimated at five thousand followed this miracle worker. They were hungry. Philip and Andrew, like good, anxious staff, reported on the scarcity of food. Jesus spied a small boy who has five barley loaves and two fish. Taking the loaves and fishes, Jesus gave thanks and had the disciples distribute enough food to feed everyone with twelve hampers of scraps leftover.

Where did the food come from?

"Claire, for me, the miracle was never a random, divine Uber Eats delivery from above. This is an invitation to relax clenched fists, resist the hoarding, and understand we have enough if we only would share. It is a story on overriding primal, basic instincts that we do not need all that toilet paper or panic shopping in the pandemic, to discover the real miracle of community that feeds all, with surprising leftovers for another day. The invitation to love freed those five thousand to share what they had. Otherwise, fearful of tomorrow, we grip tightly to what we have and hoard more."

We can all do well when others do well. It often makes no sense until we try it.

"That's all good, Uncle Rick, but, unless you are doing a miracle, I am calling Uber Eats right now."

CHAPTER 18

Peru

Greg Humbert and I grinned, sitting triumphantly on the majestic summit of Machu Picchu in the Andes Mountains in Peru. For the last fifty feet up the narrow trail, the 8,000-foot altitude felt like a lumberjack had jumped on my shoulders for a ride. We paused every step, gasping for air. The view was spectacular, notwithstanding a discarded Coca Cola can at the peak.

"Cruz, who litters heaven with a Coke can? Maybe it was an offering to the gods."

We had travelled to Peru to visit friends who were missionaries from the Diocese of London serving in Zana, located in a river valley near the Pan-American Highway in the north of the country.

"Claire and Cruz, your Uncle Frank O'Connor (brother to Jerry, Maggie, and six other siblings) was there. Machu Picchu and a visit to the capital in Lima capped a month's vacation there. We immersed ourselves first in the mission."

As a teen, I had been introduced through the Sault diocese's Guatemala missionaries to a bigger world. We raised money, heard mission stories, and learned firsthand about a country, a culture, and a church different but still ours. Later, I grasped the complicated lessons in this missionary era, i.e., a mix of good news alongside other efforts that wed the Cross to a country's flag, to capitalism, armies, and globalization.

"In the beginning [1959], our mission responded to the call of (Pope) John XXIII for North American and European dioceses to send missionaries to Latin America, probably to save it from communism," Frank told us. "The truth was that we slowly discovered that we went there to be saved. With few exceptions, we learned and received more than we gave. It gave us a chance to rediscover, or to discover for the first time, Jesus Christ in the poor and the power of his gospel to change hearts, families, communities, and the wider church."

"Special were the friends we found among the Peruvian priests, religious, and above all laity who were able to put up with our stupidity and patiently accompanied us as we learned from our mistakes. Fortunately, when we first went, we couldn't speak the language well, if at all, so we were not able to say all the foolish things we were thinking or were saying to one another in English. As friendships deepened, our respect and love for the people we served increased."

Frank had arrived for a first assignment in Latin America in 1971, around the time of the birth of a theology of liberation. People were learning to "do theology" with the help of priests like Gustavo Gutiérrez and the community centre of Bartolomé de las Casa. "They gave us tools for understanding our reality on many levels—social, cultural, economic, political and ecclesial," O'Connor told us.

"Here, I learned, in a real way, the social implications and imperatives of the Gospel of Jesus Christ and what it is to be church from the heart of the poor. Exhilarating!"

"Of course, Claire, you had your own Latin American immersion story."

"Yes, for third year at Trent University, I spent a year in Quito, Ecuador and a community along the Amazon River. I was there in September in 2001 in my first week when my host mother started crying and freaking out. 'La Virgen Madre!' I had to look up all the words in my Spanish-English dictionary. Jesus' mother was apparently appearing in a church. We piled into a car and drove six hours. People were coming down from the mountains to join cars and people walking to this church. When we arrived, people were weeping and hysterical. Inside, we saw her face with dried blood. The statue was inside this glass cage that was forty feet tall."

"In a few days, back home, everyone was upset again, but for different reasons. I looked up the Spanish words about planes crashing into buildings. It was September 11 and the World Trade Centre. It was crazy. My first week in Ecuador and, the Virgin Mary appears, and 9-11 happened. I said prayers that night to be safe, just in case."

"My only keepsake from Ecuador are paintings by Oswaldo Guayasamin, a painter and sculptor of Kichwa and Mestizo heritage. He is known for his Pan-American art capturing human and social inequalities. He once painted a soldier in a Nazi helmet with the letters CIA."

"Claire, Frank and your stories are a counterpoint to missionaries that imposed North American ways rather than let local churches flourish."

I was in Peru for the month. What I experienced there stayed with me much longer.

Rick and Greg Humbert on Machu Picchu summit, Peru, 1982.

CHAPTER 19

Hidden Talents

1982–1987

It may have been the wine, or the Catholic chutzpah Dad had bred in me. I was at a reception bending the ear of the Canadian tenor and opera singer Ben Hoeppner on MY recent recording studio experience and MY two record albums. Hoeppner was a class act, smiling, sensing the fun at play.

Years later, everyone played that party game telling three true facts and one falsehood about themselves. I usually won as few could guess the lie that I had on my list:

> I had a private breakfast with the pope.
>
> I went to two Rolling Stones concerts
>
> I released my two record albums.
>
> I was a journalist.

Sadly, I missed Mick and the Stones. The priests at The Canadian College where I would live celebrated Eucharist and broke bread with Pope John Paul II. The albums came first. The year was 1986. The Hidden Talents, a troupe of Catholic priests from the Diocese of Sault Ste. Marie, were fresh from our Ottawa recording studio session.

We had recorded our second album, *Songs We Learned at Our Mother's Knee and Other Joints*. The musical troupe of priests was another stroke of genius of Greg Humbert, a stage version of the hockey Flying Fathers. Stationed in Sturgeon Falls, Humbert knew the executive director of an ARC organization helping adults with intellectual and developmental challenges; the director wanted to boost its profile in the community. Humbert and John Balfe conjured up an informal concert by priests. During the drive to the auditorium, Humbert wrote on a napkin our seat-of-the-pants suggestions for songs. We performed to a sold out, standing room-only crowd. By the time Humbert was back in his rectory, there were three new invitations on his answering machine.

Our name came from the gospel parable exhorting disciples not to hide their light under a bushel basket but rather to use their God-given gifts for the Kingdom of God (Matt. 5:14-16). That was a faith cover for the crazy good times we had taking our show on the road. From winging that first concert, we drifted into practices and polished performances. We knew the concerts put a human face, a singing, entertaining billboard on the priesthood and Catholic faith. On an earthier note, the concerts and time travelling with anywhere from six to nine priest friends were equal parts grace and insanity. After busy weekends marrying, burying, baptizing, and preaching, we'd throw our tired bodies into a van for a mini-road tour of two or three community concerts somewhere in Ontario. We even made it to New London, Connecticut. It beat Valium for decompressing from bouts of mad ministry.

By early in Act One, when we sang the raucous beer-drinking song, "The Night Pat Murphy Died", we had the audience in the palm of our hands, clapping and tapping their feet.

There was real talent in the voices of Mark Balfe, Hamish Currie, Al McMillan, James Ketzler, and Dave Tramontini, the piano playing of Peter Moher and John Balfe, and Humbert's classic broken English, side-splitting renditions of Habitant French poems like "Ma Beeg Marie".

Unlike most of the boys in the band, my talents were especially hidden. I sang a bit off-key. I didn't play an instrument. They placed me farthest from the microphones. Nonetheless, friendship called. I was welcomed on stage, paying my dues by adding volume to the chorus, telling irreverent stories or jokes between songs, as well as writing the album jacket back covers. And, of course, I volunteered for the liquor store runs. When all else failed, I picked up my "musical instrument," a rolling pin, to wave during "Consider Yourself at Home, Consider Yourself Part of the Family".

The Hidden Talents performed forty-three concerts and raised approximately a quarter million dollars for charities. Promising "a wholesome evening of entertainment and laughs," we coughed up two acts, the first in our civvies belting tunes like "New York, New York". In the intermission, we changed into our clergy suits and collars to sing hymns like "Be Not Afraid", "On Eagle's Wings", "Here I Am, Lord" and "Matakatifu", the African Eucharist Sanctus prayer John Balfe learned while bringing medical supplies to a village clinic. Our amateur zeal threw us back on stage fast for an encore and chorus line kick singing, "Years May Come, Years May Go".

Between songs, Humbert or I might stay on stage at the microphone and sigh about seeing so many people and not being able to take up a collection. Cue the laughter and cue the fellow priests who had beat it to the back of the auditoriums to pick up their offering plates to start a fake collection.

Those were the days, my friends.

It was at the Capitol Theatre in North Bay for a sellout concert of 1,350 people when Bishop Carter was in the front row to hear me tell this story.

"I was at a loss on what I should say for a sermon on Marian devotion. A fellow priest suggested this opening. 'The bishop is in love, in love with a woman, and her name is Mary.' That might work, I thought, but my nerves did me in. I blurted out, 'The bishop is in love, in love with a woman, but I can't remember her name'."

The audience howled. I peeked to see Carter laughing. I looked out at the crowd.

"Is the bishop laughing?" I asked. "It's been fun ministering at The Pro. I hope you visit me in Manitouwadge (800 kilometres west) after the bishop assigns me there next week."

Kneeling, left to right: Al McMillan, Tom O'Connor, Rick Prashaw. Standing, from left: Dave Tramontini, Eric Pannike, Mark Balfe, John Balfe, Greg Humbert, Hamish Currie, Dennis Kennelly, Peter Moher. Missing: Jim Ketzler.

Catholics loved the performances. Protestants clapped. White-collar workers, we joked. We were vain enough to enjoy the press clippings:

"O come enjoy a heavenly evening. Show-biz priests make Sault bishop proud."[21]

"Crooning Clerics"[22]

---

21 Dunn, Joan. "O come enjoy a heavenly evening. Show-biz priests make Sault bishop proud," *Catholic Register*, May 28, 1983.

22 "Crooning Clerics," *Kitchener Waterloo Record*, Jan. 19, 1985.

"What stands out most about the Hidden Talents is their honest, almost naked sense of humour."[23]

It was fun while it lasted, two hours of laying down the burdens of people weary with daily chores. We on stage had our own weariness to shake off. At each concert, I found my quiet place in the wings to listen to Mark Balfe sing "The Rose." His languishing lament on endless aching needs stoked the embers still lit inside me. I shed tears. I was not yet fully conscious of a celibacy crisis. For now, on the road with my friends, I dodged a creeping loneliness.

Balfe later had the inmates at Collins Bay Penitentiary rocking and roaring and on their feet for his "Delta Dawn" mansion in the sky.

The concerts pulled back the veil on a life few could understand—our camaraderie, professional skills, humour, and, really, how ordinary we all were. The Hidden Talents was our manna from heaven.

"Claire, reading the album liner covers I wrote long ago, I smile and yet wince a bit. My words captured an idyllic portrait of the priesthood, words I believed in and yet were struggling to live. The words on the second cover lining only two years later mention emerging struggles."

April 25, 1984, Hidden Talents: "It is the last night of our recording session in Ottawa and the eerie midnight blackness of the nearby Corkery country sky is ablaze with the brilliant splendour of the northern lights. Another exquisite moment of divine surprise. Dancing in their freedom, shivering and shimmering from the treetops to the stars, the northern lights offer us a celestial celebration of life . . . was it our imagination or did we hear the not-so-distant laughter of a God madly in love with His earth and His children. Like the northern lights of this spring, our priesthood strives to be that celebration and witness of God's creative love. Like the northern lights, we dance with a divine partner lifegiving in His embrace."

April 1986, Songs We Learned at Our Mother's Knee and Other Joints: "Slowly we are learning that life is about choices and their consequences;

---

23 "What stands out most about the Hidden Talents is their honest, almost naked sense of humour," *The London Free Press*, June 20, 1984.

about deciding what is worth living for and what is not. God has called us, and we can never be the same again.

This is no naive joy we talk about, no Pollyanna priesthood. We are too conscious of the tensions tugging at our hearts, the vocation crisis of our friends, the pain and loneliness which becomes the scary yet wise companions of any thoughtful human journey. Our priesthood is an offering of joy and sorrow, pain, and possibility, reverencing our wounds and weakness through which God graces creation."

CHAPTER 20

Darker Days

In ministry, I seldom tired of proclaiming Jesus' radical nature of grace, i.e., love, also his denouncing religious leaders' smug self-righteousness, and his choosing to eat with tax collectors and sinners. Some days, I spotted the Pharisees in church stonewalling God's grace. I monitored the Pharisee in me as well. As good as these early priest years were, darker clouds were moving in.

Breaking Up

In 1982, there had been the abrupt breaking up of the pastoral team of Don, Tom, Bonnie, and me, a hierarchical decision with little input by those directly affected. After hearing the news, I headed to Don's cottage the next morning to sit like a lost puppy on his camp stairs until he woke up. He poured the coffee and tutored me on his life lessons on bishops, obedience, and faith. I stayed at the Pro-Cathedral while the others had new assignments. The new pastor, Rev. David Cresswell, a former Guatemala missionary, was a gifted pastor in the *Lone Ranger* model. We were friends on the golf course and watched sports on tv. I sat forlornly though on the rectory stairs that first morning watching Cresswell implement a dozen changes, recalling Father Bausch's advice to new pastors to proceed cautiously, respecting local history, traditions, and leaders.

Laity

MacLellan had asked a rhetorical question once on why a Catholic's IQ might drop fifty points opening the doors of the church. This was a "Dad talking to the Virgin Mary statue" type question. MacLellan was puzzled by otherwise smart people offering somnolent resistance to becoming active in the faith community. I was noticing how a "pray, pay, and obey" mandate to Catholics might induce a dumb-it-down passive paralysis among some of them. Don may have modelled a collaborative ministry, but the faithful also had to deal with domineering and uncompromising pastors fixated on a priest's unquestioned authority as sole custodians of the faith. There was ministry for lay people to do, but only within the grave limitations of canon law and male clergy privilege.

Anti-Abortion

I angered a few extreme anti-abortion zealots who were handing out those repulsive, dead fetus postcards. Instead, I talked about a pro-life position that cared about the born as well as the unborn and why these women might find themselves in such vulnerable, soul-wrenching situations: No birth control. Sexual assault. Health benefits withheld. Lower wages, no jobs, no viable options to say yes to life. I had listened to women's stories. On my office bulletin board were American Benedictine Sister Joan Chittister's words: "In fact, I think in many cases, your morality is deeply lacking if all you want is a child born but not a child fed, not a child educated, not a child housed. And why would I think that you do not? Because you don't want any tax money to go there. That's not pro-life. That's pro-birth."[24]

Pro-life, not pro-birth, womb to tomb.

Priests in Crisis

The priesthood was taking its toll on the lads. Father Joe Cangiano, an affable pastor at St. Peter's Church who resided at the Pro-Cathedral, went out for a

---

24 Heidi Schlumpf, "Sr. Joan Chittister's 2004 quote on 'pro-life' versus 'pro-birth' goes viral," *National Catholic Reporter,* May 23, 2019, https://www.ncronline.org/news/politics/sr-joan-chittisters-2004-quote-pro-life-versus-pro-birth-goes-viral.

jog one afternoon and never came back. He dropped dead of a heart attack. He was fifty-one. Don MacLellan would have a fatal heart attack at fifty-two. I spotted a different pattern of some priests dying soon after they retired. Priests were also resigning, taking leaves, or away on health programs to deal with alcoholism or recuperating from burnout. A popular Redemptorist retreat facilitator left, to marry, but also because he no longer believed in God.

What?

How could this be? My faith was still London-North Bay-Prashaw solid, questions notwithstanding.

The celibacy calling was far less certain. The workaholic inside bossed me, yes, still performing many good deeds that nevertheless left me exhausted at the end of a hectic week. I headed to the liquor cabinet sometimes for a scotch or two. I did reach for the bottle for an anesthetic respite from a skulking loneliness.

CHAPTER 21

St. Andrew's, Sudbury

1984–1986

In the summer of 1984, I spent a few months in Ottawa assisting North Bay's Father Dennis Murphy plan for the fall visit of Pope John Paul II to Canada. In September, when the pope departed, I headed to Sudbury as associate pastor at St. Andrew the Apostle Church. This move felt right on many counts, wrapping up five years at the Pro-Cathedral, a time to leave my hometown for new challenges. My parents would only be a ninety-minute drive away, the same distance for a Tomiko Lake cottage that six young priests now owned, our sane and insane refuge.

There was no bell to ring at St. Andrew's supper table.

Sudbury was the north's largest city, already at ninety thousand, double North Bay's size. Differences were apparent right away. With the Falconbridge and INCO mines, there were more immigrants from Europe, strong unions, and a few strikes. My thesis at St. Peter's Seminary had examined the "right to work" church teaching through the lens of the 1978 INCO strike, then the longest in the city's history. Sudbury was this ring of bulging hills set on a basin containing some of the richest nickel ore in the world. There was a proud, vibrant Franco-Ontarien community with its own flourishing arts and culture. Laurentian University, facing a financial crisis now, was growing by leaps and bounds then. Indeed, Sudbury was as well, named the regional seat for government and healthcare. The modest bungalows in subdivisions circling downtown reminded me of my Pinewood neighbourhood in North

Bay. The hard-working folk were down-to-earth, some below the earth, seventeen thousand working in the mines.

All to the music of Stompin' Tom Connors' "Sudbury Saturday Night."

My pastor was Steve Clarke, a native of North Bay, my third "boss" after MacLellan and Cresswell. One of the positives in having a new pastor and new city was to be inserted into a different circle of priests, men like James "Harpo" Sharpe and Harris Mulcahey. Sharpe was another Hollywood casting in the clan of priests. He did his good works and then relaxed at Sudbury Downs, placing a wager on the trotting horses. Story after story rolled out in his Scottish burr as we gathered in the rectory, tales on a legendary Father John "Boxcar" Callaghan, whose church was on Broadway Ave. in Wawa, Ontario. Callaghan spoke fondly of his twenty-hour car rides to New York City, "Broadway to Broadway." I enjoyed my time with Clarke. Laid back, he was not a priest to stay in uniform all day. There appeared to be mutual respect in this "arranged marriage." I worked hard not to screw up and again gravitated to ministries with youth, engaged couples, and pastoral care.

There were new families to befriend, my never-ending quest for normal, a home away from home, families like the Medinas, Piccinins, the Olivers, and a few others where it felt safe to be off duty. Good meals. Conversation. Wine and irreverent teens to keep me honest. New squash partners as well, like Fr. Mike Brehl at neighbouring Holy Redeemer Church.

Ellen Mackinnon, Gino Medina, and their family became good friends. Ellen was a gifted lay pastoral chaplain at Sudbury General Hospital. One day, we bounded down the hospital stairs towards the cafeteria. A nurse asked me how I was, and, apparently, I offered a long-winded answer over two flights of stairs, divulging personal information, everything but my x-rays. When MacKinnon and I were in the cafeteria line, she grabbed my forearm and whispered pastoral care.

"You know, Rick, sometimes when people ask you how you are, all they want to hear is 'fine'."

I laughed, a window on my Peter Pan, extrovert personality with few filters that seemed both a blessing and a curse. Make that a Peter Pan-Captain Hook personality. Once, after I sustained a concussion on a head-over-heels bike accident, MacKinnon suggested I sleep over in their basement recreation room. Kara, one of her teens, set an alarm and woke me every few hours to check how I was.

Around 1:00 a.m., Kara tapped me on the shoulder with her first skill-testing cognitive question.

"Father Rick, do you walk to school in the morning, or do you take your lunch?"

I reached for a pillow to concuss Kara.

Preaching, I was drawn to the ambiguities these good parishioners shared and tried to live. They faced many challenges: their adult children living with partners before marriage; a marriage ending; illnesses, or a materialism clashing with faith values. There in the pews were good people with few answers nor clear beliefs. I resuscitated dry or complicated ancient scripture passages, stories that broke out of the mind to emotions and whole persons, to quote Andrew Greeley.[25]

I could relate. The ambiguities were embedded in my own faith journey. I was still comfortable preaching and teaching this faith if I also acknowledged its intangibles, the doubts, and the enduring questions.

Clarke let me take a week off right after Christmas liturgies in 1984 as he had scheduled his holidays in January. This proved providential. I headed home to enjoy a late Christmas Day supper with my parents and two siblings visiting there with their young children. I inhaled a week of Prashaw fun and more cheating at cards.

"Claire, this is when I received the second worst phone call of my life."

"Poppy?"

I had planned to be back at St. Andrew's on New Year's Eve for a liturgy and parish dance. Dad had been complaining of lower back pain, spending considerable time in the bathroom on December 31, 1984. I extracted a promise he would see his doctor once the house emptied of family.

---

25 Harris, Mark, "Andrew Greeley," *New York Times,* May 6, 1984, https://www.nytimes.com/1984/05/06/magazine/andrew-greeley.html.

I kissed him goodbye on the forehead.

When I arrived in Sudbury an hour and a half later, Clarke greeted me with the news that Dad had been rushed to the hospital. I should return immediately. He may have known more. On the phone, Father Mark Balfe, who had gone to the hospital to anoint my father, urged me to hurry.

No one said he had died, but I somehow knew. I packed a suitcase for a week's visit. I brought vestments. And, in a peculiar denial, I did not hurry, keeping within speed limits on a foreboding, slow drive home. Balfe greeted me in the hospital parking lot. We hugged, and, for the first time, I heard that Dad, my best friend, had died, instantly on an emergency bed at St. Joseph's when his aorta burst. Dead in less than a minute. Now, if there's enough warning and people with those pains go to the hospital, emergency surgery is often successful. That is my brother Jon's story from a few decades later when he felt a stabbing pain while shovelling snow. In an hour, he was in an ambulance to Sudbury for a life-saving operation. The aorta aneurysms appear to be genetic, especially in males. I am booked every few years for tests.

After I hugged Balfe, I ran into Bishop Carter at the Emergency entrance doors. He had come to bless Dad. We returned to say prayers. When Carter left, I was alone with Sr. Nona Dennis, a chaplain and dear friend of Dad's. I leaned over to kiss him that second time on New Year's Eve. My tears splashed an anointing on his cold face. The leader of the band was gone.

Cruz interrupted the story.

"What was the worst phone call of your life?"

Smart kid.

"When Suzanne called me in California to tell me about Adam drowning."

"I was almost six when Poppy died," Claire said. "I remember the funeral."

I chose for the back of Dad's memorial prayer card this passage from Henri Nouwen's *Clowning in Rome:*[26]

"Slowly, I started to realize that in the great circus of Rome, full of lion tamers and trapeze artists whose dazzling feats grabbed our attention, the real and

---

26 Henri Nouwen, *Clowning in Rome* (Toronto: Penguin Canada Random House, 1979).

true story was told by the clowns. Of the clowns we say, 'They are like us.' The clowns remind us with a tear and a smile that we share the same human weaknesses. The longer I was in Rome, I enjoyed the clowns, the peripheral people who by their humble, saintly lives evoke a smile and awaken hope . . ."

The church was packed for Dad's funeral Mass on a bitingly cold January morning. I wanted to be down with the family mourning, but the blessing and burden for priests at family liturgies is usually to be celebrant; I added a few stories after Margie's fine eulogy. I tried to tame the gruesome pain with the joke that women at The Pro would now be spared his ceaseless flirting. They may have been more disappointed than relieved. Home after the cemetery and a parish luncheon, the adults were exhausted and ready for a nap when Katie, Margie's three-year-old, announced it was her birthday and asked us when her party was starting. We forgot! A young child hurtled us back into life's rhythms—a posse headed to stores for cake, balloons, and presents.

Mom was now a widow, her tears reserved for pillows late at night. Otherwise, she drew on her "grin and bear it" Beaton stoic personality for family and friends. Within days of Dad's death, she shipped his clothes to St. Vincent de Paul charities. Within months, she put the house of twenty-five years up for sale, moving into a charming Clarence Street apartment across the street from where I had swiped that *Playboy*. Worried about how she was managing, days off meant regular drives home to help her handle the business side of a modest estate, banking, and shopping. Interestingly, she bought new art and fashionable clothes as she stepped out from dad's long shadow. Our friendship grew even dearer. Still, the grief was evident, early God-forsaken days, a brave face masking a broken heart. They had been married thirty-nine years.

I threw my sadness back into ministry. As at The Pro, the social life was an essential dimension of St. Andrew's faith community. I promoted golf tournaments and curling bonspiels, the New Year's Eve dances, parish suppers, youth car rallies, and more; the social life grew the ties to the parish and one another. Roman Catholics were not alone in this. James Orr, my nephew, spoke fondly of his United Church family and youth experiences well into his university years. His memories focused on energetic ministers, youth outreach, and social events. This incarnational God dwelled in our dancing shoes, songs, sports, lives, and loves, along with worship.

Father Rick and Theresa Doiron, St. Andrew's
Ministry demanded pie-tasting

As at The Pro, there were scores of appreciated meals for mourners after funerals, back in the parish hall from the cemetery. Meals cooked, served in faith and love by the Catholic Women's League team, dishes done, and halls cleaned. Rinse and repeat. I attended hundreds of these meals as a priest, struck by this recurring miracle, mindful that this manifestation of community was happening in thousands of parish halls, synagogues, and temples across the country. There is abundant good to relish.

Bishop Carter appointed me to the diocesan Senate of Priests, sitting on the renewal committee. Carter named me the diocesan vocations director too. I spoke to high school classes, meeting lads discerning a calling, also visiting seminarians studying in London and Toronto. It was my turn to take them out for dinner. There was much good news preaching the awakening of God within us and a call to respond. Again, to be authentic, I needed to translate Sacred Scripture to real life, to acknowledge the difficulties, to speak straight from the heart, straight from the heavens too. Inevitably, each vocations' talk returned to that dual calling to be Father Rick without forgetting Rick.

This may have been my forever attempt at self-preservation, a life jacket to keep Rick afloat.

I resisted clericalism that even in the northern church could surface, minions obedient to a Rome which, with Pope John Paul II and his lieutenant, Cardinal Joseph Ratzinger, the future Pope Benedict XVI, appeared bent on locking us in wholly on Rome's version on the will of Christ. It could risk gutting love in favour of a domineering and authoritarian male clerical caste. In talking to young men responding to a vocation call, I became aware of a few seminarians then who, to use Andrew Greeley's phrase, resembled "young fogeys." Unquestionably, they possessed faith and generosity in their good works. Still, it was their rigid, auto-response reciting eternal truths that troubled me, more so, hearing it at their young age. I was not bent on cloning other Father Ricks. Nevertheless, I dreaded parishioners dealing with those priests most days. The poor folk in the pews needed a hug before scripted, uncomforting quotes from canon law or the Bible.

> Faith to them (young fogeys) is clinging to a shrine, remaining in a safe harbour, not Abraham Heschel's 'endless pilgrimage of the heart'," Ted Schmidt writes. "No 'burning songs, audacious long-ings, daring thoughts,' rather a soothing and secure bedtime lullaby before the sleep of the content and secure. Many in the advanced capitalist world would simply blend in with the herd and are buf-feted by cultural trends. Here Ratzinger is correct. The authentic self disappears. Spontaneity and creativity evaporate. In Eric Fromm's words, they have given up the 'freedom to.' Mature Christians, however, maintain their 'freedom in Christ' and maintain a loving but

critical identification with the structure of the church. In Cardinal Newman's famous phase, they toast the pope, but conscience first.[27]

Put a collar on those young fogeys, and they marched in uniformity to Rome. Put the bishop's mitre on their head and staff crozier in their hand and, as we lamented at the cottage, it seemed blood no longer sufficiently flowed to brains nor hearts. Vatican II collegiality was abandoned for a hierarchy over and above gifted laity. Women were put in their place by young men who were vowed, chaste, and chilled.

In a homily, I shared a story on the laity living their faith with this church hierarchy.

> One definition of the pope is that he is a servant of the servants of God. In a hierarchical church, that makes cardinals servants of the servants of the servants of God, bishops are servants of the servants of the servants of the servants of God. Priests are servants of the servants of the servants of the servants of the servants of God. Clearly, the laity has a servants' problem!

I then reflected on Jesus washing the feet of the disciples, a radical shift in how to be servant.

My fellow diocesan priests were much like a larger family or sports team or political caucus, meaning I could love and "hate" my teammates intensely on the same day, even the same hour. Brother priests could bring joy or grief. I was not able to share with all priests what was troubling my heart. That intimacy was reserved for a few friends at the cottage where we fuelled our "burning songs, audacious longings, and daring thoughts".

Keeping me entertained were sports, scotch, and my hard wiring to humour. One summer, three priest amigos—Peter Moher, Ray Renaud, and I—hopscotched on cheap flights across the continent to follow a Toronto Blue Jays' road trip. In Kansas City, aware that Peter's sister, Mary, was about to deliver her baby, we scrawled a sign that read, "Honey, Have You Had the Baby? Signed, The Three Fathers." We alerted a *CBC Sports* cameraman. The

---

27 Ted Schmidt, *Journeys to the Heart of Catholicism*, ((Hamilton: Seraphim Editions, 2007), 122.

broadcasting crew of Don Chevrier and Tony Kubek referred to the sign with a puzzled Chevrier, known as the "Voice of God," adding that he had no further comment on Mary's "Three Fathers."

At the cottage, after Sunday liturgies, the priests close by gathered, unmasked. Nothing was off-limits to talk about: popes, bishops, church intransigence, all on the same menu with swims, barbecues, and drinks. In this clergy locker room, we could name the bullshit and not defend the indefensible. I don't remember much self-pity then about our lot. We shared plenty of good news stories as well. Bottles disappeared, and legends grew. On one Monday, my friends told me how, at 2:00 a.m., passed out on the couch from ministry exhaustion and a wee dram, I suddenly sat up and joined a conversation in mid-sentence without missing a beat.

Ministry was still good. I experienced setbacks, failures, disappointments, all the stuff of daily life any working stiff knows.

"Claire, enthusiasm covered the deficiencies. I still loved this job."

"Hit pause, Uncle Rick. I'm making drinks, Good Friday, chocolate eggs and all!"

CHAPTER 22

Ciao, Roma!

1986–1987

Marcel Gervais, my seminary professor, was the new bishop in the Diocese of Sault Ste. Marie. A year into his appointment, he asked me to drop by his Sudbury home. I could not guess his news. On behalf of St. Peter's Seminary, he asked me to return to my studies, this time in Rome, to prepare to be a professor in London. "Ask" is the polite word for command. Gervais had already responded favourably to a request by London's Bishop John Sherlock.

Did the seminary want Rick's grounded sex talks?

"Hahaha, Uncle Rick. We could have collaborated. A whole new dating platform for me," Claire laughed.

"Seriously, Claire, they wanted me to leave parish ministry to study sacraments and liturgy at Sant'Anselmo College, a Benedictine institution on the Aventine Hill. I would live at the Canadian College, a seminary-like residence for student priests pursuing graduate studies at pontifical colleges."

My first three reactions to Gervais were predictable. No, no, and no. Acquiesce I did though, after a "for the record" plea on how strongly I felt called to parish ministry, how I thrived there.

"Exactly, the kind of priest we need in the classroom to inspire future pastors," smiled Gervais.

Are bishops programmed to deflect contrary arguments, laying everything at the feet of God?

Ciao, Roma!

"Cruz, you must visit Rome, a city you would love!"

The Eternal City. Besides the delicious pasta, the primo, secondo, and terzo course meals, beautiful people were there. I recalled Father Cavanagh's lecture about the diet celibacy imposed on priests, those real dangers arising from looking at the menu too long when you could not order. The sweet *la dolce vita* was on this Roman menu. I fell in love with its living history, the Tiber River, the catacombs. I ate at restaurants down the side alleys away from the high-priced tourist traps.

I loved stepping on the cobblestones into ancient history; the love tempered a bit in the Vancouver-like rainy season of November through January. For school days, I had a forty-five-minute walk from the Canadian College on Via Crescenzio situated near St. Peter's Square. A daily ritual was sipping a café latte at an espresso bar halfway to classes.

"Cruz, a young boy about ten, smaller than you, often came by at the same time, school bag slung over his shoulders, his head hardly reaching the counter. He ordered a coffee and then proceeded to dump an entire jar of zucchero, sugar, into his tiny cup. In one gulp, he drank it, put his knapsack back on, and headed to school."

"Claire, somewhere in Rome, I imagined parents puzzled by teacher's notes on how their well-behaved son, who had left their house calm, had morphed into this out-of-control sugar bomb in the classroom. I was in on his secret."

There were days I was late for classes, especially if I witnessed an accident in the crazy chaos of Rome's streets. It was worth the delay to find another coffee bar and sit for the impromptu street theatre unfolding. Two drivers exited the cars to examine the damage. Cue the shouting, arms waving, the carabinieri arriving to escalate the drama to its pitch-perfect denouement. Documents were thrown on car hoods. Spectators joined the debate from the mosh pit. These were three-act plays.

Daily, I observed *furbizia*, the Italian character trait for their clever "end runs" around inconvenient laws. One time, a judge dramatically announced that he was closing the entire city core to traffic because of gagging, high levels of pollution. The next day, vested business interests mailed him death threats. He relented, cuing new threats from the left. On the third day, perched firmly on the fence, he qualified his decision to say he never meant to ban every car, only vehicles without a new exemption sticker. Presto, a long, lucrative sticker queue formed! Most cars had the exemption sticker on the windshield. However, whenever a car without a sticker ventured into the city centre, the police stopped them with a theatrical flourish worthy of an Oscar. Pollution levels remained high.

Furbizia! Roma!

"Uncle Rick, I think some Canadians have discovered their *furbizia* in the pandemic."

The piazzas. The soccer balls kicked in the squares. An entire city out walking, talking, and smoking, arm in arm. The eternal flirting on the Spanish Steps. The cats that brushed by pants legs on the ristorante patios. The taxi tsunami. The sardine-stuffed buses where one quickly learned to place hands on your own wallet or purse as some passengers laid hands on you.

And St. Peter's Square, with its community of beggars, Romani, priests, brothers, and religious sisters peddling their Catholic swag—statues, rosaries, relics. Dad's "clowns" in Rome, as Nouwen had called them. They might be the ones nearest to God. I gravitated to those clowns, salvation on the margins of the holy city. Some in this circus chose the edges while others appeared to be in exile from the pungent clericalism on display everywhere. It was a teeming, breathing city of life, lust, and la dolce vita. Keeping a celibate's distance, I admired that Rome.

Sadly, Rome also meant living at a Canadian College with twenty-one priests, far, far removed from the lively faith communities I had served at The Pro and St. Andrew's. The sad part was not the priests nor the college per se; it was a shock to adapt to liturgies and studies void of a community of lay people.

"Cruz, the Canadian College where I lived was a few minutes' walk from the Vatican, the city-state that separated from Rome in 1929. It is roughly half the size of your High Park in Toronto."

I admired the goodness and intellect in those priests at my new residence. Less admirable were a handful of priests there and elsewhere perpetually chasing the pope and Vatican spectacles, single men in skirts chasing skirts, the weight of an all-male, clerical, and ecclesial world never so evident.

Among my fellow students was Father Christian Lépine, future archbishop of Montréal. Lépine and I ate our share of hamburgers at Speedy Burger. There was Father Ron Fabbro, destined to be Bishop of London.

Father Robidoux was the gracious rector from the Sulpician religious order, a perfect Mr. Rourke imitation from the first *Fantasy Island* show. Maria, the housekeeper, was a breath of fresh air. We chatted regularly about her family and pets as I practiced my bad Italian. Languages never came easy. Humour and effort gave me an audience. There were new friendships that breathed energy into this home away from home. I did not complain out loud nor to anyone in Canada. It was a comfortable oasis, capped on Sundays with a late morning, multi-course brunch after the Sunday liturgy with the aperitivo and disgetivo cocktails around pleasant chatter with clergy and diplomat guests in those back court gardens. When I was desperate, I slipped out across the city to the Sant'Egidio lay community, a vibrant place that attracted searching youth in its mission of prayer, justice, and service for the poor.

On a positive note, Rome's Catholic Church was a reminder of its universality, ethnic diversity, and unity.

I need to sort out how Father Rick in 1986 viewed Rome and the Vatican compared to later years when the judgment is harsher. Clearly, I did struggle even then in the pervasive clericalism, the dominant orthodoxy (power, control), the suffocating uniformity of Roman Catholicism practiced there. I had tolerated that Rome easier when it was half a world away as I ministered in the north.

And, far worse than anything I had experienced in Canada, women were put in their place in this ecclesial Rome. Women cooked, cleaned, and sewed for the clergy. They were not on the altar.

"Claire, Pope Francis released a decree permitting women there to be readers at liturgies."[28]

"Good God!"

At first, I thought this was the *Beaverton* satire news site mocking the church. Worse, it was factual breaking news. In 2021, Rome now permitted the installation of women readers (and acolytes) in their official doctrine even though, practically, we in North America had women readers and Eucharistic ministers immediately after the Second Vatican Council a half-century ago. The 2021 decree still banned women priests.

Hearing Pope Francis' news, some cheered Rome's progress. Others spied the trap of formalizing the great divide between the ordained and non-ordained; women were banned from reading the gospel that was the exclusive realm of ordained priests and deacons.

"Brutal, this is so medieval," Claire said.

This was my Rome in 1987. It endures today.

There was that memorable Eucharist and breakfast with Pope John Paul II. In line to be introduced, I spoke a few words to the pontiff about Bishop Carter and my work on his papal visit to Canada. John Paul II had become pope in 1978 when I was a seminarian. He would be the single pope during my years as a priest. I respected his indefatigable travel to the ends of the earth and his formidable social justice encyclicals.

However, there was no warmth nor human exuberance in him like the folksy Pope Francis who melted hearts that first night on the balcony in 2013, speaking the common greeting, *"Buona sera"* to those gathered in St. Peter's Square after the puffs of white smoke had announced a new pope. As Catholics, we pray for the pope. Pope Francis appeared to be more of a kindred spirit as he washed the feet of prisoners, personally paid his hotel bill from the conclave of cardinals after they elected him, and chose a simple, austere casa to live. John Paul II's twenty-seven years as pope with Cardinal Ratzinger at

---

28 Winfield, Nicole, "Pope says women can read at mass, but still not be priests," *Associated Press*, Jan. 11, 2021, https://apnews.com/article/pope-francis-women-still-cant-be-priest-3bdcad94325be16ee2993f61eb17c5a0.

his side had ensconced the church deeper in a safer orthodoxy. It was a time, too, when they appointed many bishops of similar theology. I had met a few progressive nuns in Canada who, in exasperation, stopped praying for the conservative Pope Benedict XV1. I humbly suggested to them the pope may need their prayers more than ever.

Living in Rome was an odd paradox of enduring this Vatican version of church versus visiting the treasures of Michelangelo's David, Bernini's sculpted bronze canopy, and the heavenly Sistine Chapel. I could stalk Michelangelo every day. I did enjoy attending the papal blessings in St. Peter's Square. Still, I clearly belonged on the periphery with the clowns, a safe distance from this gaudy, glorious, triumphal pageantry.

It was as if I had taken a time capsule back to the previous four hundred years of the church. All this inner turmoil was slow to surface. More importantly, I believed I could stomach this exile if I stayed focused on the arranged path to teach. I remained faithful to my celibate priesthood, feeding the stomach instead with Italy's food, sipping its wine, and delighting as a spectator in the passion of the menu alive in the piazzas. Again, the celibate life was assisted by a new spiritual director, Fr. Marcel Rooney, a warm American Benedictine monk at Sant'Anselmo College. Confession was still good for the soul.

Some days, on the edges of this church, I bought a bouquet of flowers from a street vendor to plant in the arid desert of my Canadian College cell.

CHAPTER 23

Game, Set and Match, Pope John Paul II

Mom visited me in Rome in 1987 along with Jude who, at the time, was a lay member of Madonna House Apostolate.[29] I was wrapping up my first-year studies, doing well while still questioning this plan to be a seminary professor. Visits like Mom's and Jude's were tonic for this exile in Rome.

Heading to Fiumicino Airport, I had rehearsed a trick to play on Mom. Planning their two-week itinerary, I had penciled in St. Peter's Basilica, the Coliseum, catacombs, and Assisi pilgrimages. Mom would be a special guest at the Canadian College celebration on Mother's Day; in our splendid courtyard, she would be a surrogate mother for the priests, bishops, even a cardinal who might attend.

However, the Italian Tennis Open for the women's draw was scheduled during their visit. Gertie Beaton had loved playing tennis. Her forehand smash, volleys, and serves had won her tournaments. And, looking at pictures of her from then, I imagined this beauty had lads interested in playing her, forty-love, double faults, and all. If she wasn't watching her beloved Blue Jays, she followed tennis and golf religiously on television. When Dick Prashaw had

---

29 Catherine Doherty, a Russian baroness and her husband, Eddie Doherty, an Eastern rite
  priest, founded Madonna House in Combermere, ON. in the Madawaska Valley
  in 1947. Madonna House calls itself "a family of Christian lay men, women, and
  priests, striving to incarnate the teachings of Jesus Christ by forming a community of
  love," www.madonnahouse.org

fought in Italy, and the lovebird letters volleyed across the Atlantic Ocean, he had noticed one picture where Gert had removed her engagement ring. He was upset. Aware of soldiers breaking up with their wives or girlfriends, he sent her a letter asking what in God's name was up. She told him, Beaton-like, to stop being such a fool because, did he not know, no boy would play her with that ring on her finger.

Mom, Rick, and Jude in St. Peter's Square, after tennis!

"Claire, match point to Gert and Beaton ingenuity!"

"I love it!"

I hopped on a bus to the airport.

"Mom," I told her, "we are going to be busy this week. St. Peter's Basilica, the pope, the Vatican. And, oh, there is the Italian Open tennis tournament. We could see Martina Navratilova play this Wednesday. Unfortunately, that's when Pope John Paul's audience is, which I will take you to . . ."

Mom smashed my lob right back.

"Doesn't the pope have other audiences?"

I pulled out the tennis tickets I had already bought. Tennis first, pope later. I had guessed right.

Game, set, and match, Mom over Pope John Paul II.

"Bahahaha," laughed Claire. "We get our sports addiction from Grandma too."

"Cruz and Uncle Rick, grandma was such a bad driver. She needed pillows underneath her to prop her up because she couldn't see over the driver's wheel. When I was little, I thought my parents didn't love me when they put me in the car with her driving."

"As a senior, Claire, I suspect Mom may have seduced a driving instructor or two to pass her road tests."

The tennis was her trip's highlight, a chance to watch the doubles team of Navratilova and Gabriela Sabatini in the women's bracket. Navratilova was the greatest female tennis player of all time, the only player to have ever held the top spot in both singles and doubles for over two hundred weeks. At the Foro Antico outdoor clay courts, we needed gin and tonics to survive the sweltering heat. When the match ended, we headed down the stairs as the announcer in broken English said a singles match would start on the same court in thirty minutes. I was ready for a siesta. Did Mom hear him? She tapped me on the shoulder.

"Are these tickets good for the singles?"

I heard that voice again.

Lie, Rick.

But you never lie to your mother. More gin and tonics. Mom might be this quiet, gentle woman, but she often outfoxed us all drawing on that stubborn Scottish streak. The Czech Navratilova and Argentinean Sabatini won the women's doubles finals.

Jude, who now lives in Vermont and is "back to the land", among other things, decided to raise three chicks. She lost two to predators. The one named Gertie has survived. I am not surprised.

Mom wrote this note to her grandchildren in 1994.

"Someday you'll have a grandchild
And you will surely see.
Why being your grandmother
Means the world to me.

My wish for the future is you will all be happy. Put your hand in the hand of God. I wish you wisdom in the decisions that you face. Learn to get along and do not let jealousy or bitterness come into your relationships. Take time to get to know people. Always bring your friends home and listen to your parent's advice. They love you and want your happiness. Don't be deceived — that money will make you happy. Happiness is found in your faith, in searching out what you're best suited to. Your hope is in your daily living, trying to be loving."

love Grandma
1994

CHAPTER 24

The God Who Does Not Care

Good Friday, 1987

I met the "God who does not care" on Good Friday on a hillside in southeastern France, in the heart of the Burgundy wine region.

"Claire, living in Rome then, but leaving Rome, in the holiest of weeks in the Holy City, that is a story."

This was nearing the end of my first year of studies in sacramental theology.

It was an exceptionally warm April, Rome coming to life after the rainy, damp weeks of winter. I had spent days in a dreary hospital with a bout of pneumonia served up by those walks in the rain. Now spring had exploded. Glorious sunshine, the luscious cypresses, azaleas, thistles, and plants were blooming beside ancient ruins, a smile on people's faces again, and more skin showing. Was there anything more "heavenly" than sitting in a piazza sipping a glass of wine and people watching?

At Christmas, I had attended the liturgies at St. Peter's Basilica before jumping on a train for a week's vacation in Sicily with a new priest friend, John Tollan from New Zealand. However, at Easter, struggling to stay the course, I felt no compulsion to join the millions of pilgrims flocking to St. Peter's for the Holy Week liturgies. Tollan and I headed in the opposite direction. I had my own special pilgrimage planned. We boarded the train to Florence and then over to France to spend four days at Taizé, a village and home to the Ecumenical Community of Taizé, founded by Brother Roger.

"Cruz, Brother Roger earlier with his sister had provided an underground shelter to persecuted Jews and others in World War II."

As the son of a Protestant pastor, he had lamented how divided Christianity had become and vowed to work for reconciliation and unity. His order had over one hundred Protestant and Catholic monks. Their simplicity, kindness, and emphasis on reconciliation were beacons of hope. Youth from around the world flocked there.

Taizé was everything I hoped for and more—songs, prayers, and fellowship, served up with wine, delicious French bread and pastries. I treasured two incidents, one that contributed towards a life-changing moment four years later. Praying the Stations of the Cross in the magnificent cathedral, I turned to see Brother Roger standing beside me. He introduced himself. We chatted. When he heard that I was a Catholic priest studying in Rome who came to Taizé in Holy Week to discover God's will for him, he swung around to a statue of Mary, made the sign of the cross, and prayed the Hail Mary in impeccable Latin. I mumbled along, forgetting some of the *Ave Maria, gratia plena, Dominus tecum* I had memorized as an altar boy long ago.

Roman Catholic prayers spoken in Latin by a Protestant monk in France. My kingdom of God was indeed stretching in all directions. My studies in church history had highlighted how fluid those first four centuries had been between Jesus' ministry and the organization of a church to be blessed by Emperor Constantine. That merger birthed a church identified primarily as the saved over and against ALL others who were damned, church leaders mandated to be the gatekeepers for the faithful, a Catholic church proclaimed to be the true church, the one and only way to salvation, and a framing of religion primarily as a set of beliefs, and far less as a pilgrim people struggling with questions and doubts. Now, Taizé and Brother Roger were fresh reminders of a big God and a Church of Christ beyond Rome.

"Claire, it stunned me seventeen years later to read the news that a woman with mental health issues attacked and knifed Brother Roger in the neck in this same cathedral. He died from those wounds."

"Really? That's awful," Claire said.

The second, finer treasure was unwrapped on the hillside on Good Friday. As a Roman Catholic, 3:00 p.m. is the traditional time to commemorate the crucifixion of Jesus.

"Right, Claire?"

Taizé had no such service that afternoon. A Stations of the Cross celebration was planned for 7:00 p.m.

So, on a glorious Friday, the weather warm and healing, I grabbed my Bible and headed to a hillside. I packed a baguette, cheese, and water. As I read the Passion readings, I asked God for clarity on this profound unhappiness I felt heading to teach. Yes, I could teach and be good at it. The bishops and seminary rector affirmed those gifts. Yes, I recognized the merit of having parish-loving seminary professors as teachers. Yes, I had bowed to sacrifice and a larger plan that I was still figuring out. On the vocation side, I was dying, an overriding ecclesial and spiritual malaise distancing me from this God I knew and loved, farther from this parish priesthood I enjoyed. It had been the relationship with people of faith, a building of community, a loving them as they were, people's precious life moments, the daily mundane conflicts too, our falling down and getting up, the encouraging, accompanying, and loving them till they could love themselves again. And now, this God of mine wanted me to step away for another calling or at least a virtual, distant pastoring of pastors.

"Like a Zoom pastor," smiled Claire.

"Ugh. Exactly!"

I had prayed. I had given great weight to people in authority—their office and wisdom of experience—to agree to these studies. And yet, in Rome at the Canadian College and the Vatican, I had found the opposite of who I was and what I believed.

What did God want of me?

Two files appeared on this hillside: professor at a seminary and parish priest. Which file, God, was yours? Which is mine?

There were tears and invocations, plain-speaking prayers as Don MacLellan had prayed in the chapel. On that warm Good Friday, while soaking up the sun, I discovered God's plan was not that precise. Other than loving me. Other than calling me to life. God did not care if I stayed or went, taught or be a pastor. And I laughed. My Good Friday memo was THE good news that God loved me, full stop. God was committed to being my companion, wherever. The choice was between these two goods. God was in both files. This was the God who did not care! About the details, that is.

Jerry O'Connor had told me his own vocation discernment, which ironically included Gervais, at the time organizing that lay community the O'Connors joined. Jerry was wrestling with a perceived call to the priesthood. Over time, he concluded it was a sense of duty more than any genuine call. Margie's sour jujubes helped clarify his discernment too! As Jerry said goodbye to Gervais after one spiritual direction, Gervais asked him the route he was taking to walk home. Jerry said he would walk four blocks south on Waterloo and two blocks east on Hill.

"Is there another way to go?" Gervais asked.

"Sure. I could go east first and then south to land there."

"Both routes bring you home," Gervais smiled.

I doubted Gervais would appreciate me telling back to him his own discernment counsel when I explained I was coming home against his wishes. I did not make any decision that Good Friday nor for several months. I went home for the summer and returned to begin my second year of studies. It would be close to Christmas before I returned for good to the diocese.

In Taizé, I savoured that scary delight of freedom of choice and its responsibility. The God who did not care freed me to care.

I did choose parish life. I reassured my Italian friends in Sudbury their beloved Roma was not the reason for my departure. At a far deeper level, I grappled with "failure" for the first time in my life. I had been fortunate, sailing through school, earning two degrees, performing well, briefly as a journalist, and then as a priest at my first two parish assignments. Quitting studies in Rome was a failure on a mission given to me. I disappointed a few bishops, a seminary, and others. The Taizé hillside meditation had brought me peace. Still, there was no getting around the failure of choosing to end the studies. We do learn from our failures, as much or even more than our successes. I was discovering more of who I was and who I wanted to be and not be. I discovered a new resilience, survival skills, and the grace of not beating myself up forever. Lessons I filed away for future "failures."

After I returned to Canada, I preached the homily at the funeral Mass of a friend, Mac MacKinnon, Ellen's father, patriarch to a MacKinnon and Medina family. Mac, who died in his nineties, had converted to Catholicism when he was seventy, joking he switched so that a Catholic would die rather than another Presbyterian. I told that story along with talking about the movie, *Chariots of Fire*. The story of Eric Liddell, the Scottish runner, who wrestled with his God in a choice between two goods, to be a Christian missionary in China or to continue running, knowing that God called him to missionary work, but God had made him fast, and it pleased this God to see him run.

I remembered the God I met on the Taizé hillside. We celebrated God's pleasure in Mac's full life, Presbyterian and Roman Catholic. I continued to celebrate God calling me forward.

CHAPTER 25

Garden River and Batchewana

1988

[WARNING: This chapter contains information on residential schools that some readers may find distressing.]

While I was still in Rome, Mom had been found by a friend in an empty bathtub at her apartment; she may have been there twenty-four hours. A diagnosis confirmed a brain aneurysm leak, fortunately not my father's life-and-death type. She had a reasonably quick and full recovery after doctors at Sudbury General Hospital inserted a plate wall to dam the leak. Heading home to Canada, the days at Mom's bedside provided a safe bubble to return to the diocese and to meet up with the hospital pastoral team of Sr. Elaine Cassidy and Ellen MacKinnon along with other St. Andrew's friends.

I was grateful to Gervais for this time with Mom. Soon enough, the bishop called. He wanted me to go to Sault Ste. Marie to be administrator of a cluster of four parishes circling the city. It would be my first assignment in the west end of the diocese. I lived at an Immaculate Heart of Mary Church rectory on Garden River First Nation. I had a pastoral charge at Goulais River Mother of God Church, a Goulais River Mission, and Batchewana Bay's St. Isaac Jogues Church.

I was assigned to two "native parishes," as they were called then. This was manna from heaven. Or was it bannock? Celebrating the Eucharist at St. Isaac Jogues while looking out at Lake Superior was breathtaking, a "nearer my God, to thee" moment. While there were no bad assignments in an eleven-year ministry, this time would be special.

On my first Sunday morning in Garden River, I threw my alb on and headed out to the church near the 9:30 a.m. start time for Mass. Only a few people were there. I approached an elderly woman praying the rosary in the front pew.

"Good morning!" I smiled. "I'm Father Rick."

"Morning-FATHER."

I would enjoy this sing-song cadence I noticed predominantly in the older women rolling all the words together, peppered with a "Father" punctuation for each sentence.

"Mass today, right?" I asked, scanning the empty pews.

"Of-course-FATHER."

What must she be thinking of this new pastor asking if there was mass today?

"How many come usually?"

"LOTS-of-people-FATHER."

"When do they come?" I asked, gazing at my watch, knowing an 11:30 a.m. service in Goulais River was a forty-minute drive after this mass.

"They-will-be-HERE-soon-FATHER."

It was my baptism into local concepts of time; a 9:30 a.m. Mass that might begin closer to 10:00 a.m. Indeed, the church filled for a beautiful celebration with a choir, readers, and ministers of Communion. I was happy to start the 9:30 Mass on their time, except it pinched my 11:30 Mass across town. Within weeks, we flipped those two services, making it 9:30 in Goulais River and 11:30 in Garden River, or whenever. This suited me as I joined the packed post-Mass meal in the Garden River parish hall. I escaped though, before the afternoon Bingo and its thick cigarette smoke that hung like a low smog cover over the players.

Garden River and Batchewana First Nations immersed me in their delightful humour and deep spirituality that, then, still embraced but would not be contained exclusively by any Roman Catholic Latin Rite. People invited me to slow down, to rediscover the rhythms of the rising and setting of the sun, to soak up what truly mattered: the land, water, people, meals, family, children, peace, harmony, and accountability.

I loved their storytelling. It was easy to spot the vital role grandmothers played as keepers of the community wisdom. A youth who had a grandmother present was richly blessed if they listened. I sat. I listened. I learned. I remembered Frank O'Connor's wisdom from Peru on who was teaching who now.

At Immaculate Heart of Mary, there were many lifelong Catholics. Those coming to services appeared then largely comfortable still in the Catholic rituals and prayers. However, some others were embracing or returning to older, traditional practices from an Indigenous spirituality. Ceremony. Sage. Smudge. Medicine Wheel. Drumming. Dancing. Sweat lodge. They told stories that honoured Creation with spirit dancers and different names for the gods. I was open to working with leaders who wanted to blend the Christian and Indigenous traditions although some in the community preferred traditional Roman Catholic rites at the church. I acknowledged it was their church and their faith walk. After I left the priesthood, the Truth and Reconciliation Commission (TRC) investigation on residential schools would dominate the news. I would hear later that far more people in these communities came to see Christianity and Indigenous Spirituality as mutually exclusive.

I had listened to Art Solomon, an Ojibwe elder, speak at Anderson Lake as he weaved good memories into the broader quilt of the long assimilation of his People.

> Art Solomon brings an immediate hush to the auditorium," Jody Freeman reported from a (different) Montréal talk Solomon gave in 1993. "Art lights sage in a traditional sacred ritual, and as he gives thanks to the Creator, smoke from the sage spirals up, slowly reaching all of us with its sweet scent. Then, with humour and simplicity, passion and humility, Art speaks of the injustices suffered for hundreds of years by Indigenous Peoples in Canada, and of the healing that is needed to restore balance within ourselves and within all Creation. The auditorium is transformed into a place of sacredness where all are honoured: the dead, the living, those yet to be born,

the land and air and waters that sustain us. We all feel it. This is a deeply heartful man whose gentle presence has great power to heal and inspire.[30]

I knew only a little of the local painful church-Indigenous history—the cutting of hair, stealing of children, the suppression of their ways. Down the road from the rectory was the property where Shingwauk Indian Residential School had stood, operated by the Missionary Society of the Church of England.

> (For food) we got mush, two slices of bread, and a three-quarter cup of what they called cocoa in the morning for 365 days a year," Jack White said at a survivors' gathering years later. "(The staff) are sitting in their room having bacon and eggs, coffee and tea, crumpets, whatever, and we're starving. There were no fat kids at Shingwauk.
>
> Teddy Syrette, an intergenerational survivor, noted that "whether it's indirectly by being raised by somebody or as a great grandchild, might hold, what we know in our culture as blood trauma. The blood from our ancestors has trickled down through the bloodlines and it can hold a certain amount of stress (and) traumatic events that occurred can be passed on through the bloodlines . . .[31]

Heading east from Garden River, I would drive by the former properties for the Jesuit-run boys' and girls' residential schools in Spanish, ON., along the Canadian Pacific Railway branch line on the shore of Lake Huron. The empty shell of the St. Joseph Girls School was visible from the highway, its ruins an apt metaphor. St. Joseph's with St. Peter Claver School next door housed one hundred eighty students, the largest residential school in Ontario.

---

30 Radio Canada International. "Walking in Beauty and with Power—the Spirit of an Ojibwe Elder, Art Solomon." Adaptation by Jody Freeman on documentary, Dec. 30, 2017, Montréal, https://montrealserai.com/article/walking-in-beauty-and-with-power-the-spirit-of-an-ojibwe-elder-art-solomon.

31 Klassen, Jeff. "Where It Comes From-10 stories from the Shingwauk Gathering," *Soo Today*, Aug. 3, 2016, https://www.sootoday.com/local-news/where-it-comes-from-10-stories-from-the-shingwauk-gathering-10-photos-348879.

In *Indian School Days*, Anishinaabe author Basil Johnston described what it was like at St. Peter Claver during World War II and then his better years at a new Joseph Garner High School.[32] Johnston was ten when he was taken with his four-year-old sister, Marilyn; he saw her once a month for an hour, she silent and hugging his leg. Johnston focused on the clever ways Ojibway, Mohawk, and Cree students outfoxed the Jesuits. To help erase identities, the priests had assigned numbers instead of calling the children by name. Johnston was number forty-three. He resisted answering to a number, waiting to hear his real name. The students resorted to Sign language to safeguard their culture.

"Spanish! It was a word synonymous with residential school, penitentiary, reformatory, exile, dungeon, whippings, kicks, slaps, all rolled into one," Johnston wrote.

In a later lecture at Queen's University, Johnston described the devastation of abuse.

"Abuse is too mild a word. It's a violation of the worst kind. It violates not only the body, the flesh, but also the spirit. And you live with this fear of death and fear of being dispatched to Hell....Little ones suffered the most, outcasts, told Jesus loved them while their experiences were being unloved."[33]

George Couchie, a cultural leader at Nipissing First Nation, said Spanish "took the spirit out of my father, aunts, and uncles. When they got home, they were defeated. The only things they were taught were anger, violence, and hate."

"Trauma is not only the bad things that happen but also the good things that didn't happen. As a kid, I didn't want to be an 'Indian.' I was ashamed of the community, but now I realize I was embarrassed of all the trauma that

---

32 Basil Johnston, *Indian School Days* (Norman, OK: University of Oklahoma Press, 1988).

33 McKegney, Sam. 2006. "Indigenous Writing and the Residential School Legacy: A Public Interview With Basil Johnston," *Studies in Canadian Literature* 34 (2). https://journals. lib.unb.ca/index.php/SCL/article/view/12711.

was caused by the schools. The last residential school closed in 1996, but the ripple effects will last for seven generations."[34]

Not all memories were bad. Some survivors told stories of friendships, education, new trades learned, and kinder teachers. Any good, though, could not possibly cancel the bad. Genocide is never good.

I try imagining what it would be like if roles were reversed, and a government or church agent had arrived at my London or North Bay home to remove a sibling and me to a residential school far away. Red hair shorn because it was of the devil, my English language forbidden, Catholic faith censured. Unimaginable, literally, because I shared the same skin colour as Christopher Columbus and Christian missionaries who sailed from Europe to exploit a new land and its riches. Once in North America, the land-grabbing also imported the settlers' "superior" culture and Christian religion to "the savages."

On May 27, 2021, officials from Tk'emlúps te Secwépemc First Nation revealed multiple unmarked graves containing the remains of two hundred fifteen Indigenous children, including some as young as three, had been found on the grounds of Kamloops Indian Residential School in British Columbia. This school was operated by the Catholic Church between 1890 and 1978. Memorials quickly sprung up across the country, two hundred fifteen pairs of shoes placed in ceremonies on Indigenous grounds or near the site of other schools. A few weeks later, survivors and Canada reeled from the breaking news of seven hundred and fifty-one confirmed graves in Saskatchewan at Cowessess First Nation. Undoubtedly, there will be more. Survivors and their communities had heard the stories of those graves or disappearances passed down from earlier generations.

Some days, I think about my oldest brother, Danny, his death, that hole in my parents' lives, and the children never born to Danny. I live too in the holes Adam left us. However, I cannot pretend to know the pain of those Indigenous families whose children were taken and never came home. My

---

34 Steer, Bill. "Residential schools' legacy lasting for generations," *North Bay Nugget*, Nov. 24, 2019, https://www.nugget.ca/news/local-news/residential-schools-effects-lasting-for-generations.

sadness washes up on their shores and those shoes. Adam's death was a tragic accident. However, cultural genocide is no accident; acts committed by the government and churches, seventy percent Catholic. (Anglican, United, Presbyterian and Methodist churches operated other schools) The TRC report said there were at least four thousand one hundred school-related deaths, although any exact number is an estimate given the incomplete historical records.

What would those children have become? What did the world lose by never knowing these children? Questions begging questions.

I have read the Truth and Reconciliation Commission report. I am learning a history lesson that for the most part was never taught at the schools I attended. Some teachers are now teaching this history.

Since 1997, tens of thousands of participants have experienced the Kairos Canada blanket exercise.[35] On an intellectual and emotional level, participants see—in a new way—the shared history of Indigenous and non-Indigenous Peoples by stepping on blankets that represent the land and into "the role of First Nations, Inuit, and later Métis Peoples . . . by walking through pre-contact, treaty-making, colonization and resistance." The hour-long exercise can be powerful and authentic without intentionally dwelling on anger or guilt-tripping. It is followed by a sacred ceremony and talking circle for self-care and further learning that might last for one to two hours. This immersion provides information and can invoke strong emotions from both Indigenous and white participants. It can be the first step in education that requires further work in reconciliation.

I have signed up, along with hundreds of thousands, for an online Indigenous Canada course offered by the University of Alberta. From an Indigenous perspective, topics for the twelve lessons include "the fur trade and other exchange relationships, land claims and environmental impacts, legal systems and rights, political conflicts and alliances, Indigenous political activism, and contemporary Indigenous life, art and its expressions."[36]

---

35 Kairos: Canadian Ecumenical Justice Initiatives, www.kairosblanketexercise.org.

36 This University of Alberta course grants a certificate for students paying the course fee or it can be taken free. Financial aid is available.

I will circle back to Basil Johnston and residential schools many years later in political staff work on Parliament Hill. In our pandemic times, I had noticed how Johnston had named the loss of the sense of duty in his community. He said the whole emphasis was on rights now, "My rights are being violated. My rights are being infringed upon," he said.[37]

"Claire, it was as if he foreshadowed COVID 19's frustrating 'dialogue of the deaf' as some demand their rights while ignoring their own corresponding responsibilities to others and their communities."

"To us, a right is '*debnimzewin*'. But each right is also a duty. And we've forgotten to teach those in our Native schools," Johnston said. ". I've also noticed that they do not teach much in terms of duties to your neighbours in the secular schools and in the public school system of Ontario. And so, we go back to some of these values: responsibility, duty, right."

Meanwhile, the St. Isaac Jogues Church where I was administrator would later close for good for many years, and then the building and property were returned to Batchewana First Nation.[38]

---

37 Ibid., McKegney, "Indigenous Writing and the Residential School Legacy: A Public Interview With Basil Johnston."

38 Batchewana First Nation of Ojibways. "102-year-old Church gets new life in Batchewana village," *Soo Today*, May 12, 2012, https://www.sootoday.com/local-news/102-year-old-church-gets-new-life-in-batchewana-village-159836.

CHAPTER 26

"Si Dios Quiere"

I was the scheduled homilist for a big Marian Day Catholic rally at the arena in Sault Ste. Marie.

I prayed the readings, read the homiletic books, and peeked at sample homilies. There were few shafts of light from on high.

Mary, the mother of Jesus, intrigued me as a faith figure. In meditation, I had walked into gospel scenes that allowed me to observe and interact with Mary. I never pictured her first as Holy Mary Mother of God. She was no "whatever you say," mummified, forever virgin. Did such a teenager ever exist? She was young, curious, and loved Joseph. No sex and pregnant, as the story revealed. An immaculate conception she would have to explain to Joseph, her family, and sort out for herself. Cue her thousand questions, the sleepless nights, the second-guessing. She would travel to her cousin, Elizabeth, to stay for months, a chance for the women to talk, as they do so well.

No, I sensed a young precocious, plucky woman with a million doubts wrestling with this God. I related to her "not knowing," her wondering, her "yes but" faith journey. I had zero doubts about her enjoying a healthy sex life with Joseph after this one-time ask from God.

"Claire, like today, her family story was playing out in the politics and empires that were crushing ordinary people. The baby she birthed grew up to denounce the injustices of the Roman Empire and the treatment of the poor and powerless. Those powerful leaders would crucify her baby."

"I like your Mary," Claire said.

Sweating the pending Marian rally, I was at a loss for words. So, I napped. The phone rang. Bishop Gervais was calling. He was in the Sault visiting Precious Blood Cathedral. He had met up with two teenagers who had knocked on the rectory door. Antonio and his brother, Carlos. Two lads from El Salvador.

Was this a dream?

"Cruz, Antonio, and Carlos told the bishop their own 'flight out of Egypt' story. They left El Salvador months earlier because their government wanted them to be soldiers in an army killing their fellow citizens, the vast majority dirt poor. They consulted with their mother and instead fled their homeland. They crossed to Mexico, waiting for a mother who never came. They entered the USA and travelled across the continent all the way to Buffalo, New York, entering Canada at Fort Erie legally because an aunt in Guelph vouched for them. They were granted a three-month visa. However, when they arrived at the aunt's home, their uncle barred the door."

"Why did their uncle not let them stay?"

"I don't know, Cruz."

The boys looked at a map. They knew they had relatives in Los Angeles. They tried walking across a bridge, first in Fort Erie and then Windsor, to return to the USA. The American border patrol turned them back each time. They were legally in Canada, but not so in the USA. They hitchhiked all the way up to Sault Ste. Marie to try crossing at a third border community. Without proper documents or anyone to vouch for them, they were turned back from crossing the International Bridge. Out of options, their faith and desperation led them to the cathedral.

Gervais facilitated a call to the American relatives confirming their mother had made it safely to Los Angeles. They could wait in Canada for a refugee hearing in the fall for permission to stay or be deported to a third country like Mexico, where they might apply to enter the United States. Neither option appealed to Antonio and Carlos. Yes, except for their uncle, the hospitality in Canada had been warm, but the weather was too cold. Mexico was a roll of the dice. They were homesick and homeless. Gervais suggested I bring the boys to the nearby Garden River First Nation community. They may have a solution.

I spent three days feeding the boys pizza and hearing their stories. I went to visit Garden River First Nation community leaders. They listened. I heard no proposals. They too fed the boys, and we left. Nothing happened instantly or in a straight line in that community. It was why I felt so at home there.

A few days later, I was asked to bring Antonio and Carlos back. I drove over to the Michigan side of the river to a place where I would meet them. I cautioned the boys about all the ways this river crossing might not work. Carlos, the younger brother, reassured me all would be well.

"*Si Dios quiere*, padre. If God wants us in Los Angeles, we will be there. If God doesn't, we won't."

Mary's faith. Elizabeth's faith. Carlos' and Antonio's faith. It happened exactly as proposed. Across the border, I took the boys to a nearby town where they bought bus tickets for their cross-country odyssey to their new home and reunited with their exultant mother in east Los Angeles.

I looked over at the blank pages for the Marian Devotion homily. I now had Antonio and Carlos' story to tell. Mary had travelled while pregnant with Jesus from Nazareth to Hebron. Anthony and Carlos were living the Visitation story.

On July 22, 2020, the Federal Court of Canada ruled it was unconstitutional for the United States and Canada to ban would-be refugee claimants from trying to enter either country at official border crossings. The judge chided Canada's complicity in the U.S. treatment of asylum seekers through the so-called safe Third Country Agreement that in fact was not at all safe for refugees.

Canada appealed the ruling, and the court granted the appeal.[39]

Good grief, Canada! There are many refugee policies and injustices to right.

"Si Dios quiere, Carlos and Antonio."

---

39 Government of Canada, April 15, 2021, https://www.canada.ca/en/immigration-refugees-citizenship/news/2021/04/government-of-canada-appeal-granted-on-safe-third-country-agreement.html.

CHAPTER 27

St. Andrew's, Take Two, a "Bloody Miracle"

1988–1991

Priests might dread calls from bishops. Not so for Gervais' call delivering good news. He wanted me back at St. Andrew the Apostle Church less than three years after my sudden departure for studies in Rome.

So much for thinking that I had never won the lottery!

Eight years into the priesthood, I had the challenge, at last, in being a pastor, "the boss" who, in fact, theologically and practically, had everyone as his boss. St. Andrew's was a golden opportunity to deepen the vision and vitality of a true Vatican II parish.

A typical assignment in those days lasted six to nine years. I would be there for only four years, not fathoming what lay ahead. St. Andrew's was the largest parish in the diocese, its budget exceeding half a million dollars. There were five permanent deacons—Randy Dussiaume, Luke Fay, John Noble, Bob Poulin, and Austin Lupton—an active parish council, Carol Noble, a valuable secretary, a genial Ed Lang as custodian, all part of the pastoral team working with dozens of volunteer ministries. I hired Dan Currie as a lay staff to bring his faith, music, and charm to ministry. Currie and I attended ecumenical Sudbury Ministerial Association meetings. We prayed one weekend at masses for the United Church of Canada as they elected a new Moderator. Currie had this Dan Fogelberg look and sound with his guitar. He was destined to play a supporting role in what waited in the wings.

Despite security concerns, we left the church doors unlocked. Shift workers in the mines or hospitals, a suffering soul or insomniac, appreciated the night sanctuary.

"The homeless might come," one insurer warned.

"I can only hope."

We erected photo bulletin boards and a wailing wall for prayer requests, reflecting the community back to themselves, hooking new engagement. We started a Lazarus Society for the bereaved, a young adult's group, and imported those all-day penitential celebrations from the Pro-Cathedral. I emptied my calendar to enjoy the recorded music and grace happening as city priests assisted. Dozens of times, I pronounced the words penitent Catholics longed to hear.

"God, the Father of mercies, through the death and resurrection of his Son, has reconciled the world to himself and sent the Holy Spirit among us for the forgiveness of sins."

"Through the ministry of the church, may God give you pardon and peace, and I absolve you from your sins in the name of the Father, and of the Son, and of the Holy Spirit."

Matthew Fox's *Original Blessing* perspective on God and faith still influenced ministry. Fox took us back to page one of scripture, before the fall of Adam and Eve, the first symbolic couple, before their bite of the apple, their bittersweet taste of venturing out, alienated from God and the divine plan. These inspired biblical myths could still reveal truths about God and ourselves.

"God saw all that He had made, and indeed, it was very good." (Gen. 1:31)

But God?

No, there were no "if, ands, or buts" in God's blessing of all. An original blessing too easily lost in rigid canon law, in the daily din of everyone struggling to get by, pay the bills, keep a roof over the family, and survive being screwed at work or by life.

We are good.

God's mercy changes everything. As a pastor, I had this supporting role in a cast watching God perform on stage. Once, I dropped a big rock in front of the sanctuary, preaching on the passage when Jesus asked anyone who had not sinned to cast the first stone. (John 8:1-11). I reworked Edwina Gately's words on the woman who anointed the Lord. People could take distributed pebbles to drop their "stone" in a container to signify the release of their sins. Parishioners relished rituals with real, tangible symbols to mark transitions in life. I cherished this unique pastoral relationship—servant healer, weaving a family of faith stitched together with our stories, laughter, tears, and praise.

The Saturday and Sunday services, along with wedding, baptism, and funeral rituals, were the headlines for a week, figuring out how we might live with one another and be all we were invited to be. The rituals were there simply to support, strengthen, and sustain this everyday engagement. Friends kept it real. Less so, the handful of Catholics who figured a priest without a wife and sex was either extraterrestrial or at best clueless earthlings, to be talked to as a child or left on that safe pedestal.

People in confession told me they sometimes felt like hypocrites, repeatedly back talking about the same old laundry list of sins. I reminded them that their brokenness was part of our human journey. We might be sinners. Few though were the hypocrites Jesus lashed out at for their loveless, feckless judgment. His words shocked his followers. It still can today. Catholics seemed obsessed confessing sexual sins, understandable from their earlier catechism and hellfire preaching. Those were the easiest for me to pronounce God's mercy. I corked any curious follow-up questions, saving those for people who muttered generalities on not being nice with the wife nor with their employees.

Pastoring was my covenant with this faith community.

I began slipping in words like "women" and "Creator" into the rubrics and rituals to replace exclusive masculine references to God or to people. Having girls as altar servers was but a baby step forward on Rome's restrictive rules.

"Claire, you know how women and girls have been discriminated against by a twisted interpretation of the Word of God."

Fr. Rick preaching, celebrating Eucharist and officiant at wedding of Leo and Nicole Duford

After six decades, former U.S.A. President Jimmy Carter finally severed ties with his Southern Baptist Convention, citing how women are prevented from playing a full and equal role in many faiths. Carter wrote, "It was, however, an unavoidable decision when the convention's leaders, quoting a few carefully selected Bible verses and claiming that Eve was created second to Adam and was responsible for original sin, ordained those women must be 'subservient' to their husbands and prohibited from serving as deacons, pastors or chaplains in the military service." [40]

"Where do we begin?" Claire asked. "Disrespect for women. Denied control over our bodies. Violence. Genital mutilation. Rape not a crime in some countries. Women, because they are women, are denied fair access to education, health, employment, and equal pay. The burden of the pandemic shouldered way more by women because of childcare demands and loss of jobs."

"Amen, Claire."

The myopic patriarchy is a given in too many churches, synagogues, mosques, and temples. A male-dominated clergy lay women's subservient role at the feet of a divine being and sacred texts. As a pastor, I appreciated how we, as a faith community, were enriched by women leaders. They excelled as spiritual directors, pastoral care, and in organizational development. Their voice, gifts, and service were sensible. At the Pro, I had witnessed the extraordinary contribution Sister Bonnie made to the pastoral team. She had gifts and perspectives so different from the three men. Topping my long list of church reforms was giving women an equal and valued role in ministry and governance, paid too the same as men. Women in that leadership might then take care of many other reforms.

The Gathering conferences in Chicago continued to inspire.

"If you're exclusively into the magisterium-institutional side, you'll try to get people 'into the church,' and obedience is the final criterion," Bill Bausch taught. "If you're exclusively into the mystery side, you'll try to get people to pause and adore where they are, and freedom is the final criterion. Both

---

40 Jimmy Carter, "Losing My Religion for Equality," *Sydney Morning Herald*, July 15, 2009, https://www.smh.com.au/politics/federal/losing-my-religion-for-equality-20090714-dk0v.html.

can go to excess, but both are needed, and only one side or the other is heresy. Most people are in-between: they appreciate the institutional side of the church, but it is relatively unimportant to them. Their pastor is more significant to them than the pope is, the local mayor than the bishops, the neighbourhood than the Vatican, and baptism more than ordination."[41]

My "magisterium and mystery" spectrum could collapse at times, focusing too narrowly on attendance. I exalted when the pews were as full in "Ordinary Time" as they were for Christmas or Easter. The good people could check-mate my zeal. One day, a woman told me it was a "bloody miracle" she was there at all! She had no energy to be a light for the world. There were other "bloody miracle" Catholics there seeking sanctuary. They wanted to be left alone to pray and then head home to take care of their kids.

Be kind to them, Father Rick. Let them be!

Jesus was a pastor's model here, taking people where they were and inviting rather than coercing them for the journey ahead. Nevertheless, his teaching could be annoying, difficult to defend, even infuriating for the faithful who gave it any thought. Seriously, what's with the prodigal son abdicating family responsibilities, off on a wanderlust lark, returning to snare a father's full forgiveness, a party thrown, instant equal standing with a loyal elder brother who never left?

What is THAT about?

Where is the justice in the crook on a cross beside Jesus, who was welcomed into heaven with a deathbed confession? What in God's name is Jesus doing eating with the bad tax collectors?

Love my enemies?

Do good to those who persecute us?

What was the point of even being good, being here in church?

This smacked of the odious unfairness of it all, a divine shuffle of the deck, upsetting rules people abided by in the public square and in their homes; life there was measured by good versus bad, rewards and punishments.

---

41 William J. Bausch, *The Hands-On Parish, Reflections and Suggestions for Fostering Community* (Mystic, CT: Twenty-Third Publications, 1989), 60.

"You know what I never got . . .," said John Shea. "Why didn't the father explain more to the older son . . . why the workers hired last got the same . . . why Jesus didn't defend himself at the trial . . . why Jesus was so hard on Nicodemus . . . why Jesus delayed in going to see his friend Lazarus . . . why Jesus called Peter Satan . . . why Jesus vanished after he broke the bread . . . why the Messiah had to suffer . . . why . . .why . . . why?"[42]

"Why, why, why, Claire? Why couldn't God be a caped crusader stopping bullets and fatal seizures in hot tubs?"

"We wanted that for Adam, no?"

This was another question I would live with, more so than ever answer adequately. Good behaviour did not automatically come with immediate rewards. Faith could be a crap shoot. I did discover, humbly, God in my suffering, more by redemption than any immediate rescuing me and my loved ones.

I loved going to Chicago for this spiritual feeding every year. Asking the tough questions seemed reasonable acts of faith.

But wait, a son dead coming to his senses cries out for a party, no? Divine energy renews us. With those demanding gospels, it was dawning on me why Jesus had a large crowd nearby, but far fewer disciples. Palpable tension between a living faith and props under the guise of religion. It would always be tempting to fashion God into our likeness.

Teresa of Ávila, a doctor and saint of the church, once admonished God as she slid down a muddy embankment on her way to enter the convent. "If this is how You treat Your friends, no wonder why You have so few of them!"[43]

"Oh my God. I like her," cheered Claire.

"Claire, the saints are cool, some quirky, with heathen pasts and then performing their God-smacking miracles. Grandma doubled up on saints when she named your dad, Martin Gerard Prashaw. As she had lost her firstborn,

42 John Shea, *Gospel Light Jesus Stories for Spiritual Consciousness* (New York: The Crossroad Publishing Company, 1998), 52.

43 Stagnaro, Angelo. "If This is How You Treat Your Friends," *National Catholic Reporter*, Oct. 15, 2016, https://www.ncregister.com/blog/if-this-is-how-you-treat-your-friends.

Danny, she invoked St. Martin, patron of her parish, and then St. Gerard, protector for pregnant women. St. Jude, the saint for lost things, finds my phone as good as Google. Superstition and faith all rolled into one."

I struggled not to weaponize the granting of sacraments. I could state Catholic teaching, invite, even challenge, and disturb those comfortable in the pews. I had figured out long ago, grace and all, that I was not God and that that revelation mattered. Who was I to judge? There were Catholics who stayed in their pews at Communion, told or believing they should not receive Jesus in the blessed bread—a divorce, "living in sin," or not Catholic, whatever. It didn't seem to matter that they might be innocent parties in the break-up of a marriage. They hurt and hungered for healing more than a wagging finger or judgment. I invited all to the altar. Those coming forward could fold their arms across their chest to signal they wanted a blessing. Honestly, if their hunger had them putting out their hands, who was I to deny them? I could state the high demands of discipleship, while acknowledging our regular shortcomings and choose never to be a barrier to their genuine yearning for the Bread of Life, God's gift no one had earned. Even the Pharisees were welcome. This was all in God's hands. I had meditated long on the equalizer of the Communion line, the one same line for privileged or poor, all races, fallen, forgiven, some wearing their go-to-church finery, others in blue jeans.

"Claire, I cheered Pope Francis for reminding everyone, 'Eucharist is not a prize for the perfect, but a powerful medicine and nourishment for the weak.'"[44]

The Catholic Church seemed to have this compulsive need to explain or defend everything when I was quite content to leave the mysteries in God's hands. God didn't need a lawyer. I let God take care of unbaptized babies without the need for this place called Limbo which theologians had invented to spare those babies from Hell. We celebrated the lives of people who committed suicide and buried them in the consecrated Catholic cemeteries. The

---

44 Pope Francis, *Apostolic Exhortation Evangelii Gaudium* [24 November 2013], 44: AAS 105 [2013], 1038, https://www.vatican.va/content/francesco/en/apost_exhortations/documents/papa-francesco_esortazione-ap_20131124_evangelii-gaudium.html.

Catholic Church would revise its teaching on these matters in the 1990s. I couldn't wait. God is Love.

Catholics knew their priests' faults. Best I kept mine in mind. My zeal was still intact but contained. Was I maturing spiritually, or discovering my job was indeed a bit like that Ford plant assembly line from the seminary summer job—dispenser of sacraments, candles, and services? I found myself tending more to my little hectare, far less to saving the whole wide world.

CHAPTER 28

Teen Talks

"Claire, the teens from my ministry years are your age now, parents themselves with their own teens or young adult children. Occasionally, new 'old' Facebook friends finish their stories about my ministry with them."

"Rick, I thought I would share with you what an impact you made on me during the tender teen years," a Sudbury woman messaged.

"I remember sitting with you at Youth Encounter and talking. You never discouraged us as teens from questioning our faith, and I always remember having a talk about sexuality and the like, which was never ever something I could discuss with my parents. Just so you know, you made a comment to me to try and wait until I was eighteen before exploring sex deeper, and you were able to reach my analytical mind advising me that, once you are eighteen, you are thinking more with an adult brain and approaching sex with a different attitude.

"I never told you I was molested as a child by a family friend and had a traumatic perception of sex.

"I did wait, and I did have a different attitude toward it when I eventually did explore. I went to therapy over the molestation (it took me until my thirties, but I finally confronted it).

"That conversation you and I had though stuck with me. I repeated it to my own daughter as she entered puberty, and I am proud to say your words of wisdom also reached her analytical brain. Although eighteen, she has quite a different attitude towards sexual activity and a healthy one as a result. She and my youngest boy are in what I call a fluid stage while they explore and learn who they are. I have often spoken of you to my husband and kids and [of] having a marked influence on my life, and I thought you should know that I am so grateful."

I enjoyed "happy endings" where I, under higher powers, served to channel grace or plant a seed to bloom later. That anyone listened to my counsel was never the bottom line. Others clearly made different choices about sex. It was simply the holy ground of listening and loving when teens had so few adults they might trust with their secret struggles, no parent they could or would talk to. There were hundreds of those talks. Not all were about sex. There were legal and moral limitations too, recommending professionals when necessary and reporting any abuse to authorities. While a few priest colleagues had become certified counsellors, my spiritual direction was more of a cheerleader, steering the youth past the perilous shoals in their latest life-and-death angst.

Was it a prelude to parenting? I did not know that at the time.

CHAPTER 29

Weddings

Even with five deacons, I was a celebrant for about forty weddings a year, investing significant pastoral time in meeting engaged couples. The first meeting put the nervous couple at ease as I inquired about their love story and news on their families. I slipped in the crucial distinction between a wedding lasting a day, and their marriage, hopefully, a lifetime. I committed to fashioning a first-class ceremony, but their married love was my focus. The obligatory weekend preparation courses offered talks by couples on finances, parenting, communication, and sexuality. I dropped by, shared a meal, and did a faith talk.

There were priests now dreading this supposed happy ministry, what with couples living together, not in church regularly, some throwing knives for those compulsory courses. Priests I knew abhorred a church wedding that was requested for exclusively cultural rather than spiritual reasons. I was not there yet, but I knew a few priests who preferred funerals over weddings. The corpses never talked back.

I could work with any couple open to spiritual growth regardless of their church attendance. Some couples resumed practicing their faith. While I was extremely reluctant to refuse a sacrament, there was this one wedding that made me challenge a couple. They arrived in a foul mood, backs up, angry at the "command performance" they felt I imposed. I explained what their wedding day and marriage meant for the church and for me as the officiant. They countered that they did not believe any of that "hogwash;" the bride's mother wanted a church wedding. I complimented them on their honesty. I asked them to respect my honesty as well.

"You don't want to be here. That is okay. This may be a time, as adults, to do what you believe in and not what others want. It's your wedding."

The young man suffered whiplash as he glanced at his fiancé. They took a deep breath and agreed to head to her mother's place to talk. I passed Carol Noble's office, telling her I would be in the kitchen for the call from the bride's mother that I expected in fifteen minutes. It came a half-hour later. She was furious that I had denied her daughter a church wedding, withholding God's blessing. I reassured her that the couple had made this decision and God would bless her daughter wherever the wedding happened. I suspect I made matters worse by praising the couple's honesty, seizing their own responsibility to make their decisions.

Mother rained a few invectives on me, threatening to write the bishop. I offered her his address.

CHAPTER 30

Good Friday

1988

Holy Week was by far my favourite week as a pastor, its processions, the palms, washing of feet, Judas' kiss, the cock crowing, Jesus alone in the agony of the Garden of Gethsemane, the drama of death, despair, frightening empty tombs, and a ridiculous resurrection winning the day.

"For the women (visiting the tomb), the only thing more terrifying than a world with Jesus dead was one in which he was alive...." warns Esau McCaulley. "The terrifying prospect of Easter is that God called these women to return to the same world that crucified Jesus with a very dangerous gift: hope in the power of God, the unending reservoir of forgiveness and an abundance of love. It would make them seem like fools. Who could believe such a thing?"[45]

A song, chrism oil, darkness, and light spoke in symbols far more than most of my words ever could. I had goosebumps enjoying the early Pro years sitting on the front pew with Bishop Carter before the Easter Vigil, listening to the choir raise the roof in glory.

This Easter, Greg Humbert found himself between appointments, available to help celebrate liturgies. Inspired by Chicago, social justice, and Peter, Paul & Mary music, we created a play for a modern Golgotha Hill Crucifixion.

---

45 McCaulley, Esau. "The Unsettling Power of Easter," *New York Times*, April 2,
2021, https://www.nytimes.com/2021/04/02/opinion/easter-celebration.html.

Humbert had been listening to Peter Yarrow's solo album and a song called "Greenwood" with the haunting melody and refrain from Scripture, "If we do these things in the greenwood, what will happen in the dry!" (Luke 23:31)[46]

The Passion was divided into three parts and the missalette that year had a psalm refrain between each section. We skipped that refrain, offering a snapshot of contemporary injustices instead. After the first reflection, Greg, sitting in the balcony, stood, and in a loud voice delivered a line from the Passion of Jesus and then sang Yarrow's refrain from "Greenwood"."

Part One:

Rick: I may not be perfect, but I don't do anything that anyone else isn't doing. Everyone is sleeping together these days, taking something from work.

Greg: At that moment, a cock began to crow . . .

Rick: I want to stop pollution but come on, the ozone layer. Greenhouse gases. Acid rain. Rain forests disappearing. I am one person. I can't make any difference.

Greg: At that moment, a cock began to crow . . .

Rick: I'm against pornography. Women deserve respect, but gee, everyone buys a magazine now and again. A video won't harm anyone.

Greg: At that moment, a cock began to crow . . .

Rick: That's it! I'm giving up on my brother. I've tried to reason with him. He can come to me.

Greg: At that moment, a cock began to crow . . .

Greg (singing "Greenwood" refrain):

The second act covered worldly judgments, AIDS patients "getting what they deserve," "useless" government sanctions against South Africa and apartheid, and refugees taking Canadian jobs.

At each pause, Greg shouted, "Crucify Him. Crucify Him."

46 Peter Yarrow, Greenwood, Solo Recordings, 1971-1972. The New RSV Bible verse now is, "For if they do this when the wood is green, what will happen when it is dry?"

Act three reported news on the Sudbury Soup Kitchen feeding two hundred hot lunches daily and three Campaign Against Poverty walks happening in communities in Ontario.

Rick: And in Calcutta with Mother Teresa this day, and for hundreds and hundreds of believers in Sudbury, the Kingdom of God is being built.

When I was homeless, you opened my doors.

When I was anxious, you calmed my fears.

When I was little, you taught me to read.

When I was sick, you cared for me.

Seeking employment, you created jobs for me.

When I was old, you smiled at me.

When I was restless, you listened to me.

When I was happy, you shared in my joy.

Greg: And this testimony has been given by an eyewitness, and it is true.

Greg (singing "Greenwood" refrain)

CHAPTER 31

Clergy Abuse

[WARNING: This chapter contains information on clergy abuse that some readers may find distressing.]

In 1989, I read the *North Bay Nugget* news stories reporting on priests in the diocese facing criminal charges.

I had no direct evidence on the nature of the assaults or the extent of the police investigations. It is deeply troubling now to discover how police and prosecutors, for decades, routinely deferred to church authorities to handle these incidents internally. The movie, *Spotlight,* poignantly portrayed the systemic cover-up in the Archdiocese of Boston that went far beyond the acts of a few fallen priests. The offending priest might be rebuked and shuffled off, silently, to a new parish and, sadly, to more victims.

The worst-case in the news was Father John Sullivan who had sat across from me at the Pro-Cathedral dining room table when I visited as a seminarian in the late 1970s. Sullivan served as vicar of the Matrimonial Tribunal on the chancery side of the church. Sullivan was this convivial, charming, bright guy with his Irish bent for conversation and humour. He was also a pedophile with a record of incidents unknown to me and most people in the faith community. One of his victims called Sullivan a "serial molester." In writing this memoir, I learned that Bishop Carter and a few church officials knew of Sullivan's record as far back as 1960.

Sylvia's site, a victims' website,[47] reported testimony from a case in 2015 when AXA Insurance, the then diocesan insurer, contended that they should not have to pay claims of the diocese's previous insurer to victims of diocesan priests because of a church pattern they labeled as "bad faith," i.e., the diocese not dealing directly and effectively with those priests. While that case involved abuse claims against sixteen priests, there were significant details on Sullivan's diocesan history.

"The plaintiff (Diocese of Sault Ste. Marie) takes the position that it is insured by a policy of insurance in place," reads the Ontario Superior Court of Justice summary. "The defendant (AXA) takes the position that it is entitled in law to deny coverage based on material misrepresentation, material non-disclosure and bad faith. The position taken by the defendant is that the policy is void ab initio."

"In March 1960, the then Bishop of the plaintiff Diocese, Bishop Alexander Carter, received a report that Father Sullivan had sexually assaulted two boys in the parish. Father Sullivan admitted to the misconduct, was reprimanded by the Bishop, and sent from the parish for a period of one week to do penance. In January 1961, Bishop Carter received a further report from a father of three boys that Father Sullivan had sexually assaulted his three sons.

"In light of the repeated sexual assaults against minors committed by Father John Sullivan, the plaintiff Diocese, under the direction of Bishop Carter, conducted a Diocesan Tribunal, *Processus Criminalus* essentially an internal trial within the Roman Catholic Church. This "Diocesan Tribunal" was conducted according to church Canon Law, and, in particular, under Canon 2359, paragraph 2. This trial within the church was conducted under an "Oath of Secrecy…"[48]

"Claire, one week to do penance. This felt like the Dark Ages, not my childhood years."

"That's unbelievable," Claire said.

47 Sylvia's Site, https://www.theinquiry.ca/wordpress.

48 Ontario Supreme Court, Roman Catholic Corporation for the Diocese of Sault Ste. Marie v. AXA Insurance, 2015 ONSC 838 (CanLII), http://canlii.ca/t/gg844.

I had no idea what this "nice man" passing the roast beef had done, or was still doing, abusing children, including some altar servers he courted with a sick befriending and seduction of them and their parents.

He was a priest, "a good man," no? How could anything bad like this happen?

Sullivan was charged in 1989 and faced thirty-two charges related to allegations of sexual abuse involving nine boys aged nine to twelve between the years 1958 and 1979. There are a different number of counts and years cited on the victims' site. He pled guilty. He was sentenced to two and a half years in a federal penitentiary. The diocese defrocked and dismissed him as a priest in 2015. Sullivan died in 2016.[49]

Those are the cold facts. However, the experience of these children and their families can never be told merely by statistics and dates. I feel sick thinking of the violations to innocent kids at the hands of these predators whose modus operandi included their hallowed priestly entrapments. I occasionally ate with the one priest who may have been the worst priest pedophile in the diocese. There were those three priests I had lived with at the seminary who had since been imprisoned for crimes against children or women.

Of course, there were many good priests who did not abuse.

News of clergy abuse began to surface elsewhere. There were Sullivans in other dioceses and countries. There would be far more cases and media coverage in the years after I left in 1991. It was a first, unnerving experience to look evil in the eye and be hoodwinked myself. It has taken a long time to begin to understand how this happened, to better appreciate the power imbalance of adult to child, the coercion, bribes, gifts, threats. How a child cowered against an all-powerful universe and even the threat of God, invoked by the abuser, should the child dare speak to anyone about what was happening.

Your parents know, the priest whispered. Your parents will be in big trouble. No one will believe you. God blesses what we do.

Priests hunting and cornering victims. The abuser's gifts and specialness of their relationship. Then the lies, bribes, and threats of what might happen if their secret was ever disclosed. The further real physical danger the

---

49 Ibid., Sylvia's Site, https://www.theinquiry.ca/wordpress.

children faced. The not being believed, and the consequences and shame for themselves, for their parents and families, the twisted blessing of what was demanded by the priest.

The guilt the children felt, shame, blaming themselves, alone afterwards lost in their tortured thoughts, the secret driven deeper and deeper. They were kids, for God's sake! Those children did not stand a chance. And, with the credibility of the church and its priests intact, the victims and their families were sidelined. Priests were like God, sometimes their parents' friends, all-powerful. Who believed a kid over and against these "superheroes"?

"Those kids would be Cruz' age, younger. So sick. So evil," Claire said.

"I'm glad he's biking with friends," I said. "Yes, appalling, that innocence and that evil, together."

A good number of Catholics who had their priests on a pedestal were hard-pressed to fathom this happening. "Father So and So" is a good priest. He married us. He baptized our children. I have never seen anything bad happening. Why did it go on for so long? Why had the victims remained silent? There was little grasping of what victims, and their families, were up against, this "next to God" figure, this universal, Holy Roman Catholic Church. Why did police officers, detectives, and crown attorneys disappear after interviewing us? Victims tell stories of police not showing up as promised for meetings with church officials. Some victims were invited to give depositions or meet church officials on the very grounds where the abuse had happened. They saw the clear care wrapped around the accuser.

Some came to hate priests, the church, and God. If the accused or convicted priest had not left the diocese, they might face lynching parties. Parents who had not the slightest suspicion might beat themselves up "for being so stupid." Anger and rage followed.

I understand human nature, the heart, the hell people can dwell in. There is no judgment of any victim or their family response. The damage done is cata-strophic. How ruined was their innocence—suicides by some, many crippled in any normal, healthy maturing to adulthood, their own relations with women or men estranged, monstrous fears about having their own children; might they continue the abuse in new generations? Some did. Other victims somehow discovered healing, a few publicly even offering forgiveness. There is no one path that every victim chooses. I respect their stories. I admire their courage in dealing with their pain and fears.

Some Catholics rushed to the defence of bishops, citing hindsight is 20/20. Some argued it was another era, so little was known then about pedophilia or abuse. I still have questions.

Yes, the abusers are a minority, albeit a significant minority of all clergy. Yes, abuse has surfaced elsewhere—Boy Scouts, coaches, police, doctors, lawyers, Hollywood directors, billionaires on Wall Street. There has emerged a crisis of disclosure exposing abuse in society. All true, and a perspective, I suppose, but frankly, it rings hollow to defend or rationalize clergy abuse by citing similar abuse, some with comparable frequency, in other professions who deal with minors. Clergy abuse was singularly horrific. It appeared point-less to scatter the church problem elsewhere or to reduce the story to some average, like a hitter in baseball. One victim is one too many. And there are thousands and thousands of victims at the hands of Catholic priests.

How could this happen? I suspect most bishops believed or certainly wanted to believe these priests. Still a new bishop in 1960, Carter likely sought counsel from other bishops. They followed Vatican directives in place, canon law dictating ecclesial tribunals and sanctions being administered in secret. Non-disclosure agreements would bind both sides; some dioceses are only now voiding longstanding confidentiality clauses. Often, neither the police nor Children's Aid Society would be called or, if they were, advised the church would handle matters internally. It was clear which principles drove this process. In the best interpretation possible, a church wanted to preserve the faith of believers and the dignity of the priesthood, avoiding scandal, wherever possible, that might hurt the faithful. The worst interpretation was a cover-up, a lame addressing of wrongdoing, a cataclysmic failure to protect children as abusers received minimum church penalties and then continued their offending in new appointments. The priest was back in the diocese or elsewhere, still a pedophile and corralling new victims.

The secrecy and overriding fears of scandal only made matters far worse.

There are victims' groups, and lawyers convinced it was more sinister than "well-meaning but ignorant" prelates defending Holy Mother Church. They chronicled priests like Sullivan with early, repeated offences staged over several years that became known to a bishop. Yet, the priest continued to serve in new assignments, and parents were kept in the dark on the wolf in their midst while more children were put at risk. The priest would eventually be sent to another bishop's diocese, all followed by poor handling of their victims. It doesn't look good because it is not good.

Those abusing priests were cons and good at it. Pedophiles bluffed their way through the allegations or convinced church officials of their deep remorse and commitment to not offend again. Diocesan vicars and treatment centre counsellors have commented on the chilling lack of remorse in the abuser, their victims completely ignored as the priests in treatment told their stories.[50] Once caught, the priest might appear cooperative, express remorse, promise anything to avoid prosecution, and keep the perks and perps of their wayward office.

There may be historical context to consider but, unquestionably, there are no excuses. It troubles me greatly how otherwise smart bishops made decisions that did not adequately deal with the abusing priest. A damning 2020 report on the Archdiocese of Montréal's handling of Rev. Brian Boucher, sentenced to eight years in prison, detailed how the diocese shredded documents to cover any paper trail.[51] However, the archdiocese's auxiliary bishop, Thomas Dowd, received accolades in the media for believing and assisting Boucher's victims in seeking justice. In October 2020, Pope Francis named Dowd the seventh Bishop of Sault Ste. Marie.

I credit Carter for the way he grew my and others' faith and influenced my pastoral approach to ministry. In our youth, he was like another father figure to some of us. In his early years as a bishop, he dived into an enthusiastic, unreserved renewal of the Catholic Church. So, how could this happen? In those same years, he was conducting those secret hearings. Was he duped?

---

50 Donald Cozzens., *Changing Face of the Priesthood* (Collegeville, MN: Liturgical Press, 2000), 38.

51 Gloutnay, Francois. "Reports says Montréal Archdiocese covered for abuse priest for decades," *National Catholic Reporter*, Dec. 2, 2020, https://www.ncronline.org/news/accountability/report-says-montreal-archdiocese-covered-abusive-priest-decades.

Some answers are buried in graves and non-disclosure agreements. Can we ever know? Despite the polarized perspectives on clergy abuse, I wanted to understand the complexities of an ecclesial system that was insensitive to the trauma in the lives of clergy-abused children and adolescents, its negative impact on the faithful, and mistrust in the institution that publicly professed gospel values. I contacted an old friend from Pro-Cathedral days. Dr. Maryann Fraboni is a psychology professor at the University of Western Ontario. Back then, when I was a priest there, Fraboni practically lived at the rectory and chancery as her parents, Ralph and Frances-Clare, were leading church renewal programs and building the Catholic Education Centre for the entire diocese. She had a front-row seat with her parents to the Cathedral priests, good and bad.

We talked about cognitive dissonance to help understand the confusion we felt.

"Cognitive dissonance is a theory that refers to this mental conflict that happens, along with feelings of unease and tension, when a person's behavior does not line-up with what we think or believe about that person, as one example." Fraboni explained. "Take Carter: he was a great leader, I mean, he was my philosopher king, brilliant, a lover of wisdom, a bell-ringer of the new age, of truth and reconciliation, of ethics. Then, simultaneously, Carter who some say did not do enough to stop the abuse. This made no sense. He cannot be both in my head because that is exactly the dissonance. To relieve this tension, I must believe one or the other about Carter because he cannot be both, and that causes me discomfort. Naturally, we try to resolve these facts so that we have consonance/harmony in our thoughts. So, to do that, we rationalize these inconsistencies. We explain them away. I do not want to believe that Carter allowed the abuse to continue. I mean, I can't believe he did that with full awareness. I think it through under my theory as applied to Carter and believe he was persuaded by colleagues, superiors, and Sullivan himself that this was curable. But what really happened here to sway them in that direction? People trusted this man, Fr. Sullivan – and, oh my gosh – there it is, that's exactly what happened.

"I think it through as an adult and as a psychology practitioner understanding now these abusive priests were highly predatory. Easily classified when the pieces came together: sociopathic/borderline personalities. Most were very narcissistic. They were smart, charming, seemingly normal, and often highly attractive individuals. They were the bring-home-to-mother type. We trusted them.

"Indeed, cognitive dissonance was pervasive—the perspectives on Sullivan, Carter, the diocese moving Sullivan around instead of defrocking him sooner, the community confusion. We had a shared archetype of a priest, and it did not include pedophilia; evil is the opposite of good—a moment of shock."

My personal dealings with Carter when I was a seminarian and then priest covered ten years from 1975 to his retirement in 1985. Earlier, when I was a student and altar boy, Carter as a religious figure was equally a real person and a larger-than-life persona. Without personal knowledge, I find it hard to believe Carter had any intentional malice or criminal behaviour to ignore the abuse or deliberately perpetuate it. He did apply the grossly inadequate Vatican directives. From my experience, and I could be wrong, minimally Carter had to want to believe, as others did, that Sullivan could and would change. I completely understand some victims and families thinking otherwise.

Adulthood can give us a new perspective on those "good old days" that were also "good old bad days." We are mindful of our own development in sexuality and relationships. I grew up in so-called times of innocence thinking things were perfect and the church was perfect. Adulthood opened my eyes to the human condition, to my human condition. It's an awakening that seeks understanding while never excusing crimes.

But nothing fully computes here. I am stunned at a church and bishops' lack of awareness on the impact of this abuse of children. There is the pressing demand for criminal, civil, and moral justice. Sadly, rather than right the wrongs, the episcopal corporations initially veered into crisis management. There were concerns for image, assets, at risk solvency and financial reserves. Call in the lawyers and the accountants. Most chose crisis management over any profound, deep examination of the issue of clergy abuse and what it was revealing to the church and society.

In later work for The Church Council on Justice and Corrections, I was to learn how inadequate the legal, adversarial criminal justice system can be dealing with the profound hurt crime causes. Verdicts render judgment on the evidence deemed admissible and presented. Courts are the domain of professionals where ordinary folk become a supporting cast. Ironically, it's not advisable to always "tell the truth, the whole truth, and nothing but the truth, so help me God."

In an interview with the *Sudbury Star's* Carol Mulligan, Jean Louis Plouffe, the Sault diocese bishop from 1989 to 2016, spoke about the limitations imposed by the courts or settlements.[52]

"That legal process can sometimes be restrictive," Plouffe said. "You can't do at times what you would like to do."

Plouffe said "in the best of worlds," he would want to sit with the accusers and the accused and "see what we can do to help these people in a practical way without having to go through a process which is, at times, very painful." Plouffe said the goal would be to "alleviate the hurt as much as you can, be as fair and honest as you can so that people can move on."

The tide is turning. There needs to be swifter compensation, resources for healing, solid protocols to deal with allegations, including the immediate suspension of the accused priest, and reporting these complaints promptly to civil authorities.[53] Some of this is happening. The protocols will need to be assessed on how effective they are.

In 2019, Pope Francis abolished the pontifical secret prevalent in clergy sex abuse cases after mounting criticism that the high degree of confidentiality has been used to protect pedophiles, silence victims, and keep law enforcement from investigating crimes.[54] It was clear such secrecy also served to keep the scandal hidden, prevent law enforcement from accessing documents, and

52 Mulligan, Carol. "Stories go to grave: Bishop Plouffe says full stories of abuse allegations may never be known," *Sudbury Star*, Jan. 30, 2008.

53 The Roman Catholic Diocese of Sault Ste. Marie, Guidelines for Dealing with Complaints of Sexual Abuse Against Children and Sexual Assault Against Adults, September 2016, https://dioceseofsaultstemarie.org/complaint-guidelines.

54 Puella, Philip. "Pope abolishes 'pontifical secrecy' for sex abuse investigations," *Reuters News Agency*, Dec. 17, 2019, https://reut.rs/2XD3Fvx.

silence victims, many of whom often believed that the pontifical secret prevented them from going to the police to report their priestly abusers. Some families experienced great harm precisely because the abuse damaged their deep faith and love for the church.

The accused deserves the presumption of innocence, a fair trial, and resources for treatment.

I am back to Sullivan, shaken even in the little contact we had at not seeing what he was up to. I knew some of his victims. They were good kids. Of course, no one, good or judged as bad, deserved this abuse. When the official church did not protect their children, Catholics who had heard a story or rumours stood guard. They whispered a circuitous code to talk about the elephants in the room.

Don't let your boy go serve mass there with "Father So and So."

Angela Pace, a mother of ten kids, told me at a party once that, when one of her sons came home wanting to go on an altar boy trip to a Blue Jays game, she asked them which priest was going.

"I signed when they told me it was Father Rick."

That was good to hear. It had to infuriate parents to listen to stories of abuse and yet see the offending priest continue to serve in his ecclesial protection cell.

I spent time with several priests when I was young as an altar boy and guests at the Prashaw supper table. I went on several trips with priests to Stratford Festival and Montréal Expo. I joined a dozen altar boys as we jumped on Brian McKee. It was all good. I was not abused. I saw no abuse. As a young priest, I organized Saturday morning flag football league games. I felt comfortable then putting an arm around a boy or roughhousing with them. It was that good "man-to-boy" relationship that, for me, substituted a bit for no family.

Those days are gone. Priest friends tell me they are never to be left alone with students. They walk school halls, eyes straight ahead. There are the good priests who suffer in silence as their priestly identity has taken a nuclear hit to forever change a vocation. The demands of the priesthood, its waning prestige in the eye of some, and the relentless bombardment in public circles leave many weary and disheartened. Some priests talk about low morale and spirit. Fewer young men decide to devote their lives to the church. Some parents are reluctant to foster a vocation in their family. In a dominant secular culture, I suppose some priests might burrow in their religious foxholes.

There are plenty of good priests, those serving who are witness to a life of profound service. I respect those priests, their sticking with it.

The priests in prison or defrocked need visiting too if they welcomed it. I am grateful for treatment centers working with abusing priests. Jesus' love of sinners or criminals is an altogether different "scandal". Father Pedro Arrupe, a Jesuit superior, was severely criticized for visiting Father Daniel Berrigan in jail. Berrigan and his priest brother, Philip with the Cantonville 9, had been convicted for stealing draft records and burning them in the street with homemade napalm to keep young men from serving in Vietnam.[55] Arrupe answered his critics:

"Matthew 25, I was in prison, and you visited me." (Matt. 25:39)

Where does this leave us? For some rank-and-file Catholics, there is dissonance that will never be resolved. They grieve what has been lost. There had been considerable good in a church and ministry that is gone for some. People forge a justice that will do a far better job to protect children and anyone who is abused.

What will be found or fashioned anew? Regardless, we need to tell these stories.

---

55 Rivera, John. "Siblings still protest after 3 decades Activists: In 1968, the Berrigan brothers, both Catholic priests, were leaders of the Catonsville Nine. Today, they continue to engage in civil disobedience," *The Baltimore Sun*, May 18, 1998, https://www.baltimoresun.com/news/bs-xpm-1998-05-18-1998138018-story.html

CHAPTER 32

The Lighter Side of Heaven

I dreamed up an NHL hockey playoffs draft for a parish fundraiser. Parishioners formed teams to pay the entry fee for a pub night, food, and draft their players, recruiting as well non-churchgoers. Sports mixed in with church—God's mysterious ways made straight.

"Claire, it was not the weird 2020 COVID-19 schedule playing the Stanley Cup playoffs in August, so this meant staging the draft in the few days between the end of the regular season and the first series, in Lent! I seized on Don MacLellan's Chicago dispensations 'for the greater good'."

"I'd go to your church, Uncle Rick."

The hall was packed. The parish raised a few thousand dollars. Former Sudbury MP Glenn Thibeault told me it was a fond high school memory.

With their pastor an avid Boston Bruins fan then, parishioners arrived at Sunday liturgy to see votive candles surrounding a mannikin wearing a Boston hockey sweater. Still, the Montréal Canadiens had their own gods, winning most series.

The youth group with Mary Rosset and other leaders was busy with rallies, garage sales, and dances. There were baseball games and taking altar servers to a Sudbury Wolves Junior A hockey game where, after the home side scored, a mangy, stuffed wolf sailed across the arena on a zip line. Oh, the perks of being their pastor.

Once, I brought a case of beer to the pulpit and then promptly ignored it for a parish budget talk. People stayed awake, wondering what Father Rick was up to. When I finished, I asked them if they had noticed the beer. A chuckle. I reviewed the price of a case of beer and a large pizza with three toppings, suggesting they compare that amount to their weekly offering in the collection plate. Catholics were not schooled on generous Protestant tithing, ten percent of wages then. We'd spend money on beer and pizza in a heartbeat. Might we give that same amount to support what this faith community wants to accomplish?

I had a sign near my office desk telephone, "What am I here for?" It was a personal reminder to separate the gospel demands from petty complaints. One parishioner who spotted my sign quipped, "God help us all if you don't know why you are here!"

I once left a parish council marathon meeting still going at 11:30 p.m., stating I was going to bed, deputizing God as chair. I baked a devilish "sex in the pan" dessert, requested by families I visited. They enjoyed telling their neighbours about the priest's dessert.

None of this is what my older nieces and nephews remember about their "favourite uncle," Father Rick.

"Right, Claire?"

"Cruz, remember at the Glad Day Bookshop reading when your mother regaled the audience by retelling that family visit she and her cousins had to Uncle Rick's castle?"

It was Christmas 1988. Margie, my sister, had Jules, her sixth child, still in her arms. Meanwhile, nine other double first cousins in Marty's and Margie's families aged three to nine years old roamed this palace. On the rectory side, there were three floors with five bedrooms, stairs, a large kitchen, and a dining room, a laundry room, and an indoor garage. The kids slept on mattresses and bedrolls in a meeting room, with its tempting doors and admission to the parish hall, church, and more adventures. It was not long before the kids discovered in the laundry room the end of a chute that began two floors up. They raced upstairs to begin dozens of squealing rides from the second floor into a basement laundry bin.

Rose Frizzell, the housekeeper, raced into the living room to alert the adults. Whether it was the happy hour underway or the family rapture with the orange shag rug a former pastor had laid, the non-plussed parents shrugged and dispatched the celibate uncle to check it out.

"It was the magical kingdom," Claire picked up the story, "So many rooms and floors, passageways out to the church."

For a Gibson's & Company cafe audience in Collingwood two weeks later, Claire's sister, Emily, unwrapped that Christmas visit further. The kids picketed the final Christmas Day noon Mass because the adults had decided not to open presents until I was done.

"Imagine, Cruz," Claire interrupted. "Ten of us kids together, seeing, under the Christmas tree, the biggest mountain of presents we had ever seen because of two families and five adults there, and NOT being allowed to open one present until 1:00 p.m. on Christmas afternoon!"

"Remember, Rick, how you had us take turns to process baby Jesus to the front to lay him in the crib that was the manger? One of us carried the baby. The others were in the procession."

"Cruz, it began all right. In the first Mass, we were slow, happy, and loving. We were gentle with Jesus. I felt I was a bride walking down the aisle."

"We were good the second Mass too, but the novelty was wearing off. We wanted to open our presents. By the third Mass, we practically ran Jesus to the crib, express like, and then, for the final Mass, one of us launched Jesus thirty feet from the centre aisle over to the manger. We looked at you at the altar and tapped our watches."

"Claire, that football Hail Mary pass with baby Jesus HAD to be you!"

For the final liturgy, a few of the older kids did scrawl signs protesting "Uncle Rick Ruins Christmas" and "No Fair, No Presents" and stood at the parish doors to greet parishioners. Shades of my childhood picket outside the Cowards' home. I reassured parishioners what was going on in the rectory before anyone called Children's Aid.

If I complained too loud of my sacrifices as a priest, a family member kept me humble. Hearing me mention the meagre priest's salary, Jerry O'Connor, deep in a mortgage with six kids, offered to swap lives for my modest income that came with free housing, free food, a cook, and housekeeper. Indeed, we priests were landed gentry, kept, salaried, and fed.

CHAPTER 33

The Lone Ranger and Celibacy

I laughed out loud on a Google search, reading this question about my childhood masked hero.

"Why was the Lone Ranger called "lone" if he always had his friend, Tonto, with him?"

According to the fictional television and comics series, the *Lone Ranger* was the sole survivor of a group of Texas Rangers who were ambushed by outlaws. Tonto and he joined forces to fight the bad guys. I had already figured out the racist stereotype of Tonto. I now saw that the solitary Lone Ranger who watched over me playing priest as a kid might not be the most positive role model for my priesthood.

In a 1988 homily, I reflected on the state of ministry in the Roman Catholic Church.

"The church is in crisis, with tensions, which can be problems or opportunities to evolve. The priestly identity is part of the confusion. The priest was never meant to be all ministers in miniature. Ordinations confer a particular ministry, not all. Priests today are called to leadership, an affirmer of gifts, presiding over the church here gathered. But ordination is one ministry among many, all baptism and confirmation based. All who are baptized are called."

I was still keen to evangelize, to draw lay people into parish work. I situated everyone's ministry, mine too, first in our baptism. Laymen and laywomen who ministered were not mini priests. Nonetheless, it was nearly impossible to shake off the strict dualism of clergy and lay ministries codified at the Council of Trent from the sixteenth century. An insidious male clergy club prevailed. Some parishioners were sitting passively in their pews, preaching back to me, satisfied to pray, possibly still pay, and decide for themselves what to obey.

Serving on priests' renewal committees, I was cognizant of burnout emerging among fellow priests. Overworked, isolation, and loneliness were evident, not so much the quantity of our work as the quality. The cottage offered relaxation and renewal. We craved nourishment for the long haul.

It seemed too few bishops wanted that genuine conversation with priests on what mattered. Once, at a priests' retreat, the topic of celibacy came up. It may have been when the Canadian bishops, in a curious move, welcomed as Roman Catholic priests several married Anglican priests. This was nonsense to a few of us who, while happy welcoming new (older) married priests, wondered, "Why not us?"

Gervais dismissed our plea for a dialogue, cryptically defending celibacy with an odd comment on the hardships married couples faced. Something about the grass not being greener on the other side. Another time, Bishop Bernie Pappin happily confessed he would marry if church law permitted but, since it did not, he would not marry.

So there, end of discussion!

I respected Pappin. I did wonder what antifreeze he injected in his body. Maybe that is what I needed to live this celibate life. In truth, I did not shop for that antifreeze!

Serving on the diocese's Senate of Priests, I attended Ontario and national conferences. I was aware of studies on priests who chose a relationship with a partner under the covers of celibacy. Richard Sipe, a former priest and psychologist, devoted most of his career to studying celibacy, priests' sexuality, and clergy abuse. Based on one thousand five hundred interviews—priests in treatment, or who volunteered information, or from individuals in relationships with priests—he estimated more than fifty percent of priests secretly had a partner.[56] I did not. I knew enough priests who, from all appearances, did not. Of course, that did not exempt us from the struggle. Clearly, there were priests leading what literature called "a double life," a partner or family tucked away, far away likely. I wondered how that played out for the couple, especially for the partner who chose or felt obliged to live this secret life. Some relationships were with other men. There would be priests who consciously distinguished the call to priesthood from the obligation of celibacy. The phrase, "double life," seemed literally accurate, and yet somewhat judgmental. Some priests followed their conscience. I heard stories of widespread skepticism in Africa and Latin America on priests being celibate, either because celibacy was foreign to their culture or the faithful knew or suspected the priests had a partner. The bishops knew all of this and yet, for the most part, kept their heads in the sand.

Jesus never mandated celibacy although he offered praise for it in a specific discussion with his apostles on marriage and divorce.

"For there are eunuchs who have been so from birth, and there are eunuchs who have been made eunuchs by others, and there are eunuchs who have made themselves eunuchs for the sake of the kingdom of heaven. Let anyone accept this who can." (Matt. 19:12).

"St. Peter was not celibate. Much of the clergy for the first 1,000 years of Christianity were not celibate," wrote Father Peter Daly, a retired priest in the Diocese of Washington. "Celibacy was not mandated for diocesan clergy until the First Lateran Council (1123) and reaffirmed by the Second Lateran Council (1139). Both of those decrees were brought on as many clergy, especially in rural areas, had wives or concubines. Often, they gave church property to their families. Celibacy then was honored more in the breach than the observance." [57]

56 Rodricks, Dan, "Richard Sipe and the secret lives of priests," *The Baltimore Sun*, Aug. 24, 2018, https://www.baltimoresun.com/opinion/columnists/dan-rodricks/bs-md-rodricks-0826-story.html.

57 Daly, Fr. Peter, "Celibacy advances the priesthood's culture of compromised truths." *National Catholic Reporter*, July 22, 2019, https://www.ncronline.org/news/accountability/priestly-diary/celibacy-advances-priesthoods-culture-compromised-truths.

I knew celibacy was not essential to the Catholic priesthood. It is mandated in only two of the twenty-four autonomous churches in communion with Rome, the Latin Rite, and the Ethiopian Rite. All the other rites—Ukrainian, Syrian, Maronite, Coptic, etc.—allow their priests to marry prior to ordination.[58]

As far back as 1971, Bishop Carter, on behalf of the Canadian bishops at a synod in Rome, had called for the option of married priests. Belgian Cardinal Leo Joseph Suenens then presciently noted the day was coming for the Roman Catholic Church to choose between the Eucharist and the charism of celibacy as more faith communities had no resident priest and therefore were denied Eucharist. That day has long come, tens of thousands of Catholic priests choosing to marry, the church opting instead for stopgap measures like importing priests from Africa or India. A tired clergy is assigned multiple parishes. In that 1971 synod, Carter referred to the unhealthy obsession with compulsory celibacy. The gift, a charism given to some, is shackled as an obligation. Carter said that "Canadian bishops are nearly unanimous in favor of ordaining matured married men where there is need, and a small majority are in favor of changing the present discipline to provide for the ordination of married men independently of need. And 90% of our priests are of the same mind."[59]

In the creative non-fiction movie, *The Two Popes*, Francis and Benedict are at loggerheads between their reformist and orthodox views. As an exasperated Benedict inquired into Francis' progressive beliefs, the then cardinal and now pope answered.

"Celibacy can be a blessing and celibacy can be a curse."

As a celibate priest, I had loved people in a healthy manner. However, from my years living it, I believe compulsory celibacy is fundamentally unhealthy. I am convinced that optional celibacy is the right decision for healthier priests, a partial solution as well for the fewer vocations. Of course, allowing priests to marry is not a cure for all that ails clergy. Married people can suffer burnout, addictions, and abuse children too.

58 Ibid., Daly.

59 Ibid., Carter, *A Canadian Bishop's Memoirs*, 217.

Rome continued to ignore the lived experiences of many priests.

"Claire, in 2020, despite genuine anticipation, Pope Francis reiterated his doctrinally conservative views, disappointing many in not relaxing the married clergy ban even for certain remote areas in the world.[60] This was fifty years after Bishop Carter's intervention in the synod. A Vatican and Curia abetted by enough conservative cardinals still ruled."

Citing Pope Paul VI, Pope John Paul had said celibacy was the way "a priest configures himself most perfectly to Christ, manifesting and reflecting Christ's own love for his church."[61]

That configuring, I believed, was intended to imitate Jesus' love, mercy, and compassion. Rome's configuring rather settled squarely and narrowly on Jesus as a man who was not married.

Configuring?

Go figure.

60 Horowitz, Jason, and Provoledo, Elisabeth, "Pope Francis Sets Aside Proposal on Married Priests," *New York Times*, Feb. 12, 2020, https://bdnews24.com/world/2020/02/13/pope-francis-sets-aside-proposal-on-married-priests

61 Catholic Review, "Married priests? For the Vatican, still an exception to the rule," Jan. 19, 2012, https://www.archbalt.org/married-priests-for-the-vatican-still-an-exception-to-the-rule/.

CHAPTER 34

Suzanne

The best "missionaries" who drew others to St. Andrew's were those talking about us at their work. For example, a Monday morning office coffee with someone mentioning a good homily, a joke, or a teen youth event. Suzanne Corbeil had heard from a colleague that the new pastor was a storyteller with a good sense of humour. She was a mother with three children, an Ontario government manager delivering social benefits.

Corbeil brought her family, enjoying the weekend liturgies—the spiritual feeding, a whole congregation rocking a thundering chorus, "And the Father Will Dance." Like other parents, the loud celebration could be good cover for noisy kids; before the readings, we invited the children to the front for a blessing, sending them off with leaders to a children's liturgy. Catholics pining for quiet chose the earlier 9:00 a.m. Mass.

Corbeil was dealing with the acute pain of a marriage ending, she not wanting it to end. Crisis like hers might be moments of grace, as priests with parishioners explored realistic options, help if the husband and wife both wanted to work on a better, different marriage where they stayed partners or to separate in a way they remained friends. Better to reach heaven apart than hell together. I met with Corbeil three times. Her marriage did end.

She had company at St. Andrew's, parishioners, mostly women, who were suffering through a marriage ending while finding solace in a strong faith community. They may not have always been appreciated at home, yet in this community they were loved, their skills and leadership welcomed. Corbeil volunteered to help with the busy youth group. She invited me for supper a few times where, inevitably, she found me playing in the backyard treehouse or a recreation room with her three children, Lindsay, Lauren, and David. We clicked easily, my recognizing another family where I was not full bore on duty as Father Rick. I left those homes refreshed for the parish calls again.

Corbeil skipped a team I was on for a parish curling bonspiel. We won because she is a good curler. Her daughter, Lauren Mann, is a skip in national women's curling, already competing in two Scotties Tournament of Hearts. At that parish bonspiel, I won several movie passes and joked I would take her. I took other friends instead, and she never let me forget it. Corbeil hailed from North Bay. She was six years younger than me and had played high school volleyball against my sister-in-law, Nancy Prashaw (Armstrong). Corbeil was smart, progressive in her church and social views. I liked her.

In September 1990, she facilitated a Visioning exercise for St. Andrew's, drawing on her organizational development skills. Interestingly, after a Rita McNeil concert that a retreat group attended, I brought her back to the rectory, knowing three priest friends were visiting. I did want them to meet her. There was talk on the Visioning experience, its team building, personality testing, and communications. Two other parishes invited her to do workshops.

My close priest friends began to hear about Suzanne. One recalled a lengthy chat about how impressed I was by her story, perseverance, return to church, and how I hoped to introduce them.

The way I tell this, it would be a mistake to surmise anything happened fast. All the above was spread over more than two years. I had no sense of any real attraction. She was a good friend without alarms yet sounding on my celibate commitment.

Late in 1990, a hernia flare-up, surgery, and a holiday in California kept me busy.

It was now 1991, three years of knowing Suzanne, starting my fourth year back at St. Andrew's. I was still shocked whenever any fellow priest left. Not me, I vowed, *sotto voce,* eyes though wide open to prevalent struggles. For those eleven years, I never thought of myself as a Catholic priest out to marry.

One Sunday morning, between liturgies, I was in the kitchen grabbing coffee with Currie. Out of the blue, he casually asked me how I was doing living a celibate life.

How do I deal with it?

He confided that this was a huge issue for him. I was in a rush and not keen between masses for a heart-to-heart celibacy chat. I dodged his question with Matthew Fox's line on being okay with celibacy most of the time. I mentioned the strategy of a good confessor.

"Suzanne likes you," Currie interrupted.

"I like her too. She's nice."

"Rick, SUZANNE REALLY LIKES YOU."

Did someone vacuum the air out of the kitchen? I looked at Currie and smiled.

Suzanne Corbeil likes ME?

Corbeil had chatted with Currie about her feelings. A Catholic woman attracted to a priest might have few people to turn to. I learned later that Suzanne spoke about her feelings with a few friends, some that did not attend church at all. A Catholic girl attracted to a priest. Catholic guilt. She figured she would live with those feelings and not talk directly to me. Currie mentioned his talks with Suzanne, of her sharing her feelings.

"Well, you two should talk," Currie commented, washing his mug before heading back for the next liturgy.

I parked this information for a few days, smiling whenever the phrase bubbled up.

Suzanne Corbeil likes me!

For the first time, I became conscious of feelings for her, transcribing "I like Suzanne" to more precise language. Suzanne was pretty with dark, dark hair and soap white skin. Earthy. Sexy. From chats, it was apparent she was positive, fun, thrived in a good circle of friends, and was a good mother. I liked playing with her children. I guess I REALLY liked her.

On Wednesday, I took a deep breath and telephoned her, vaguely mentioning Currie's conversation. One get-together was scrubbed. I wondered what she had planned for that Friday night. I suggested we ice skate at a rink near her house.

That Friday, I bet I changed my shirt three times, brushed my hair a half dozen times, looked in the mirror more than I had in a long, long time. There was an excitement and a wonder, like a spring thaw warming a long, harsh winter—many winters. I brought skates even though it was raining by supper time. I had not a clue what we might say to one another. That did not bother me.

Her kids were with an aunt in town. We had the place to ourselves to talk uninterrupted. Corbeil poured me a B & B as humour sailed us past the opening, awkward lines. We sat on a couch, talking. I was comfortable to share feelings, my thoughts on compulsory celibacy, my living as a priest alone, my eternal struggle in giving up my own family and not being a Dad. Corbeil shared her feelings, her questions about the church and priesthood. We probably talked for three hours, easily, effortlessly. We were talking, but not yet talking.

She filled my glass. On her stereo, Suzanne played Blue Rodeo and then Dire Straits, "Brothers in Arms".

We were sitting on the rug by then. The frank conversation with this pretty lady and song references to mists, destruction, baptisms, and fire had me in a good place.

I felt this strong desire to kiss Suzanne. I did not, not yet anyway. It may have been why I suggested we see if it was still raining or if we might be able to skate. By the time we reached the outdoor rink, the rain was heavy again. We were the only ones foolish to be outside. I was getting deliriously happy. I looked over, and I kissed Suzanne, once, twice. Reaching over to her again, we tumbled into a snowbank for a long embrace.

Rick and Suzanne.

When we stood up, we were wet and laughing. We headed back to her place. She said she had sweatpants I could wear. In her bedroom, changing, I went over to kiss her again and we fell on the floor for another embrace. It was not long after that when we stopped. I suggested it was time I head home.

I work weekends!

When I laid my head on the rectory pillow, I was smiling. I had no idea what tomorrow would bring, how I would feel, or what this all meant. All I knew is that I had feelings for Suzanne unlike anyone else, ever. There may have been two or three other women I met in ministry where I had recognized an attraction, but I never spoke with them. This was quite different.

The next morning, awake in bed, I was still smiling. A quick check of the room confirmed no locusts, boils, lice, hail, nor other swarming biblical pestilence of any kind had visited me during my sleep. I knew the next talk with Suzanne might be life changing.

Even before Currie's heads up and the kiss, I had suggested to Suzanne to join several others on the pastoral team who were heading to the Gathering in Chicago. Was my subconscious in overdrive? I was not aware of any special relationship developing at the time I proposed she come. However, as a single mother responsible for three children and work commitments, extra days off were not simple to come by. The kiss may have sealed the decision, though. Come to Chicago, she did.

Once again, Chicago did not disappoint. She was on a separate flight from other parishioners who had booked early. I would share a room there with Father Ray Renaud. He would join us Friday.

On a Thursday afternoon before the conference began, I discovered Suzanne had checked into the airport hotel. I knocked on her door. It was an immediate kiss and embrace. The clothes tumbled to the ground. Was I crossing the Rubicon, one part reckless, yet resolute, and unsure where this would end? Julius Caesar had defied the Roman Senate in crossing the Rubicon River to start a civil war. I was not sure at all if I, too, had reached a point of no return. Conscious of what I was doing. Repeatedly choosing it. Thursday night, in longstanding Sault Chicago customs, the Canadians found Lawry's Prime Rib Restaurant. I made sure to sit beside Corbeil and slipped a hand into hers under the linen tablecloth. This time, I was oblivious to the servers' cocktail dresses, though still savouring the prime rib.

Back at the hotel, many of us hit the lounge for a nightcap and another Chicago tradition of dancing. I valiantly tried to dance with all the women there from the diocese. Really, I wanted to dance with only one. Friday, we skipped out of the conference, a first for me in nine Gatherings, as I played guide to Suzanne for Chicago: its Grant Park, the Golden Mile, and the St. Patrick's green dye in the Chicago River. We held hands. We talked nonstop all day. Like two lovers, we bought identical pullover jerseys to wear. We made it back late afternoon for a liturgy. We participated in plenaries or breakouts all weekend, thriving on the spiritual feeding. We found each other each night in her room. Sunday, her flight left early. She laughed telling me later her seatmate was a priest from the Gathering. Booked for a Monday departure, I knew Sunday night would be a reckoning of sorts with Father Renaud. I went to our hotel room, which I had hardly been in. I pleaded exhaustion and said good night. Ray was having none of that. He was upset and mostly concerned for me. He let me share my feelings for Suzanne and my deciding to pursue this friendship, clueless on where this might go. I told Ray I had kissed Suzanne first. She was no harlot stealing a poor, innocent priest from the church.

Put down those stones.

I told him many stories about her and the kids. He knew it was serious. He was imploring me not to leave the priesthood, affirming my gifts and our long friendship. He urged all kinds of remedies. I was deaf to them all except one, sensing a major retreat might be in order.

We talked all night. It was a harbinger of the numbness, anger, and melancholy my news triggered in close priest friends. I loved Ray.

Monday, flying back to Sudbury, I heard Blue Rodeo was playing a local concert Tuesday night.

Providence, no?

I bought tickets and picked Suzanne up. I could not wait for the lights to go down to slip my hand in hers. We talked that week, although parish work kept me busy and away from her home. In a few weeks, we were deep in friendship, talking about everything. Soon, prayers and talks to a few priest friends confirmed that I faced a major decision. I needed time and space.

I was not ready yet to talk to Bishop Plouffe, who had succeeded Gervais in 1989. I did call a friend and Jesuit priest, Bernie Carroll, to learn he could make room for me in Guelph for a forty-day retreat. The Redemptorists at Holy Redeemer Church graciously would cover liturgies.

On the way to Loyola House in Guelph, I told a few siblings the headlines on my secret. Their initial reactions hinted at how deeply embedded my priesthood was in them. Calls to a sister in London and brother in Collingwood had not gone well. There would be no family blessing right way. No, they did not want to meet Suzanne nor her family. The problem, as Marty acknowledged, was not Suzanne but themselves. The Prashaws were raised in a traditional model of what it meant to be Catholic.

"Perhaps we are jealous to share you with someone else and not a parish," Marty confessed.

They had questions, doubts, some harsh language to hear that did not sit well with me. I was their Father Rick, their pride and joy, and in some way, their frayed and fragile lifeline to a church they were scrutinizing themselves. Was I their surrogate priest as well as a brother? They judged. I lashed out. Brothers and sisters "in arms." It took time to reconcile fully. Thank God, we did. Dick and Gert had taught their children well.

"I remember I was thirteen when you told the family you were leaving the priesthood," Claire said. "All I could think of was that big palace we wouldn't visit and play in anymore. I never heard this story before. Thank you."

The sibling I chose to tell in person was an odds-on favourite for blessing my news. Jon lived close by in North Bay. Mom had her Catholic worry for Jon, what with him living with a girlfriend at the time and not going to Mass. I had repeatedly reassured Mom that Jon was fine. His goodness and character would see him through. He has long since married that girlfriend and is a fabulous dad to Lindsay and Marci. I had joked once with Mom that she should worry more for her priest son, not Jon.

Oh, well!

When I told Jon how much I loved Suzanne, he was incredulous. He may have had a soft spot for his brother, the priest.

"You're a fucking priest," he exclaimed.

Those words hung in the air for a few seconds. Then, Jon let out a long belly laugh. I grinned at his choice of words. I postponed a foreboding visit with Mom until after the retreat.

CHAPTER 35

Forty Days and Forty Nights

Spring 1991

This is the point in the story where my non-believing friends gather damning evidence on the perils in a faith journey. Thank God, I have a few agnostic and atheist friends keeping me honest. Over beers we duel, my teasing them on forcing their "beliefs" on their children, my noting neither of us will ever know if they win the wager on there being no life after death. We will both know if I won. The fun fencing on faith buys us another round of drinks.

Why didn't I simply leave right away and marry Suzanne?

Good God, the curse of being so Catholic!

In truth, I was a loyal son, dutiful, desiring a clean, certain exit if that was the decision. I would not go gently or quickly into the night.

The retreat would last forty days and forty nights. The nights not all for sleeping, as one spiritual exercise had me wake up intentionally in the middle of the night and off to a chapel, weary, supposedly ripe for divine grace. Or to sleep in the chapel.

Forty days, all in silence, except for a daily liturgy and a talk with Carroll, my spiritual director. Classical music played in the dining room as retreatants ate, lost in their thoughts. In pre-silent days, we introduced ourselves. People were here from eleven countries.

"Claire, you remember the symbolism of this number, forty—days in the desert, days between Jesus' resurrection and ascension into heaven."

"Am I getting a certificate for this course?" Claire asked.

I gazed over at my "fellow inmates", wondering what life crisis had brought them here. There were no last names, no identities except for the directors. Besides the chapel and dining room, a cornfield, a farm, and woods with a few deer became go-to special sanctuaries. That, and a large oak tree where I wrapped my arms around one night, wailing.

"Oh, dear," Claire sighed.

I did talk, to myself, to God, and to Bernie. I heard no cock crow. The dog-eared journal I kept gives up the secrets of what happened. Retreats had been special gifts during the seminary and then as a priest. That was part of the collar's privileges, to leave for rest, renewal, and inspiration. Without ever imagining when it might happen, I had suspected there would be an Ignatian retreat.

"For over fifty years," their brochure stated, "Loyola House has been offering a forty-day experience of prayer and daily guidance with a spiritual director as one journey through the Spiritual Exercises of St. Ignatius of Loyola. This experience is helpful for anyone seeking a deeper relationship with God. It is an inner "Camino" pilgrimage with Christ. It can be particularly beneficial for someone on a sabbatical or a person deciding of any kind."[62]

If the El Camino walks had been in vogue then, I may have headed directly to France and Spain. As I unpacked, I put my ordination holy card, its "All my words for The Word," on a side bed table. Next to it, I put a picture of Suzanne and the three kids. There would be no contact with Suzanne for the month. I remembered a poster that illustrated a rag doll being squeezed through a wringer washing machine with the words, "The truth will set you free, but first it will make you miserable." That rag doll was kin.

---

62 Ignatius Jesuit Centre, The Full Spiritual Exercises Experience, Guelph, https://ignatius-guelph.ca

Would this be a return to that Taizé hillside, its two files, where I might discover God in both choices? Would God sweat the details with his celibate priest tempted to bolt?

"I believe; help my unbelief!" (Mk. 9:24)

Carroll was a friend from Jesuit ministry in Northern Ontario. We could be honest with each other. His "loving ambivalence" as a detached director would guide my decision.

Right away, he lifted a pressure I felt, noting that any decision I made would be tentative, to be tested afterward and implemented. Most important, Suzanne and I would talk. I relaxed a bit, fears subsiding of a retreat deadline coercing a priest out of me. Carroll was grateful I had shared the real reason for being here with family and a few priest friends. He felt such honesty makes me more pliable to the Spirit of God. We shall see! I was conscious of the privilege of being there while Suzanne could not do likewise.

Suzanne was not the only reason I came to Guelph. Suzanne in the flesh revealed a deeper crisis of faith, ministry, and my relationship to the Roman Catholic Church. What I had preached to others, I needed to hear myself. God's abiding love. God loving me through these dark nights of the soul.

On the wall in Carroll's office, I spotted the words of Cardinal John Henry Newman's (d. 1890): "In the higher world it is otherwise but here below to live is to change, and to be perfect is to have changed often."

I should be perfect in no time with all these changes happening! Would unchangeable Rome ever heed Newman's words?

"God does not want our submission," Carroll said. "God wants our freedom." This is a radical, freeing love. Carroll reassured me that God would not harm me. God never tested us beyond our capabilities. Right, I needed those reassurances. Nonetheless, I noted all the exit doors in the building.

I felt angry about the deep wounds and sadness growing among the priests. We deserved no exemption on life's headaches, but it was distressing to witness too many good men who were sick, some growing cynical, and intolerant. I vowed not to go there.

The retreat began with a review of my history with God, reaffirming that God called me to become a priest. The Seattle vocation was carved in stone. I questioned the celibate part of this life, its foreign nature for me. What does it mean to be a man in the world now? Sam Keen, a leading writer in the men's movement, insisted there could be no homecoming without leave-taking. To become a man, a son must first become a prodigal and travel solo far into a foreign country. Then, in becoming oneself, it was pivotal to embrace your identity first, and, knowing who you are, figure out who to live that with.[63] I was back to the Rick-Father Rick conundrum.

I knew some of that prodigal story, first leaving the sphere of the Prashaws and the north for Carleton University, later heading west to the *Vancouver Sun* and still later across an ocean to Rome. Was there another leave-taking to happen, to come home to myself?

I was back to the two files: stay a priest or marry. Might there be a third file, an option to grow into celibacy again? Did God have other surprises?

As a Prashaw and as Rick, I felt I could never be separated from God. Does God want me to remain a priest at all costs, and can I accept that? Where will I be happiest? Is it guilt or shame that keeps me from Suzanne? Questions begging questions.

Early in the retreat, Carroll suggested I write my father. Yes, he had been dead for seven years. Carroll suggested a hot pen technique, pen staying on paper to yield a genuine stream of consciousness from deep inside, sidestepping the self-editing we all do. True, unguarded thoughts could surface. And, Carroll added, write my father's reply. This idea intrigued me. It did stun me how a letter appeared out of nowhere. I introduced Suzanne to Dad. I identified the longstanding fear of disappointing him, my father, the closet priest, proud of his priest son.

> Dear Dad:
>
> Funny that I have not written you these seven years, not talked in the heart-to-heart way I need too, son with his father.

---

63 Sam Keen, *Fire in the Belly, On Being a Man* (New York: Bantam Books, 1991).

I guess from your perspective you know all that I am going to tell you. I miss you more than anyone can imagine. Tears come writing those words. We were friends, good friends. We did not talk as deeply as I wanted. There was a given though, your constant love. You protected me and then you let me go when it was my time to fly.

And how you loved! You so filled my life. I am who I am because you were my dad. That is not to forget or diminish Mom's love. There is something special for fathers and sons. You were Dan Fogelberg's "Leader of the Band".

My news may hurt and disappoint you. I have been courting your approval for a long time.

My real fear is disappointing you because I know what you feel about my priesthood.

Dad, I love a lady named Suzanne Corbeil from North Bay. Between you and me, I am going to marry her someday. I suppose I should qualify that and say I sense I am going to. It surprises me to say that I am going to marry Suzanne. I have not said that yet to Bernie or even to myself. The retreat is for freedom, for peace of mind.

I wonder from heaven what you make of this, with your own freedom? Heaven has a whole new way of loving, living, and seeing, no?

Suzanne is so pretty. You would flirt with her as you did with other women. Had I brought her home before ordination, you would do somersaults. The ending of my priesthood, that is the problem, no? You probably know there will be married priests in a couple of generations. I never did have good timing. Dad, I need your help. I have hurt our family with the decision without meaning to. Please help us keep talking.

I need to give myself totally to Suzanne as you did to Mom. Can I let my first love, priesthood, go, knowing, as they say, that I am still a priest forever, but not in the way I have been one? That will hurt, and it scares me to make a commitment if I thought I was incapable of giving it my all. I cannot marry her until I find that freedom. Dad, I want your blessing. I will marry Suzanne regardless, but your blessing means everything to me. Suzanne is the first lady I have loved with forever written all over it.

Dad, I am a good priest and want to remain one. That cannot be, and that is the church's folly. I bring to God eleven wonderful years. I am proud of that.

In your reply, be honest as I know you will.

All my love,

Rick

I jotted a quick postscript, pen still on paper.

> P.S. In case I do not marry Suzanne, for whatever reason, not imaginable right now, hold Suzanne close, protect her, and bring someone to love her to wholeness and heaven. She deserves that.

As tired as my hand was, my father's reply came instantly, shorter, for the scribe in Guelph to record.

> Dear Rick:
>
> Do you have any idea what postage costs from heaven? Never mind!
>
> You doughhead! Of course, I bless you. I am your father, and you are my son, and that is what fathers are supposed to do for their sons. And I want to bless you, especially in our desire for you one day to be here with our happy gang. Close your eyes and think of the happiest moments of your life and that is but a drop in the ocean of heaven.
>
> Sounds as if you are going to find out for yourself about the meaning of fathering, like the wedding vows, "good times and bad, sickness and health, all the days of our lives."
>
> My father and I have worked it out. There are powerful new glasses to wear here. It confirms so much and yet changes all. God is a God of love and healing. Trust me on that.
>
> Rick, life is simple here. There is not much to figure out. God, the God of love, is the one absolute. Everything else is relative.

Your words about me as a dad are wonderful. I sure wish they had given me a manual to help along the way. That may have taken all the fun out of it. You learn as you go, and you learn the most right here and now. I do not miss Mom because there is no missing anyone here in heaven. It may be hard to grasp this, but Mom is here with me already. All my love and all my loved ones are here already. Your whole life of love comes with you. Nobody does it better than God!

All will go well as you put your trust in God. Pay attention to those concerns you have about making a full commitment to a marriage with Suzanne. I am not hinting at choices here. There is no right or wrong in this choice. I see two goods. For God's sake (we use that term a lot here), be free, so you can embrace Suzanne or priesthood fully. Yes, you will always be a priest, not because of some mark on your soul but because God called you, and you answered God's call. You will discover how you will live that priesthood should you marry Suzanne.

I am proud of my family in sticking together. Through all the fights, the hurts. Keep talking. Keep loving. Keep forgiving. We all rub each other the wrong way, searching to discover who we are. In finding our true selves, we find God.

Choosing to remain a priest or marry Suzanne will never determine if I love you. I do. Period. Always. I respect your life. It is your life. Be happy. Make sure they are your choices. I was so blessed happy when you became a priest. But it had to be you and your choice. And I could not see you sticking to it now to keep someone else happy or to be faithful for fidelity's sake. Fidelity to God is what counts. I do love priests. I hang with some. You know some of them. I have seen plenty of good priests and a few bad ones. Believe me when I tell you that you are a good one. We are all praying for you.

Let us keep in touch. This heart-to-heart helps me too!

Love you, my son. Dad xxoo

P.S. You could pray a bit more.

There was something authentic, earthy, in these letters with heaven, especially Dad's reply. I smiled, happy he and his father were talking. I laughed out loud hearing "Doughhead" again and grinned at his "pray more" advice.

Still, while the son and pleaser-accommodator needed those reassurances, the decision was pending. It had surprised me, though, to be so explicit in telling Dad I would marry Suzanne. Something was bubbling up inside, but the freedom to do so was not totally there yet.

For the next four weeks, it was to hell and back, heaven too, waves of anguish, lamentations, pleas, that oak tree, silence, and circling this call to the priesthood. Dry desert days, spinning of wheels, emotional, gazing from time to time on a young married Catholic couple there who were flesh and blood to a ministry I sought, anger at a pope, imploring Christ to do something. Alas, I gazed at Jesus, crucified. He seemed to have the patent on injustices.

It was off to the cornfields, the deer, and mosquitos. Sobbing. I needed to uncouple from attachments, from Suzanne too, from a deep fear God was commanding me to stay as a priest. I put Suzanne's picture away. I stopped penning a side diary for her. God did call me. I am not mistaken. Could God call someone to be a priest for a certain number of years? Is the church frustrating God's will?

I was as certain as ever I was called to be Rick.

I prayed in this detachment from Suzanne for a real revisit of vows I took seriously, embracing the passion for my priesthood, reminding myself of the growing shortage of priests. I cherished this brotherhood. Should I stay unless clearly shown otherwise? This is not Suzanne versus the Lord.

Still, my love for Suzanne on retreat grew by leaps and bounds. So, too, knowing that God would not abandon me. Near the end of the retreat, marrying Suzanne became a pleasant thought. The external, unjust law of forced celibacy loosened its grip on me.

My immediate retreat choices were to somehow remain Catholic, to stay in ministry, to not marry Suzanne right away but to be open to our love, and to focus on whether I could leave the priesthood. It had been hard work. It was all worth it.

I met Suzanne after the retreat in southern Ontario. We needed time by ourselves to debrief. I was interested in her four weeks apart and how her family was. My resolute yes to pursue this love seemed to scare her a bit. We talked. I wanted Suzanne to take all the time she needed. However, I suspect we were soon to make an honest mistake if that is even the word. My energy and enthusiasm corralled Suzanne, pushing us forward quicker than she may have wanted or needed. We would discover all this later. Of course, neither of us could know the hidden calling to be Adam's parents that was mysteriously and indelibly caught up in our love.

Back in Sudbury, I thought about continuing as a pastor while seeing Suzanne. A summer discernment might be okay, but longer, no. A long-term double life was out of the question for me.

I made an appointment to see Bishop Plouffe. He is this pleasant, orthodox, loyal prelate. The church has a few. Sharing my retreat, its real purpose, I told him that as far as I could discern, God was okay with these two loves even though the Catholic Church obviously was not.

"All the good ones leave," were Plouffe's first words.

I thanked him for the compliment. In truth, we both knew there are good and bad priests who either leave or stay. I felt sorry for the man. It was not the best time to be a Catholic bishop—clergy abuse, residential schools, lawyers, and lawsuits. Plouffe acknowledged my love for Suzanne had to be genuine because I had been happy as a priest. He said I was not a crisis waiting to unravel.

I offered (naively?) to remain at St. Andrew's for the summer or, if he preferred, to fill in for priests on holidays. Instantly, Plouffe jumped off that fence, stating I should begin a leave of absence after the next weekend.

Leading up to the final liturgies, I began telling a few people. It was like a dress rehearsal for the full disclosure coming on the weekend. Parish council heard my "happy, sad" news. I made calls to a few priests. Father Brian Dixon, a thoughtful pastor across town, called. He was upset yet kind. Did I understand how devastating this will be for the priests and diocese? It was another compliment, a sobering check on what lay ahead. Friday night, I went for supper to an older couple who were good friends. What happened there was a startling wake-up call for what to expect. While the husband remained silent, his wife lit into me on a long, angry tirade. I obviously had not prayed hard enough. I went to the retreat with a decision to marry already made. I was not listening to God. I was selfish. When her denunciation was done, I stood and, in a whispered hissing, reiterated the forty-day-long searching, praying, anguishing, and being loved by God. I left angry. We never spoke again.

Another conversation for heaven.

On my way home to Sudbury, I had stopped at Mom's apartment. I poured us drinks. I had rehearsed that speech a hundred times to no avail. There were no right words to tell a mother her priest son was leaving the priesthood. I told her about the retreat, my love for Suzanne and the children, plans to announce this on Sunday, and to take a leave. She listened. I detected the obvious sadness, and the instant cross she would bear. Her stoic faith faced another test. And then she did what no other friend nor family member had done. She asked if I had a picture of Suzanne and the kids.

God bless "go with the flow" Gertie Beaton.

CHAPTER 36

Final Homily

June 1991

This would be my final homily as a Catholic priest. Final, in a peculiar, four-act sense since, as a pastor of a large Catholic parish, I chose to say goodbye at four masses.

"Too bad Zoom wasn't an option," Claire winked.

As the parish tom-toms spread the pastor's news, attendance grew at each mass well beyond the typical, smaller summer turnout. Drawing on Dad humour to ease my angst, I joked at the 11:00 a.m. Mass that Easter lilies should be in the sanctuary with so many people in the church.

Peculiar too, in my steadfast choice to face this community I had served in two appointments, 1984 to 1986 as associate pastor, and then as their pastor from 1988 to this weekend. Love demanded nothing less. It had been tempting, though, to leave in the middle of the night, to pin news on the bulletin board while making a getaway.

Whenever I preached, I usually felt a good nervousness that energized me. The alb could cover shaky knees. Prayer and the grace from a magnificent retreat helped calm the worst nerves now. Reading the farewell message thirty years later, I again both smile and wince a bit, recognizing in the love note to them some defensiveness, anger, and the plea in vain for a different church. There are one or two lines I pronounced on the church that I no longer believe. In truth, though, I would not change a single word. It testifies to the intimacy of that farewell, a blessed pastoral relationship, a frank openness, an eye-to-eye, and soul-to-soul leave-taking done with honesty and humour, straight from the heart.

I need to stand down here among you tonight as I share a painful announcement. Sometimes, the sanctuary is too distant.

This will be my last weekend with you. The bishop has asked me to announce a leave of absence; he and I have agreed [that] I am to take from the parish, the diocese, and priestly ministry. It will be up to one year as I make a final decision whether I remain as a priest. Regardless of that decision, I must say goodbye because, even if I were to come back to the diocese, it will not be to St. Andrews.

I want to explain this decision, to share my retreat experience which was about my vocation crisis and to tell you the new priest who will be coming here to serve you. This will not be easy, so please pray through this.

All the reasons for going on a retreat that I shared publicly were true. It was a once-in-a-lifetime opportunity to address questions about Rick, Father Rick, my identity, and what my ministry was about. Except for family, a few priests, and friends, I had left out THE reason I went. It was simply too personal and painful yet to talk about from the pulpit. I must do so now, for you to understand what has been going on in my life and why the leave of absence is the correct next step in my discernment process.

I am deciding whether to marry a lady I love very much. The bishop asked me this past week whether I would mention the reason for the leave of absence. I said I would. There was nothing to hide or to be ashamed of; I told him I wanted you to know how normal I was. In these troubled times, when a handful of priests damage the reputation of the rest, I wanted parishioners to know why I am going. This decision whether to marry or not cannot be done properly while I stay on as parish priest. I love you too much. I love this lady too much, and I love my church and [the] priesthood too much for that.

What I share with you may be painful to hear, in the sense either we do not see eye-to-eye on the laws of the church with respect to mandatory celibacy or simply because this news about leaving may be hard to hear. I stand before you today as one who wants to remain a priest and serve the church he loves. One who has been strongly reaffirmed on retreat in his priestly identity and vocation yet, and this may be difficult to grasp, I stand here as one who also loves this woman, a love from God and a blessing for us and a love that is so much of who we are. For forty days, these two loves were in my heart, stayed intact and, to my surprise, blossomed. For some priests and enough Roman Catholics, there is no contradiction in these two loves. Rome disagrees, as do our laws. They find these two loves mutually exclusive, and so a decision is forced on me, a decision which, after prayer and dialogue with God and others, I find unnecessary and unjust.

Before going on retreat, I spoke to family and close friends. It was the hardest thing I have ever done. I learned valuable lessons about people's reactions and how I must, as a friend says, trust the process and let people feel what they feel and react the way they react. Some were happy but sad for what they were losing and what I had to sacrifice. Some were angry, angry at me or the church or this lady or God or whatever. Some felt betrayed. Some did not know what they felt. I believe, through this sharing of my news, that healing can and will take place. While part of me wanted to be in New Zealand this weekend, leaving the news for the church bulletin, I could not do this. Because of our relationship, it was important you hear this firsthand from me.

This has been, and will continue to be, a serious process. There has been complete and frank honesty with the bishop, with spiritual directors, and especially in the retreat. This is not done rashly. On the retreat, I wrestled through dark nights of the soul, false images of God, beating up on myself, wondering about failure and all else we tend to do to ourselves in crisis. I felt close to God and felt a deep, deep peace within about these two loves. The God of my retreat had no problem with these two loves.

To the parish council the other night, I described myself as happy-sad. Personally, I was happy because of this love yet sad and angry at a church which, in my judgment, violates God's will.

I want to say something about this lady who, contrary to what some may conclude, happens as a Catholic to feel much of what you feel when you hear this news, that is pain, loss, guilt. Some Catholics can make cruel and vicious judgments about her and others in her situation. Be prepared to explain your judgments to God, who alone judges.

This is not a lady who steals me from the priesthood. This is not "poor Father Rick" who is tempted. This is two adults making graced and adult decisions about something that is of our human nature and something of our spiritual nature as well. Friends who were personally happy when they heard the news this week made the comment, "Well, Father, you are only human."

And I wondered, deep down, what we mean about being "only human." Is it said as a positive recognition of who I and we all are, or do we as Catholics denigrate ourselves about our humanity and specifically our sexuality? Our choosing to love one another is of our human nature and our spiritual nature. This is not a lesser choice than priesthood, not against the priesthood. This is a blessing. On retreat, I grew in respect and admiration of celibacy as a charism for those called to live it freely. As a mandatory law, it loses its grace and becomes unjust. And some who God calls today are refused priest-hood. And some who respond and do their best either leave or stay, living lesser lives than God intended. Jesus weeps about this. We need courageous bishops and laity to speak out and open the closed doors where they tell us they too question the wisdom of the law. For 1,200 years, a church had married clergy. The Eastern Church has married clergy. Our Protestant friends have married clergy. And we will have the option again someday, but I am afraid only when the crisis is so great it cannot be ignored any longer.

To those who do not agree with what I am saying, know I say this in the deepest respect for you. We do not need to agree. May we love one another and keep talking. Try to understand this is my last time here. I want to share what I have embraced in prayer and ministry.

While I suspect enough Roman Catholics are sympathetic to the option of married clergy, we are on another level of exchange here. We are talking [about] Father Rick and our relationship we have developed. I hope Dan will continue to serve with you and be part of this healing process. I told him to keep his appointment book empty and the coffee pot full.

While my plans are unclear, I have been accepted tentatively for an intensive year's course in prison student-chaplain ministry located at the Ontario Correctional Institute in Brampton. So, you can tell others Father Rick is going to prison. Please explain the details! By the end of this year, I hope to make a final decision. Either as a layperson or priest, I will serve God in some form of ministry.

Let me close by asking for your prayers. I guess, in any separation, as this [sic] some may blame themselves wondering why this happened. No one is to blame. This is about choices we are making, about integrity. Here I grew and grew up in my faith and love of God. I leave more in love of God, of life and myself than when I came. I thank you. You are responsible for that.

For those angry at the church, may you love and stay. As the writer Anthony Burgess says, it may be found wanting, but our church is our mother and is the only mother we have. I love the church and I respect it. May any anger be positive anger that energizes the prophets in our midst.

I looked out at another group of people who I know I have offended by our different visions of church. I am sorry for hurting anyone. I knew you had God in your heart. I hope you understand that I did too. I was speaking the gospel as I prayed it and tried to live it.

And I speak to a group of people who I have been privileged to know as we experienced the miracles in our lives, the extraordinary ways God has, and is, touching you. Know God has used me in grace as the instrument for God loving you. There is a temptation to have our faith weakened or scandalized or to doubt the experience of faith that you have had through me. Do not doubt. It has been of God. Those new or back to their faith, listen to the stories of the older, wiser Catholics who have endured their share of curves in their faith journey. It may have been my words or example or ministry that God used, but others will come, and God will use them as well. I thank the young people, who are not only our future church but our present church. You are my hope. Be the church. Challenge it. Take the best of its traditions and transform the rest to God's way.

I have kept you a long time, and on a summer day too. Please forgive me. Pray for the bishop, for his life is not easy. He has been loving and compassionate. Trust yourselves, this faith community, who you are and what you can become. Life here does not start or and around any person other than the Risen Lord. I love you, and I bring to God my profound gratitude for having served you.

There were standing ovations at the end of each of the four homilies. When I had finished, I went to the altar to continue celebrating the Eucharist.

"This is my body broken for you . . ."

"This is my blood poured out for you . . ."

Long line-ups formed outside for hugs. I had few illusions all cheered my news. There would be no meet-up tomorrow to storm Rome. In fact, dozens of friendships with people in the parish and diocese fractured instantly, a few by way of their scarlet letter judgment but mostly because their real friend had been Father Rick, who was about to vanish.

After the final Mass, Carl O'Grady, president of the parish council, a miner and rock-solid Catholic, whispered to me to be in the parish hall Monday night for a farewell. There, in a packed hall, I said my personal goodbyes. People hugged me, some finishing stories on life events we had shared.

On his day off, Father Mark Balfe came to stand by me all night. I treasured his presence, recalling his singing "The Rose", "Delta Dawn" to those prisoners, and hugging me in the parking lot the night Dad had died. He found his blackest clergy suit and widest clerical collar to wear. My strapping bodyguard, all six feet and broad muscled shoulders. It was as if he was saying, "You have a problem with this, friends? Talk to me." I loved Mark.

Sister Bonnie Chesser took in the room, the loud conversations, and celebration. She said it reminded her more of a wedding than a funeral.

Indeed, it did.

Later that week, she wrote Bishop Plouffe. Noting how the crisis among priests must weigh heavily upon him, she shared all that she took in, the positive comments on priests as she remarked how the bishop must hear negative ones often, too.

> Last Saturday, I went to Mass at St. Andrew the Apostle to support Rick in the difficult task he had to perform—announcing his leave of absence. Bishop, he did a beautiful job. The whole process was so healthy! He was honest about the issues and honest in sharing his feelings. In doing so, he invited that same honesty from his people. I was so moved to see the people give him a standing ovation with tears streaming down their cheeks.
>
> I also attended the farewell celebration in the parish hall last Monday. I heard some 'die-hard' Catholics sharing with me that optional celibacy for clergy would be worth considering. I felt as if I was witnessing a historical moment in the church, not because a layperson suggested this, but because Rick's honesty set in motion a process for hearing about an issue from another person's perspective.
>
> I wish you had been there, Bishop. I think you would have felt encouraged by the spiritual maturity of some of the members of that parish.
>
> Rick's leaving is a great personal loss to me, as I'm sure it is to you. My faith tells me that this "death" we are experiencing will be followed by some sort of "resurrection". I think I saw a glimmer of the light of Resurrection a St. Andrew's in this past week.

Bonnie was on the Pro-Cathedral team when this all began. She was there as the curtain came down. I loved Bonnie.

PART THREE

Father

CHAPTER 37

Jailhouse Jesus

1991–1992

After the parish hall farewell celebration, I was alone Monday night in the rectory. It still felt like home. My bones were weary. Packing could wait. I thought of a speaker from a Youth Encounter years earlier. I'll call him Chris. He was a beautiful young lad who shared his painful past—drinking, drugs, school suspensions, petty crime, all while running from an alcoholic father, and his physical and sexual abuse. Chris told other youth how he climbed down from a suicidal ledge. He bared his soul to help other kids find their way forward.

When Chris finished, he ran out of the gymnasium. I found him at the end of a long hallway, sobbing. I slid down the wall to the ground.

"I felt like I took all my clothes off in front of my friends in there, and I couldn't face them," Chris sighed.

"Chris, put your clothes back on. Go see your friends. They want to hug you. And, Chris, remember, always love the man in the mirror."

This Monday night, I recognized Chris in the flesh. Four times this weekend, I had shed my clothes, baring a life crisis and my love for a lady. I, too, had the urge to bolt. I needed to heed my own counsel. Many had hugged me already. How do I still love this man in the mirror? It would not be easy.

If I was not a Catholic priest, who was I?

If no longer Father Rick, what is there?

I was back in my philosophy classes, the words of Kierkegaard nudging me towards this full-blown existential crisis. I would struggle to live, love, breathe, be, and certainly become Rick all over again, a faith groaning and growing in new, unimaginable ways.

As I had joked, I would work this out in a one-year "prison sentence" at Ontario Correctional Institute (OCI) in Brampton, ON. I enrolled in a supervised course to become a specialist in institutional ministry with the Canadian Association for Pastoral Practice and Education (Now the Canadian Association for Spiritual Care). Half the day, I served as a student chaplain in a multi-faith setting, offering worship, counselling, and group work with offenders. My congregation were fellow lost souls—young and adult offenders, many with mental health, sex, drug, and alcohol issues—at this two hundred and twenty-bed facility northwest of Toronto Pearson International Airport. We ministered too next door at Vanier Centre for Women, another prison.

In the afternoons, six student chaplains from different denominations attended classes for intense, personal work: theological and psychological seminars, pastoral counselling reviews, bioenergetics, and supervision. What lie ahead might be chaplain ministry in a hospital, prison, or other pastoral care setting.

Putting Humpty Dumpty back together again.

This seemed like a year-long version of the forty-day, excruciating "truth will set you free" squeeze through my retreat's wringer washing machine. Christians love the "Amazing Grace" hymn, the "I once was lost, but now am found" story. Well, I seemed to be going backwards, first found but now lost. It meant "taking the clothes off" weekly with other priests or ministers also in transition for intimate discussions on who we are and who we want to be.

Sure, Rick, let's have another root canal!

"Claire, the good news was a surprising intact faith in God, the gods, and Rick."

My supervisor was Rev. John Roberts, a wise, wry Anglican priest whose accent and soccer stories betrayed his Liverpool, England roots. I lived downtown in Toronto with Tony Martin, who was in his first term as Sault MPP after that election shocker of an Ontario NDP government. Some nights, I caught up with Martin and his colleagues at a pub or theatre. On the few free weekends, I headed to Sudbury to be with Suzanne and my new family, unless she visited Toronto.

OCI's "Jailhouse Jesus" was no stranger. There had been that seminary summer at Cecil Facer Youth Centre. Then, those weekly North Bay District Jail visits as a priest, mass attendance soaring when I brought young women with guitars. I was "a guest" at Collins Bay Penitentiary near Kingston, ON. for a Cursillo weekend.[64] We slept on mats alongside the prisoners in the gym. I had looked in vain for the guards with rifles. I had watched too many Hollywood movies. On the first night, knowing the names of two guys beside me, one sentenced for murder and the other rape, I pondered who I should give my back to. I quickly fell into a deep sleep. At breakfast, they razzed me for snoring loudly.

There, but for the grace of God, goes I.

There goes I.

At OCI, I needed to claim a new pastoral identity. I weaned myself slowly and painstakingly from a priest to a pastoral minister, to sieve the golden nuggets of my Catholic DNA within this broader ecumenical faith. I was still comfortable in the Christian faith that anchored itself in a social gospel. I admired the person and teaching of Jesus, believing the doctrine on who made us, and a call to communion with one another. I was not yet aware of how Jesus was being misrepresented by some Christian churches and pastors. I am now.

As a minister, could I abide by the authority of God and the gospel rather than my customary assigned authority of priesthood? I had rejected a celibate priesthood. However, I didn't see myself walking away from ministry altogether, recalling my vocation call, twelve years of ministry, the positive influences of the gospel and kingdom of God, and a faith confident yet stirred and shaken.

---

64 Cursillo is Spanish for "a small course," a three-day weekend introduction to Christianity with talks, witness, and song, "The Cursillo Movement-What Is It?" www.drshirley.org.

Roberts was equal part healer and devil's advocate, hugging and clubbing me, pushing discernment on whether priesthood was my bottom line. If so, he grinned; he had applications for his Anglican Church.

Yes, the Roman Catholic Church taught that, even though I had left, I was a priest forever according to the order of Melchizedek (Ps. 110:4). The sacramental seal from May 9, 1980, could not be erased. In the absence of a priest, canon law decreed I still could anoint someone gravely ill and hear their confession. However, Roberts urged me to quit playing the mind game of being this married Catholic priest the church refused to recognize. That might drive me nuts, and others too. "You left the club when you chose Suzanne," he counselled. We could debate the status of my priesthood to eternity, but Roberts nailed my feet to the ground.

Ah, the club . . .

I knew its membership privileges well. One night, as I pulled out of the Pro-Cathedral parking garage, I slowed down but did not stop at the immediate first two Stop signs fifteen feet apart, leading to the busier Algonquin Ave. A flashing red light appeared in my rear-view mirror. The police officer looked at my identification.

"Father, next time you land at a Stop sign, say a complete Hail Mary and then proceed."

"Bahahaha! Do you still have the white collar?" Claire asked. "I'd like to try that for my next roadside chat with the Ontario Provincial Police."

"Slow down, Claire!"

"No ticket" favours were peripheral privileges. Far greater was the unquestioning deference shown to you, at least back then. The welcome mats out. The pedestal, the gifts, and other freebies. A crown prince. There was little scrutiny or supervision. A few priests enjoyed their luxury vacations or lifestyles. Was it their compensation for a life without a mate? Was it the gift-giver's insurance for their own salvation? Up north, truly, I had not seen much luxury.

Club privileges came then with too few checks and balances on pastors who had access to parish funds; this changed after news stories reported on a few priests with gambling or other addictions who helped themselves to the till.

I was cognizant of the club's abundant blessings too, its unique life. With my personality, it felt like being handed this Disney Pass for limitless rides, forever. Most days, it kept me humble and grateful.

Bishop Plouffe visited me when he came to Toronto. He alluded to the anger in the diocese among the priests about my leaving, diffused anger directed at him, church, Rome, pope, and me. He questioned if I could be genuinely happy without priestly ministry. It was a fair question. He hoped that I, "for the glory of God," might re-choose celibacy. I told him, "for the glory of God," I chose Suzanne. These were painful conversations. I was angry at the church. I was angry at this nice man who shrugged at his own impotency to change the rules. I was slowly weaning myself from a Catholic hierarchical universe. I minced few words on all I found wanting in my Catholic Church. It still felt like mine. After I told him how the church had failed God, he wisely ordered drinks. The bishop and I kept talking. Roberts steered me to own the consequences of making choices in this imperfect world and imperfect church.

Nevertheless, in leaving the priesthood, I discovered it would take an exceptionally long time to leave me. I craved approval. After the startling de facto ex-communication by that older couple, politer messages arrived in cards and comments. On how I still might be salvaged.

"We are praying for you, Father Rick."

"Turn around and come home!"

I welcomed the prayers and wondered if some were truly praying for me or praying rather that I be what they wanted me to be.

A priest friend who I respected wrote a beautiful seven-page handwritten letter where he acknowledged loving a few women, his own desires for intimacy, and longing for children. Noting his "shortcomings," he shared that choosing celibacy over again was choosing Jesus as his life. "Difficulties became bearable and life-giving as our relationship is renewed and deepened." He referred to Jesus again as "becoming his bottom line." Ordination had not made him someone else but that, as a man with feelings—emotions, body, mind, and spirit—there was "loving obedience in Christ." He underlined those words. This obedience freed him to love more freely, intensely, and respectfully.

I felt his love, and yet I disagreed. Jesus was not my bottom line, or, may I rephrase that, a God emerging through new stories and names, including Jesus, was becoming my bottom line alongside Suzanne. This other priest had rediscovered the charism of celibacy. I read other stirring defences of celibacy, aware that some priests lived that commitment well. Left unsaid in an apologia was celibacy's mandatory nature, exacted from priests by a church, but not by God.

Prayer was the one prescribed remedy to fix me. Writers seemed to discount my forty days and forty nights. There was some righteous judgment. With their hotline to God, they let me know who was to blame. I was weak. I had broken vows. I took solace again in letting the zealots demonizing Suzanne know I had kissed her first. *Chariots of Fire* pleasure! I seethed when Mom, still trying to protect me, let slip a few gross comments she endured from "good Catholic friends." She had bit her tongue more than a few times while listening to gossip spoken in her presence.

The year at OCI compelled me to own a second major "failure" in my life. No matter my views or peace I would come to in my choices, the real world stamped a capital F scarlet letter on my forehead. It was no surprise my picture came down at St. Andrew's. There would be lessons, positives again, in this "failing." As dramatic as this taking leave of Father Rick had been, my resilient faith endured. I chased after the resurrection, wounds and all. Healing was happening, a reaffirmation in core beliefs of life as a celebration, a dance of passion, pain, struggle, and journey.

Suzanne and I chose a wedding date for April 1992, towards the end of OCI studies. We married at St. Andrew's—no, not that parish. The celebration was at St. Andrew United Church in Sudbury with Rev. David Mance as the officiant. In the congregation were a dozen Roman Catholic priests and religious sister friends. Peter Moher, Tom O'Connor, Bonnie Chesser, Roberts and his wife, Roberta, came north. Ray Renaud, too, friendship winning the day. Mom was there with siblings to celebrate their brother's new vocation. The dinner was in the cavernous Science North auditorium. A mob of children escaped the speeches, racing the five floors through the museum built mostly underground. This was their consolation prize for losing my palace to visit. The dinosaur display seemed a rather appropriate backdrop for my leave-taking.

Roberts excused me the next week as Suzanne and I went to Jamaica for a splendid honeymoon. This love filled a gaping, unsustainable hole in my life. It would take longer to learn the web of intimacy—the couple-ness, pillow talk, making up, and those secrets behind closed doors. It was quite a new adventure.

Still, there was the urgent, practical matter of finding a job that paid. In chaplaincy, ecclesial standing in one's denomination mattered. For example, Catholics hired in a multi-faith pastoral care facility needed their church's blessing. On leave from the priesthood, limbo did exist for married priests within their Roman Catholic Church.

First, I applied for a spiritual advisor and pastoral care job at the Smith Clinic Drug and Alcohol Rehabilitation Centre in Thunder Bay (now the Sister Margaret Smith Centre). The timing was not the best, though, for Suzanne and the family. I successfully competed for a Roman Catholic chaplain position at Warkworth Institution, a medium-security prison near Peterborough, ON. Despite serving prisoners of all faiths, the job called for that irksome ecclesial approbation. I needed a dispensation from Rome to receive any church blessing as a chaplain. I was lukewarm at best proceeding down that road, finding the laicization process a Roman Rubik's Cube. I shared some married priests' objections to a dispensation that "reduced me to the lay state," which both fudged my enduring priesthood and sullied the baptism-anchored equal status of the laity. God had called me to the priesthood. The Catholic Church had ordained me. My ordination was not a mistake. They could not unordain me, although they could and did withdraw my authority. Nonetheless, I might need to put water in my wine. I objected to parts of getting a dispensation for its process, language, and its judgment. However, I needed the dispensation to work in pastoral healthcare or corrections settings. There were practical demands as the breadwinner for the family, alongside Suzanne.

Theologically and pastorally, Roberts brought me through the wringer washer to an identity as minister based on my new reality, and past this "I am, but I am not, a priest". On December 31, 1991, I wrote my "Dear Holy Father" letter asking to be dispensed from promises of celibacy as a diocesan priest to marry Suzanne. I was honest with the pope.

We know our love to be of God.

I was never called to celibacy, even though I was ordained in the Catholic Church.

I had a strong vocation calling. While I am sure the church sees matters differently, my experience then and now is that celibacy is quite a different matter than priesthood.

By the end of my retreat, I was at peace with this love for Suzanne and my love of priesthood co-existing simultaneously. For Suzanne and me to ignore or deny this love was a violation of ourselves and our natures and, therefore, our Creator. This is what we have concluded through prayer and honest dialogue.

A dispensation is also important for working in prison ministry, for my future in the church and for our family and their faith development.

It has been our love, including her children, that tells me that forced celibacy is contrary to who I am. The church would counter that it was not forced, but a choice asked of me, which I accepted. But, when one knows God is inviting him to be a priest, then I do not see the real choice. I wanted to be a priest enough to accept celibacy and prayed all would work out even though I was anxious about how that could be.

Throughout the process, I worked with the diocesan chancellor, Father Norm Clement, who stayed a priest for fifty-six years even though he appeared to be the heartthrob of many a St. Joseph College girl where he was chaplain. Clement was pastoral with me, knowing the psychological profiles that opened Rome's doors for laicization. When in Rome, be a Roman!

"Furbizia!" Claire chuckled.

My dispensation to sign arrived in 1994. For months, it sat on my desk. It was granted in 1995. The slow response on Rome's part may have had something to do with the tens of thousands of priests leaving to marry. On one hand, the dispensation was never more than a piece of paper, albeit an important piece of paper to institutions, some family, and friends. I wrote to Clement: "Life and ministry continue to be a blessing. The Holy Roman Catholic Church moves further and further to the edges of faith, community, and life's daily, throbbing needs. My regret is to know its beauty and potential and yet experience its irrelevance for many people. I fear the Lord disappears in its laws."

"Claire, those are my views, even more so today."

"You were a good priest, Uncle Rick," Claire said, leaving to make Kentucky bourbon Manhattans. My parents had poured rye in their Manhattans. I never liked them until Claire made me hers.

"Two to one, good bourbon and good Vermouth with a dash of bitters and slice of orange."

Plouffe wrote a "To Whom It May Concern" letter re: Mr. Richard Prashaw recommending me for ministry as a lay chaplain in correctional institutions. I appreciated his referring to my pastoral gifts "with a special rapport with people with the facility to reach out in compassion for those in need." However, his most significant line followed, "The Bishop of the Diocese in which he obtained employment would approve his ministry within the confines of his diocese."

Suzanne joined me for a Toronto holiday in July to wrap up my studies. On July 12th, there was a parade outside for Protestant King Billy, William of Orange. I suspect a baby was conceived there. The Protestant parade lovemaking felt like a proper exclamation mark on my emerging Roamin' Catholic faith.

CHAPTER 38

Leaving for Good

1992–1993

As a priest, I had never imagined leaving until I left. As the bishop noted, I was not a crisis in waiting. However, when I had packed up at St. Andrew's, I did sense it was over.

Some priests who leave find new communities to pastor, to celebrate Eucharist and other sacraments in their circle of close friends. The Vatican blessed none of those new ministries, although pockets of Catholics might approve.

"Claire, not judging their choices, I walked away from this priesthood. How do I say this? I was glad I had been a Roman Catholic priest, and now I was ready to leave."

Clearly, the Roman Catholic Church would not change its rules anytime soon. In that letter to my father I penned on retreat, I may have been overly optimistic on the church permitting married priests. And, by 1991, there were other significant church practices disturbing me as much or more than no married clergy, i.e., the ban on women priests; women generally devalued; the Church's views on homosexuality; a hierarchy forgetting, at times, its fundamental role as servant to the People of God; and far less attention being paid to social justice. Tragically, the spirit of the Second Vatican Council had not been fully realized. Worse, the Council reforms have been deliberately undermined by the Roman Curia, the government of the Roman Catholic Church. In a revealing comment, Pope John Paul II once said the Curia, not he, is the pope.[65] Vatican observers noted Pope Francis' talk to Italian catechists in 2021 when he seemed to be talking to the Curia as well, stating one is not "with the church" unless one accepts the magisterial authority of the Second Vatican Council. He said there could be no concessions nor selectivity on what to believe in that Council's teaching. "Nowhere have the deliberations of Vatican II encountered more resistance and prejudicial reinterpretation than in the papacy itself," a *La Croix International* journalist wrote. "Nowhere has the lack of respect for the authority of the Council been more apparent than in the actions and inactions of the Roman Curia."[66]

I had to resolve whether, as Anthony Burgess had written, this church might still be my only mother. I had doubts.

"By the way, Claire, so did Burgess as he headed to a life first as a lapsed Catholic and then non-believer." [67]

"Rick, he's not alone."

On a positive note, my passion was channelled into being a husband, a stepdad, and then, in the fall of 1992, the giddy excitement when Suzanne announced we were expecting her fourth, and my first, child.

Woah!

I prepared to be a dad, a deep, longstanding desire coming true. This family needed me. I had no prevalent energy to change the Catholic Church. My enthusiasm as a new husband and dad meant a dive into a mortgage, bills, financial advisors, making meals, cleaning, laundry, daily commuting, and juggling the routine of parenting. Almost everyone knows this life. I was not complaining. I had this foolish grin, ear to ear. This new life in the red with debt made me better appreciate my brother-in-law's offer to swap lives after

65 Kennedy, John O'Loughlin. "Is Pope Francis Warning the Roman Curia?" *La Croix International,* April 29, 2021, https://international.la-croix.com/news/religion/is-pope-francis-warning-the-roman-curia/14207.

66 Ibid., Kennedy.

67 Sandford, Christopher. "The restless soul of Anthony Burgess," *America Magazine,* New York, July 13, 2018, https://www.americamagazine.org/arts-culture/2018/07/13/restless-soul-anthony-burgess.

I had complained about priest salaries. Of course, Jerry and I wouldn't trade this married, family life for anything. I would try hard. I made my share of mistakes. Now married, with three children and expecting a fourth, I had little time to cling to a furtive priesthood.

As a family, we attended Mass in Russell, where we had moved, forty minutes east of Ottawa. I found it awkward at first in the pew rather than in the sanctuary. There were days of judging the homilies or liturgies, wincing at conservative priests or sterile words that seldom kissed real lives.

For years after marrying, I woke up from variations of a reoccurring dream sequence of me failing as a priest. The dreams were mundane, equal parts annoying and funny. I'd never get to celebrate the Eucharist or preach at The Pro because I lost the keys or found myself locked out of the church, or the lights went out, the PA system failed, vestments disappeared; a Catholic comedy of errors sabotaging ministry. Years later, a spiritual counsellor flipped those dreams to the failure of the church to let me in to minister.

Who was failing who? Who silenced the PA system, took the vestments, and locked the doors?

Much later, in 2017, dealing with the death of Adam—its unfairness, my helplessness—I laid on a table for treatment by Atherton Drenth, a spiritual clairvoyant and energy intuitive who had helped several I know release blocked energy. Drenth asked if all was okay between God and me. Without hesitation, I said yes. She then asked if all was okay between the Catholic Church and me. It surprised me how quickly I said, "That's good, too." I meant it. Of course, I could talk for hours on what I wish that church would do or become, However, Drenth had asked about my energy fields and relationship with the church.

I had moved on. It had taken several years. There was a new, healthier detachment from the exclusive Holy Roman Catholic Church.

CHAPTER 39

CCJC and The Mandorla

1992–2004

I had spotted a *Globe and Mail* job ad for communications coordinator and youth justice lead at a national ecumenical church coalition based in Ottawa. I knew of The Church Council on Justice and Corrections (CCJC) because of its stalwart work opposing the death penalty. They, with allies, had printed "Don't Kill for Me" postcards and developed a resource kit asking Canadians, "Why kill people who kill people to show that killing people is wrong?"

"Claire, I suspect you know the death penalty in the United States is a thinly guised killing of mostly people of colour, poor folk, too often badly represented legally, some wrongly convicted. Opposing their execution is not exonerating nor excusing any heinous crime; no one is going free unless proven wrongly convicted."

In an encyclical and catechism update, Pope Francis had cemented Catholic Church opposition to the death penalty, which he said is wrong in all cases, "an attack on the inviolability and dignity of the person."[68]

Sister Helen Prejean, author of *Dead Man Walking*, rebuked the National Catholic Prayer Breakfast for giving then U.S. Attorney General William Barr its 2020 "Christ-like behaviour" award.

---

68 Death Penalty Information Centre, The 2018 Revised Catholic Catechism, www.deathpenaltyinfo.org.

"Barr has presided over an unprecedented spree of federal executions this year," Prejean tweeted. The final three individuals were executed during President Trump's lame-duck period, at the same time as he pardoned dozens of his colleagues.

"Did you hear Sister Helen on the *Criminal Podcast?*[69]" Claire asked. "A friend summed up her message: humans are more than the worst thing they have ever done; it is okay to love someone, even if you don't love all of their actions; every person deserves love and dignity; and man, oh man, life is hard and complicated."

"Claire, life is indeed complicated. This may be why some people swayed by fear or anger opt for simpler solutions."

Knowing CCJC's good work, I wanted this job. To return to Ottawa, eighteen years after Carleton, to a healing ministry practiced at a systemic level, ironically working for eleven church or religious bodies instead of only Catholics. Coalition members included the Canadian Conference of Catholic Bishops, Anglican, United, Baptist, Presbyterian, Lutheran, Christian Reformed and Evangelical Lutheran churches, plus Salvation Army, Mennonite Central Committee, and Quakers.

CCJC hired me. I lived alone in Ottawa those first six months as Suzanne wrapped up her government work in Sudbury. The kids finished their school year. I made it home for Adam's birth after Easter.

On my CCJC desk, instead of that "Why Am I Here?" pastor message, I had this prose from Russian writer Aleksandr Solzhenitsyn:

"If only it were all so simple! If only there were evil people somewhere insidiously committing evil deeds, and it were necessary only to separate them from the rest of us and destroy them. But the line dividing good and evil cuts through the heart of every human being. And who is willing to destroy a piece of his own heart?"[70]

---

69 Sr. Helen Prejean, "Sister Helen", in Criminal, podcast, Episode 156, https://thisiscriminal.com/episode-156-sister-helen.

70 Alexsandr Solzhenitsyn, *The Gulag Archipelago*, Abridged Edition. (New York: Harper Collins, 2002.)

From his Gulag cell, Solzhenitsyn was not advocating for any "bleeding heart" justice. Instead, his words drilled deep through my "There goes I" message to those Collins Bay prisoners, to all in the pews. and on the streets.

Frankly, this was wisdom Canadians, and many people of faith, resisted mightily. Who wanted to look inward when we could opt solely to punish the bad guys? "An eye for an eye and tooth for a tooth" prevailed, equally a "pound of flesh" in the courtrooms. We were addicted to punishment. Most politicians gladly pushed those "law and order" fear buttons. It won them elections.

As I arrived at CCJC, there was still an appetite to consider transformation, an openness to question and re-think justice—among the NGOs, academics, and people in key policy positions in Canada. The times were changing though. Jean Chrétien symbolized the shift right. In 1982, as Minister of Justice, he had signed the forward-thinking White Paper, *The Criminal Law in Canadian Society*.[71] However, "tough on crime" laws surfaced by the second half of the Chrétien Liberal government years and then dominated the Stephen Harper Conservative administration. Even a few NDP prairie governments drank the Kool-Aid, wary of getting too far ahead of voters. An exception was Saskatchewan's Justice Minister John Nilson, an Evangelical Lutheran appointee and former president at CCJC, who coined a "not tough, but smart on justice" political policy. Canada was influenced though by American politics with its three-strikes law, primarily a war on drugs that had snared, disproportionately, people of colour, laws that Republican and Democrat presidents pushed. Bill Clinton would much later offer a "mea culpa" for his 1994 crime bill. Still, there was little political capital in criminal justice reform.

Coming to CCJC, I had a surface appreciation of Canada's criminal justice system. I had read stories of wrongly convicted individuals, of too few prisoners rehabilitated, and high recidivism rates. Sentences meant to deter added instead to criminal records, increasing the likelihood of further crime.

---

71 Government of Canada, *The Criminal Justice System in Canada*, White Paper, 1982, https://johnhoward.ca/resources/.

It was my new CCJC colleagues, especially Lorraine Berzins and Rev. Jamie Scott, a United Church minister, and working with a dazzling array of whip-smart, system savvy board members, that immersed me into a PHD on the prison industrial complex; that policy had married government and industry interests to a massive incarceration policy over and against real solutions to economic, social, and political problems. Communities welcomed the jobs and money prisons delivered. Less apparent was a pervasive over-incarceration of Indigenous Peoples, injustices to women prisoners, and the neglect of victims. Combine a few of those demographics, for instance, Indigenous women, and injustices magnified greatly. Our retributive system was broken, but it was the main attraction in town.

Berzins had been a social worker in Canada's corrections system when a harrowing hostage situation she survived hurdled her deep into a reflection on justice, how woefully inadequate a punitive, adversarial system was. Grounding her and us was her marriage to Andrejs Berzins, Ottawa's senior crown attorney. While Andrejs cheered CCJC's progressive views, he and his colleagues needed practical, immediate help for the court's long assembly line of cases.

Collaborative Justice Program

In 1999, we launched a visionary Ottawa Collaborative Justice Project, now the Collaborative Justice Program (CJP),[72] offering rare reparative and restorative processes at the pre-sentence stage in cases of serious crimes.

New caseworkers worked directly with offenders to help them gain a better understanding on what led them to commit a given crime and its specific impact on the victim and others. Collaborative justice gave victims a real voice in the process, helping to ensure they feel heard and acknowledged not only by the offender but by the larger justice system that can suffer from an impersonal and disconnected approach to prosecuting the crime.

---

72 The Collaborative Justice Program: Restorative Justice Ottawa, www.collaborativejustice. ca.

Collaborative Justice Program handled armed robbery, assaults, and a bomb threat to a school. It resolved a high-profile, hate-motivated graffiti rampage,[73] and a man who impersonated a soldier at a Remembrance Day ceremony.[74]

When Lorraine and I were not "saving the world," we regaled one other in the lunchroom with the latest shenanigans from home or our families. We never lacked for material. Scott teamed with Lorraine to deliver church family violence projects. In 2019, he was named an Officer in the Order of Canada for his leadership in advancing reconciliation with Indigenous Peoples in Canada and for his advocacy of restorative justice.

Against this rolling punitive tsunami, I told justice stories on national radio and at healthy communities' workshops. We critiqued justice legislation in appearances before Parliament.

Why Do You Want to Know My Name?

Young offenders were the whipping boy for politicians and the media. If a major crime hit the news, a predictable outcry ensued with little interest in the rationale for the publication ban on their names or that most youth crimes were non-violent, a fact we cited not to excuse the offender but rather to shift a conversation to a justice that heals.

I appeared before Parliament with Rita Scott, a British Colombia crown counsel and board member, as legislators undertook a review of a new Youth Criminal Justice Act.[75]

Mr. Rick Prashaw, Communications Coordinator, Church Council on Justice and Corrections: "You had a witness recently. He was part of our workshop in Prince Albert, Saskatchewan. This

73 Yogaretnam, Shaamini, "Teen vandal apologizes to communities for racist graffiti," *Ottawa Citizen,* Aug. 23, 2017, https://ottawacitizen.com/news/local-news/teen-vandal-apologizes-to-communities-for-racist-graffiti.

74 Dimmock, Gary. "Phoney soldier Franck Gervais Sentenced to probation, community service," *Ottawa Citizen,* Aug. 28, 2015, https://ottawacitizen.com/news/local-news/phoney-soldier-franck-gervais-sentenced-to-probation-community-service.

75 Bill C-3, Review of the Youth Criminal Justice Act, Open, Parliament, Feb. 16, 2000.

exchange happened there between him and a citizen who was exasperated with the Young Offenders Act . . .

"I can't understand why someone does something like they do but they don't have their name made public. I am proud of my name. They should be proud of their name too," the man said.

The young man in the circle had a history with corrections. He said he would like to speak to this gentleman.

"I'm proud of my name. It is my grandfather's name. But I am not proud of everything I have done. The truth is, in my small town, everybody did know my name, at school, on my street, they knew what I had done. But in moving to another community, had everyone known my name, I would not have got the job that I got at the convenience store that helped turned myself around. I would not have got back in the school and got the education that also made a difference. And my parents, who already were suffering enough grief, may well have been at risk [at] what others would say and do to them. So, sir, I must ask you, 'Why do you want to know my name? Is it to show me your care, your compassion, your help? Or is it to make me move away, or never be hired, or ever get a fresh start in my life.'"

I pose that question to legislators and Canadians. Why do we want to know the names? Are we here to help them, or are we here to harm them further? After their crimes, are they members of our community or not?

In our Judeo-Christian tradition, the prophet Isaiah says, 'everyone who is called by my name, whom I created for my glory, whom I formed and made." (Isa. 43:7) This, we believe, is our ultimate dignity and the ground for how we relate to and are called to respect one another. God did not say, "I have called you by name. You are a young offender." We can turn away from labels or scapegoating that further alienate youth and do not deliver on any genuine, ultimate community safety. In trying to be righteous, it seems we do greater harm to each other. We need someone to blame so we can feel better, and we particularly do this to those weak, different from us, or people we don't know or don't need."

Satisfying Justice

Sentencing circles, family group conferences, and other forms of community justice emerged that, when properly resourced, gave victims and communities harmed by crime a voice participating in proceedings. These circles offered the potential for real accountability, moving lives forward better than courts or prisons might.

We published *Satisfying Justice*,[76] a story-based compendium on credible, safe community programs that reduced the use or length of imprisonment. We told stories about programs on mediation, diversion, and northern sentencing circles. We profiled a young man in Windsor who had been convicted of dangerous driving causing death when impaired. Working with both sides, the judge created a seven hundred fifty-hour speaking tour. It was tough on the offender, life tough, his taking responsibility. (There were reports though on harm to the mental health of this vulnerable youth retelling and reliving that story.) Those sentences could benefit more people and at far less cost than if he sat in a prison cell. No sentence could bring the innocent back to life, but those sentences might draw new life from deaths.

For CCJC's overall contribution to the development of restorative justice in Canada over decades, the staff won the inaugural national Ron Wiebe Restorative Justice Award. Named after a late Ferndale, B.C. Institution warden, the award recognized "ways of transforming human relationships, by enabling and promoting communication and healing between people in conflict, be they victims, offenders, colleagues, families or neighbours."[77]

---

76 Church Council on Justice and Corrections, *Satisfying Justice*, (Ottawa: Church Council on Justice and Corrections, 1996.)

77 Correctional Service of Canada, National Ron Wiebe Restorative Justice Award, https://www.csc-scc.gc.ca/restorative-justice/003005-3000-eng.shtml

Conversations at the Well

We had our work cut out for us, influencing even what those in the pews believed.

I wrote *Conversations at the Well*, a three-act play featuring a faith conversation on justice between a "right-wing, hang-him high fanatic" and a "left-wing bleeding-heart liberal."[78] My unredeemed side fancied playing that right-winger at one CCJC Annual General meeting. Both characters quoted the Bible to support their beliefs. For people of faith, the subject of crime brings up other profound matters—on one hand, suffering, evil, and punishment and, on the other hand, healing, forgiveness, even reconciliation. The conversation took place at a community well where they had come to draw water. They discover common ground between them, and God's living water offered to both.

Act One

(Steph already at well, sitting.)

Steph: Hi, how are you?

Rick: (audible sigh) Aaahhh. Well, I've heard everything now. You won't believe what happened.

Steph: What's up?

Rick: I am back from church. The pastor announced at the end of the service that we have a special speaker next week, the kid who burned down our church last year!

Steph: Hmmm. That should keep everyone awake.

Rick: I don't think I'm even going to go! The pastor says the kid's sorry, and he's going to tell us. The kid burns down the church my grandfather helped built with his own hands, and all he has to do is stand up and say he is sorry? What kind of a sentence is that?

---

78 Rick Prashaw, *Conversations at the Well*, Church Council on Justice and Corrections, www.ccjc.ca, 2001.

Steph: Is he going to apologize in front of the whole congregation? That's incredible!

Rick: Yep (sarcastic), you got that right! It's unbelievable! (turns to the audience and mimics the kid's speech) 'I'm real sorry, folks, for inconveniencing you. Promise not to do it again, so help me God.' (Turns back to Steph) I'm sick and tired of everybody using the 'sorry' word to avoid responsibility.

Steph: Are you sure he's avoiding responsibility, or might he be taking responsibility? I'm not sure that that's going to be all that easy for him. Are you sure that's his whole sentence? Wasn't that fire over a million dollars in damage?

Rick: Oh, yeah, he's met with the parish council, and he's gotta put the chairs up and take them down every Sunday for us for the next year in the gym and do some other service but give me a break! Whatever happened to punishment? God's punishment, you know, 'an eye for an eye'.

Steff: Well, I think that gave way to turning the other cheek, the one without sin casting the first stone, didn't it? What do you think he should get?

Rick: Maybe time in boot camp or jail, you know, some time to smarten up and think twice about what playing with matches does.

Steph: I don't know . . . I'm not sure jail ever fixed anybody.

Rick: What do you mean? Didn't one of the churches start prisons in the first place, you know, separate the good apples from the bad apples, make the bad do penance in a penitentiary or something like that?

Steph: I don't know about that. Might be hard figuring out who's good and who's bad.

Rick: I'd be glad to help anyone figure that out. I don't burn churches down. That kid did. Yet look what we do to him. I think a good dose of God's justice might do him some good.

Steph: You're back to an eye for an eye?

Rick: Well, yeah, and what's that guy in the Bible who killed his brother and God put a mark on him so everybody would know he was a murderer?

Steph: Do you mean Cain and Abel? I think that mark on Cain was to protect him, not punish him, and to stop others from killing him.

Rick: Whatever. Everybody saw that mark and knew what he had done, and God kicked him out of the community. He got exiled and punished. God treated some people harshly when they broke the law.

Steph: So, you want this kid to suffer some?

Rick: A million-dollar fire. Church statues and icons gone forever, its memories burnt to the ground, no place but a gym to worship for a year, that's serious. I don't think God would excuse his behaviour.

Steph: Well, we agree on that. I don't think God would excuse his behaviour either. The kid, I guess all of us, gotta face up to what we did or do and make changes and amends. We can't go on doing the wrong behaviour.

Rick: (leans into Steph, whispering) You know Steph, just between you and me, when I hear people who are ready to forgive when someone they love has been murdered, I admire them a lot, but I'm not there. I don't think many in my church are there either. God must be mighty particular about who he makes forgiving and who he doesn't. I can't forget what those kids did to my church.

Steph: I'm not sure you have to forget. I guess we do have to move on somehow. I never burned down a church but (laughs to herself), when I was twelve years old, I burnt our neighbour's field and barn down by mistake.

Rick: You did what?

Steph: Me and some friends wanted a field to play baseball, so we thought a little fire would clear the bush behind our place. We didn't factor in the wind and whoosh! There was the fire in their field and burning a barn.

Rick: You young offender you!

Steph: Yeah! Well, my parents' justice was a face-to-face meeting between us kids and the family next door and, believe me, I would have taken any punishment rather than do that ever again. It was the hardest thing I ever did, to talk to them and find out how much damage and hurt I caused and the tragedy that nearly happened. I had to work the whole summer on the farm to pay them back.

Rick: So, you don't play with matches anymore?

Steph: Nope. And another thing. The neighbour hired me the next summer, and I worked for him for all my high school years.

Rick: Hmmm, Steph the arsonist. Who would have known? Well, I got to run. Give me some water.

Steph: (drawing water for the bucket) So, are you going to church next week?

Rick: I don't know. I know a lot of people are upset. Some said they're not ready to forgive. Maybe I'll hear what he has to say.

Steph: I guess it can't hurt.

(Rick leaves, and shortly after, Steph stands up and leaves in another direction.)

In later acts, Steph learns her Uncle Joe is accused of abusing a niece. Rick and Steph struggle to figure out the demands of God's love.

The Mandorla and Nova Scotia

One day, Lorraine brought in her dog-eared, yellow sticky-marked copy of Robert Johnson's *Owning Your Own Shadow*. Johnson, a Jungian analyst, urged his clients, like Solzhenitsyn had, to look inward at their unpleasant, darker side and shadows. If people instead chose to sweep that all under the rug, chances were good to excellent they would subconsciously cast their unwanted "piece of their heart" onto others, to hate that part of themselves in them rather than deal with it themselves, even scapegoating the other.

Berzins was intrigued by a remedy Johnson prescribed, the concept of "the mandorla", an Italian word for an almond sliver, precisely an almond-shaped segment visible in two barely overlapping circles or multiple overlapping circles in a community. It was a medieval symbol capturing a path for healing.

"Take this, and take that, and make a mandorla."

For CCJC, the "this" and "that" were victims, offenders, and communities, the split caused by crime, the mandorla the sliver of space to begin the healing.

"The overlap generally is tiny at first, only a sliver of a new moon but it is a beginning. The mandorla binds together that which was torn apart and made unwhole. As time passes, the greater the overlap, the greater and more complete is the healing."

"... where all our different circles overlap – that sliver in the middle where all are joined equally, and all are included without any one circle being any more or less dominant or powerful or important than any other. This space of the overlap is the most reliable grounding for true community safety: a space where everyone can feel equal in the sense that 'what is good for me, and my family, is as important as what is good for everyone else.' Our goal is to widen that overlap..."

It was not lost on us that the early sign by which Christians secretly recognized each other was the fish--the same shape as that overlap between circles.

We travelled for a community safety workshop to Cole Harbour, Nova Scotia, in the news for race-based violence in high schools. We invited Cherry Brook and Eastern Passage Baptist communities filled with African Canadians to join other faith communities to dialogue about their fears. Interestingly, the Black residents traced their Africville roots in Canada back to two hundred years. Black and white seniors met in discussion groups, seemingly worlds apart, yet soon bonded by conversation and prayer on their shared fears about ageing alongside concerns for their youth. The sliver of the common ground grew, and they connected with one another as a start in healing communities split by fears, racism, and a system incarcerating too many Black people.

Every community in Canada torn by racism, fears, and crime could benefit from this approach. We couldn't be everywhere. Our pilot projects with evidence-based proof of success never substantially moved the government to real, permanent change. Justice by and large continued in the courts—with its robes, scripts, and theatre. The symbolic Lady Justice wears a blindfold, supposedly representing the criminal justice system being blind to a person's wealth, power, gender, and race. As I saw who was pronounced guilty and jailed, as victims went unaided, I wanted to rip that blindfold off Lady Justice so she and we could see what was really happening.

My thirteen years at CCJC proved a remarkable blessing for this former priest who still believed and felt called to this work, on the margins, often in the minority, but steadfast witnesses to a healing justice that works.

As funding dried up, I was now alone as executive director, tasked to keep the doors open. One day, David, my stepson, tagged along for a "take your kids to work" day.

"Rick, you're the boss, right?" David asked, surveying the empty offices. "Who exactly do you boss?"

I told him I oversaw the board and CCJC regional clusters scattered across Canada. David, unimpressed, vowed to shadow his mother next time. Meanwhile, it was apparent Suzanne's skills were suited for a bigger stage like Ottawa. She would travel the country with new colleagues, delivering federal-provincial ministerial conferences and, later, research dollars to universities and health institutions.

In 2000, Mom was living in the most independent wing of a Cassellholme care residence in North Bay. A series of strokes confirmed she could not live on her own anymore. Like so many families, we faced difficult choices whether anyone could look after her or was it necessary to move her to the long-term care wing. We knew she would be happiest with her family.

Mom began a tour of siblings' homes. She first arrived at my sister Margie's in London.

"Mom came to us for all of December," Margie said. "I taught half time, and Katie, between gigs, was home to make sure that mom was safe in the mornings. One day, for lunch, I brought some African students home. They wanted to meet 'my people.' Mom saw them and, stereotypically, thought they could drum. So, I had to pull out every drum we had in the house, and they drummed for Mom. They told her that her daughter, me, their teacher, was a ten-cow woman. In their village, if a woman was a real catch, you'd paid ten cows for her. Mom relayed this story to Jerry at night as they did dishes. Jerry said to me later, 'I notice your mom is failing as she was talking about cows.' I said, 'No, that was actually a moment of clarity.' We had one final Christmas with Mom. We went to Marty and Maggie's in Collingwood, and I had dolls made for everyone. The aprons on these dolls came from clothes of Mom's, one was an actual apron she used, another was material from her golf shorts."

Pati, a nurse, stepped forward next to offer her home if Katie would fly with Mom to California. Those remaining behind in Canada kissed Mom, sensing this was a final goodbye.

The report forwarded to Pati indicated Mom was on/off confused and in a diaper and a wheelchair. When they arrived, though, the warmer sun and new family were good medicine. Mom began walking up the stairs and using the bathroom.

"We had an awesome month with her, and then she stroked again," Pati said. "I took her to the hospital for a few days and then took her home with supportive care. This was when Jude flew out with Alec, who was two. We would all be in her bedroom downstairs, and we would play cards on her stomach."

"Alec had a whole farm on her bed," Jude added. "Plastic horses, singing *Old MacDonald Had A Farm* at the top of his lungs."

"She hadn't talked for a few days, slipping into a coma," Pati said. "We mentioned there was cheating at cards going on even on Mom's death bed and joking about that, and Mom's stomach started moving up and down like she was laughing. She died peacefully a few days later, in no discomfort."

Mom died on January 26, 2001, at the age of 86.

The sisterhood playing cards, cheating, on our dying Mom while sipping drinks and telling stories. My family. My faith. A perfect sacrament.

The Prashaw sisterhood: Jude, Mom, Pati, and Margie.

CHAPTER 40

Adam's Dad, A New Vocation

I was born for this gig.

Lying on Adam's bed after reading a story, we turned off the lights to gaze at the moon and the stars on the bedroom ceiling. We whispered our secrets to each other. Magical. As he slept, I tip-toed back into his bedroom to watch his breathing, as holy and as mysterious as those early morning silent meditations at The Pro. I swooned the first time he slipped a hand into mine as we crossed a street.

The stinky diapers and excruciating homework supervision have long faded with the passing of years. More easily remembered are the bike rides, campfire smores, family trips to California, Virginia, and Atlantic Canada. All his hockey games, too, as a goalie, as I sat in the stands absurdly kicking out a foot to assist Adam to stop those pucks.

On my book tour, the "Father Rick to proud father of Adam" story intrigued listeners, dad to this roguish kid, including his gender identity journey home to the boy he knew he was but could not see.

"You're the best dad. You should win an award," one listener told me.

"Ha, NO! Read the book, all my mistakes I told!"

It was unconditional love, punctuated by 10,000 parental screams, especially during those teen years with his latest tattoo, budgets blown, quitting a job, and multiple Facebook snafus. Parents know this story. His love me or leave me karma had me hanging on for dear life. Indeed, "fastening the seatbelt" for this twenty-two-year ride was the best dad metaphor. I screamed on the rollercoaster while my Adam kept laughing.

At forty, I had become an instant stepdad to Suzanne's three children. Even though I had baptized hundreds of babies, this would be my shock initiation into parenting 101. I knew nothing, except no one could wipe that smile from my face; well, except when I wiped those bums. My enthusiasm needed curbing when I might overstep step-parenting of Suzanne's first three. Lindsay, the eldest, was a voracious reader, smart, and curious about everything. Entering her bedroom was an admission into endless questions and adventure. I now laugh about my worries for Lauren, her early shy, tentative stance on life misleading me on how strong she would be. As a competitive national curling skip, she barks commands to her team, handling with ease the media questions afterwards. David, the youngest, was full of love and mischief. He, too, shone in sports in a community football league and then as an adult coaching college volleyball.

A year into the marriage, I became an over the moon, first-time dad to a child identified as a girl at birth, a kid we legally named Rebecca Danielle Adam Prashaw. We had called the baby Adam during the pregnancy, as Suzanne had sensed her pregnancy was like David's.

Rebecca Adam was a tomboy. Think of Scout, the kid in *To Kill a Mockingbird* or the girl pitcher Tatum O'Neal played in *Bad News Bears*. Adam was typical of the kids at many of our supper tables or that we spot in the malls or school halls. His ball cap was on backwards, phone glued permanently in his hand, Batman shirt, Habs fan, end runs around the rules.

Adam knew best who he was. We were not surprised. We listened. We learned. We loved.

Being a parent scared the hell out of me: the responsibility, the teaching, the not knowing the answers. As Dad had confided, there were no parenting manuals. It all happened on a wing and a prayer, walking with Adam through the years of uncertainty, resilience, worry, trying to control, and finally letting go when Adam wanted his independence.

Rick's favourite Adam picture, 2015, surrounded by earlier childhood pictures and his Justin Bieber Pride look.

Oh, my pride, deep joy, and blessing. With Adam, it would be running after him, not walking. His mom's seventeen-minute labour had hurtled the boy into the fast lane where he would stay all his life. I chased after him from the moment he was born.

Most parents know this script by heart. This was my true, complete calling, a vocation as certain as my years as a priest. Parents thanked me for this recognition of parenthood as a vocation, its holiness dumped into those shitty diapers, teen rebellion, and those break-your-heart tender and terrible moments life dished out.

It's strange my father never knew Adam because I swear, they were twins in another life—comedians, rays of sunshine, making everyone feel comfortable, happy-go-lucky characters taming the darkness they faced.

When my first book came out, with its inevitable labelling by reviewers and the media, it ended up in biography or gender studies. However, Heather Down, an author and podcaster, aptly called it "a love story." She was thinking primarily of the unquenchable love for Adam by parents, family, and friends. That was half of the love story. I admired Adam's unrelenting love for himself, a courageous and indomitable quest through the teenage angst and early adult years to be who he was and to love who he loved.

I was my son's "Friend" on Facebook.

Yikes!

Click "Like" and resist calling 911!

"Bahahaha," Claire laughed.

"Cruz is a teen soon, Claire. Fasten your seat belt."

You help with the homework. You do the homework. Hell, that is half of my mark in his report card. From all those seizures, Adam had struggled mightily at school, as enough young people do. He felt he did not have the answers the teachers wanted or that life demanded, and he was not one for tests in the framework of today's education system. His school's Individual Education Plan that he started in Grade 7 was a lifeline.

Still, Adam excelled in most of life's challenges. After reading *Soar, Adam, Adam,* his cousin, Brian O' Connor, Margie and Jerry's second youngest, emailed me this note.

> We are all tested in this life, Uncle Rick. Some would argue they were/are not prepared for their tests, their tests are too hard, or they do not have the answers needed. I believe we will never be ready for the tests that life puts in front of us, but the tests will be ready for us! They sit stacked high on the desk of eternal life, given out randomly or not so randomly, depending on what one believes. These tests find their way into our daily lives one by one, or sometimes in threes. It is my belief these tests are smarter than we are. They know the final marks we will receive from completing them far outweigh the original "us" we once were before sitting down to "write" them. I know what it feels like to not have the answers as Adam must have felt, as we all feel at certain points in our own lives. That said, Adam passed many tests with flying colours! The important tests of life. The tests that can make people cower and run at times. Following one's heart and being true to yourself is one, if not the most important test of all. Adam passed this test without exception. I would even argue that he rewrote the rubric for others to refer to on how one needs to fulfill the necessary requirements to pass.

Brian knew. So many kids and families knew. Many navigate the difficult daily tests, all part of life's exam. It was my greatest life lesson and privilege to choose to love Adam, to discover how that love might be stretched beyond belief. I had counselled and preached love. I was learning every day how to live this love as his father.

CHAPTER 41

I Am Adam!

On September 13, 2014, Adam came out as Adam on Facebook. Now his name, soon his body, would align with something he always knew.

"For a while, and I do mean awhile, since I was a baby in my mother's womb, I always considered myself a boy. I got used to Rebecca or Becca because that is what I was born with and called. As I grew up, it just sounded odd, and inside I always loved boy things: playing with boys, playing video games, being prince rather than princess, hated Barbie, built forts, and played Lego with my bro, power rangers, etc.! It has been difficult for me to speak my mind and what my heart wants. And [I've] been afraid of losing people and making people laugh at me...."

In truth, Adam came out as Adam the day he was born. He now publicly proclaimed who he was, his true identity. This God making us exclusively male or female, or something along this gender spectrum, and what those terms meant, needed further unpacking,

On a book tour, I had met two eighty-five-year-old women in separate towns who confided they knew their gender dysphoria[79] at age five when teachers formed two lines for boys and girls. They were in the wrong line. Like that St. Andrew's mother who shared her teen and now her own parenting memories

---

79 Gender dysphoria refers to psychological distress that results from an incongruence between one's sex assigned at birth and one's gender identity. Some notice the dysphoria quite young, while others do so later.

with me, many parents tell stories on the gender fluidity their teens go through as they sort things out. I grew up confusing sex and gender, assuming everyone was either male or female, two binaries defined exclusively by genitals. Boy. Girl. Announced at our birth. It took time to figure out sex was anatomy while gender was this bigger social, cultural, and universe term, something one was trained to perform, and policed if one doesn't perform it the right way. My new teachers were science, medicine, and especially being Adam's parent and listening to others' stories.

"Claire, weeks before Christmas 2020, I read the personal news of Halifax actor Elliot Page. 'I love that I am trans. And I love that I am queer. And the more I hold myself close and fully embrace who I am, the more I dream, the more my heart grows and the more I thrive.'"[80]

"Adam is in good company," Claire said.

Adam's heart had also soared after his announcement. He grew, magnificently, before our very eyes. I saw this wonderful trans son who delighted in being himself. Does it not make sense we can grow as one "holds myself close, and fully embraces who I am?" I had feared what lay ahead for my son. I wanted to protect Adam. There was a lot I didn't understand that I had to learn. I am okay with people who don't get it right away, who don't understand. We grew up in different times that determined identities and roles based on dominant male and female stereotypes. Non-binary might be an unfamiliar term for some. It means that an individual is neither male nor female, but something in between or other. It refers to how people see themselves and express that gender. Adam wanted to be a boy rather than the girl he was identified as at birth. Some transgender people express gender in conventionally masculine or feminine ways while not all gender-nonconforming people are transgender. They do reject male or female binaries. I was slowly understanding how disparate this "gay community" was I thought I had figured out in the seminary.

"Queer" had been a pejorative word in my faith and the broader community. There were spoken slurs in locker rooms and high schools. Spurred by fears and prejudices, queers faced judgment, a violence that may be physical, legal,

---

80 Specter, Emma. "Elliot Page Comes Out as transgender in a Moving, Open Letter," *Vogue Magazine,* Dec. 1, 2020, https://www.vogue.com/article/elliot-page-trans-open-letter.

ecclesial, or economic, all denying them equal protection under the law. Long ago, Hollywood had portrayed transgenders as crazed serial murderers.

No, queer people were not the problem. What was, and is the problem, is what I had learned in a dominant homophobic and misogynist culture. As a father to a trans child, I especially caught Page's reference to his "fragile joy." Transphobes were loud and fierce on social media denouncing his news even though thousands more cheered him on.

I read Page's personal news as Parliament studied legislation to ban conversion therapy, this pseudoscience targeting especially LGBTQ youth to change their identity or orientation(The next Parliament passed the law to ban conversion therapy). I winced reading several transphobic submissions, some faith based. I submitted to Parliament this one-page brief, "I Am Adam."[81]

> Adam taught me, reminded me, of core values. Be who we are. Love who we love. This is what I wanted in my life, what most I know want. What we desire for ourselves, we gift to others. At no time did we, as parents, impose any other treatment or therapy other than listening, learning, and loving. We appreciated the international tests, social workers, and doctors that were integral partners on his gender journey. It is a serious and lengthy process.

> Transgender is a label. There are the extraordinary individual human beings in the trans community. Some I meet reminded me of Adam, while others had quite different stories. Some sought surgery, some did not. Some were quite public. Some were not. Some changed names. Some had not decided. I came to appreciate the diversity in this community, the rainbow within the larger Rainbow Pride community. And I heard about the hurts and hate they had endured in their journey home to themselves. And I witnessed the stereotypes, myths, and ignorance. I learned about the alarming number of suicides, self-harm, homelessness, and other forms of injury and discrimination.

---

81 Rick Prashaw, "I Am Adam", Parliament of Canada, Justice Committee, Bill C-6 (Conversion Therapy), 2021, https://www.parl.ca/LegisInfo/BillDetails.aspx?billId=10 871883&Language=E.

Too many choose to play God and judge, in this case, wrongly. Faith is never a license to hate . . . I have never once in my heterosexual orientation or marriage and family felt threatened by the differences in others' gender identity or orientation. I have felt threatened by those who hate and hurt others for religious or political reasons.

In the fall of 2019, there was "Breaking News" in Picton, ON. in Prince Edward County, where I had enjoyed a moving Trans Quinte fundraiser hosted by Stacey Love and Stacey Croucher. Songs, poems, stories, music. The love in the room was palpable. However, less than four months later, *CBC News* reported that a community protest of more than four hundred people had sprung up around St. Gregory's Roman Catholic Church, one protestor carrying the sign, "I Love You. I Love All of You."[82] A Prince Edward County community page on Facebook had encouraged families to join a peaceful protest outside St. Gregory's in support of Pride. The protest was in response to a church bulletin notice from the previous week that was tucked between news for a pot-luck supper and gratitude for donations for a new church door:

"A reminder that Catholics and all other Christians should not attend LGBTQ2 (Lesbian, Gay, Bisexual, Transgender, Queer, Two-Spirit) 'Pride Month' events held this month. They promote a culture and encourage activities that are contrary to Christian faith and morals. This is especially harmful to children because it could lead them away from God's revealed Truth. Even in 'The County' there are Pride flags and banners flying courtesy of the Government. Think. These are your tax dollars at work!"

Kingston Archbishop Michael Mulhall intervened to state he "did not sanction this (pastor's) message, and it does not reflect the spirit of accompanying charity and compassion that should always characterize our faith. The Archdiocese has spoken with the pastor of the parish. He regrets any hurt that his inappropriate comments have caused.'"

---

82 Ireton, Julie. "Anti-Gay Message in Catholic Bulletin Sparks Outrage,"
    CBC News, June 15, 2019, https://www.cbc.ca/news/canada/ottawa/
    picton-catholic-church-pastor-bulletin-homophobic-comments-1.5176341.

Within weeks, the archdiocese announced the pastor was placed on administrative leave pending an investigation into abuse allegations from decades earlier. Although I took no pleasure in anyone's problems, this news did not surprise me. There had been other clerics and politicians loud in hateful judgments, some done in by their personal demons. As Robert Johnson wrote, it's best not to sweep part of oneself under the rug.

Five minutes on Google traced the pastor's anti-gay message to a high profile, conservative Rhode Island bishop.[83] Five more minutes on Google located this quote on love from St. Gregory himself, the church's fifth-century pope and doctor of the church. "The proof of love is in the works. Where love exists, it works great things. But when it ceases to act, it ceases to exist."[84]

My gifted nephew, Kevin, teaches me daily on these matters. I enjoy friendships with several same-sex couples. They demonstrate "great things" in their love. It can witness to the same joys, sacrifices, struggles, and failures as heterosexual couples experience. I sided with St. Gregory's views on love, not the pastor's.

Not lost on some was the irony of how those prelates who had not dealt with clergy abuse of children now warned about the pseudo threat from gay people. In this regard, Pope Francis has been an enigma to some, one hopeful step forward and then three steps back. On the one hand, Pope Francis had welcomed Pride advocates to the Vatican, spoken warmly of the place of gays in the church and supported national civil laws for same-sex marriage. "If someone is gay and is searching for the Lord and has good will, then who am I to judge him?", Pope Francis told journalists during an in-flight press conference on his way back to Rome from Brazil.[85] Michael O'Loughlin,

83 Perry, Jack. "Bishop Tobin: Catholics Should Not Support Pride Month." *Providence Journal,* June 1, 2019, https://www.providencejournal.com/news/20190601/bishop-tobin-catholics-should-not-support-pride-month.

84 Catholic News World. "The Proof of Love is in the Works," http://www.catholicnewsworld.com/2020/09/quote-to-share-by-st-gregory-great.html.

85 Mickens, Robert. "Pope Francis 'attitude adjustment program » Is Gaining Traction," *La Croix International,* March 27, 2021, https://international.la-croix.com/news/letter-from-rome/pope-francis-attitude-adjustment-program-is-gaining-traction/14043.

a correspondent and gay Catholic, was shocked to receive a personal reply from the pope to a letter he wrote about AIDS and compassionate ministry. "Thank you for shining a light on the lives and bearing witness to the many priests, religious sisters and lay people, who opted to accompany, support and help their brothers and sisters who were sick from H.I.V. and AIDS at great risk to their profession and reputation...Instead of indifference, alienation and even condemnation," Pope Francis continued, "these people let themselves be moved by the mercy of the Father and allowed that to become their own life's work; a discreet mercy, silent and hidden, but still capable of sustaining and restoring the life and history of each one of us."[86] This was all better treatment than any previous pope had offered. However, he would ultimately side with doctrinal conservatives on both a narrow definition of marriage and the gender binary, condemning any deviation.

In 2019, the Congregation of Catholic Education released *Male and Female He Made Them*, a thirty-one-page document decisive in defining of the gender binary.[87] It states that a person claiming identity beyond cisgender—when personal and gender identity is the same as birth sex—they are trying to be "provocative." The document did condemn any bullying and discrimination, and there was a throwaway line on dialogue that seldom seems to happen in any substantial fashion.

Provocative? Jesus could be provocative. *What would Jesus do?*

In March 2021, the Vatican, in a brief letter, reiterated priests could not bless same-sex unions because they are "not ordered in the Creator's plan" and "God cannot bless sin."[88] Still in play was a catechism that restricted sex for

86 O Loughliin, Michael. "Pope Francis sent me a letter. It gives me hope as a gay Catholic," New York Times, Nov. 15, 2021, https://www.nytimes.com/2021/11/15/opinion/pope-francis-lgbt-community.html

87 Congregation for Catholic Education, "Male and Female he Made Them," Rome, June 10, 2019.

88 Harlan, Chico and Pulliam Bailey, Sarah. "Pope Francis says priests cannot bless same-sex unions, dashing hopes of gay Catholics." *Washington Post*, March 15, 2021, https://www.washingtonpost.com/world/europe/pope-same-sex-unions-licit/2021/03/15/8c51ee80-8581-11eb-be4a-24b89f616f2c_story.html.

straight married couples and viewed homosexual acts as contrary to natural law and being "of grave depravity." This is wrong. Their love is human love, not sin. The pontiff who still urged no one to judge reiterated a doctrine that judges.

"Claire, I know of no gay person who chose to be so in the way the Vatican describes it. It's who they are. So, morally, sin is not in play here at all. On a lighter note, can you imagine that meet-up of gay people who intentionally chose a lifestyle that courted such hate and discrimination?"

"Masochists, right?" Claire sighed. "Sign up here for your papal and pulpit damnation, social media hell and Friday night attacks. There's no life like it!"

Some people of faith pushed back. Sister Margo Ritchie, with The Congregation of The Sisters of St. Joseph in Canada, invoked the childhood nursery rhyme, *Sticks and Stones*, and how, in fact, attacks can make victims quiver and words indeed hurt. She referred to the careless projection on to God of words like "illicit" and "sinful judgment" to describe homosexual behaviour.

"So, let's try some words that heal, that celebrate, that helps one relax into who we are," Ritchie wrote. "Let's begin with love which makes us whole. Let's follow those words with generativity that cares for others and for the future. And, while we are at it, throw in courage and steadiness in the face of shaming, And why not include acceptance and appreciation of diversity. And maybe end with simple humanity in all our vulnerability and beauty."[89]

After the Vatican released the statement, Bishop Greg Rickel, from the Episcopalian Church Diocese of Olympia, wrote: "To all our LGBTQIA+ (Lesbian, Gay, Bisexual, Transgender, Questioning, Intersex, Asexual, Two-Spirit, Others) fellow sojourners with Christ, we do not see you, or your relationships, as sin. We see you and experience you as true blessings, reflections of our living God. Thank you for the inspiration and the many ways you show us how to love.

---

89 Congregation of The Sisters of St. Joseph in Canada Facebook, March 25, 2021.

Thank you for the gifts you bring to our collective Body of Christ. Thank you for how you have blessed me, and you bless this Church."[90]

Ironically, Jesus had so little to say about our sex lives, and yet, so much to say about those who judge and condemn others.

I have spoken at a few *Affirm United* communities of faith. Affirm United is a partner of The United Church of Canada, with over two hundred fifty communities of faith or ministries completing a one-to-two-year process to be recognized as embracing and understanding all gender identities and sexual orientations. There is a rainbow welcome mat out in the Episcopal Church in the United States and in some Anglican parishes in Canada. I know a few Roman Catholic pastors or faith communities doing their best to be more open.

In Catholic seminaries and courses, the faith taught wove together scripture, tradition, intellect, science, conscience, and lived experience. I would learn, too, that credible theology had to be immersed in real life and real people.

Here, with respect to gay or transgender people, we are talking about living, loving human beings who are part of our families, work colleagues, and neighbours. For Christians, no single Old Testament verse of damnation nor one line from a New Testament epistle could eclipse God's revelation in the person and teaching of Jesus, especially over and against dated cultural edicts. What did matter was the profound love I witnessed in friends in same-sex marriages and transgender communities. One's sexuality or orientation was one and only one aspect of their life. I observed their faithfulness, sacrifices, struggles, and tender mercies.

We seemed back in the Dark Ages. While some Catholics were not giving any attention to the latest Vatican decrees, it rightly bothered those harmed and their advocates. On my social media, there were Catholics who quit the church over this personal rejection of who they are. Some remain open to real dialogue.

---

90 Paulsen, David, "Episcopalians rally support for LGBTQ community after Vatican refuses same-sex blessings", *Episcopal News Services*, March 27, 2021, https://www.episcopal-newsservice.org/2021/03/17/episcopalians-rally-support-for-lgbtq-community-after-vatican-refuses-same-sex-blessings.

I wanted here to bring a faith lens to my Adam's gender journey. I vividly remember Adam's longstanding desire to shed all the labels and be himself, to find the "normal" he chased after in his life. I was reminded of that reading this tweet from a Midwest individual who is a queer seminarian. "I am tired of Christians reducing my entire humanity as a queer person to an 'issue' they feel obligated to argue about."

"Catholic meme time, Uncle Rick," Claire shouted from the kitchen, reading from her phone. "Any Catholics out there this Lent, giving up hating the gays or is it just ice cream again?"

I was now a confirmed Roamin' Catholic.

CHAPTER 42

Ken from Orillia

2019

He was the second caller on an *Ontario Today* phone-in program on CBC Radio that had me on as a guest. Rita Celli introduced this tale with its twist of a Catholic priest who goes from Father Rick to proud father of his transgender son.

"In the Bible . . ." was Ken from Orillia's first words. I slumped in the guest's chair.

Ken identified himself as a born-again Christian who needed to say that, in Genesis, also in Deuteronomy, it is clear: "God made us male and female. Marriage is God's law. Not the state. Not ours."

The producer vets callers, a pre-air chat on what they intend to say. Ken may have fudged his intentions. As he warmed up on his damnation, Celli motioned to end the call. I waved at them to let Ken talk, sensing he might be a "Godsend."

Ken decreed that God made two, and only two, genders—male and female exclusively—and that they are the only kind of love blessed, the love of a man and a woman. Friends later told me they leaned into their radio to hear my answer. I dodged any biblical ping pong.

"Ken, we need a coffee and a long chat, I'd listen to how you came to believe that, and then I hope you would listen to my theology and Bible studies. That is not the God I know or love. Especially when we discover Jesus, who, for Christians, is the exclamation mark on God, THE revelation. Jesus is slow to judge and big on forgiveness, acceptance, loving, and inviting us all to grow."

"Some Christians and churches speaking in his name have forgotten this."

The next seven callers rained their love on Adam and me. Four callers cited positive faith community experiences while transitioning or for their transitioning family members. Rod in Kingston identified himself as transgender. He said trans kids needed this recognition, and conversations like this were important. "Trans youth are real people with real families and real lives trying to make their way in life."

When Celli asked me to comment, I said:

"Amen, Rod."

A Muslim caller said he respected all religions; what he had learned is to live, love, learn, be. The will of God, he said, is to enjoy life. "Adam did exactly that. God says that he passed the test. Come and rest in peace."

I was smiling again.

Celli asked this caller what had influenced that faith perspective. He said a family member had undergone a sex change in Turkey thirty years earlier. When Celli had asked Ken how he might react to someone in his family transitioning, Ken retreated behind a phrase that, "God tests us all."

Celli quoted Adam's Facebook post on January 21, 2016, the day before his hot tub accident.

"Death is not the greatest loss in life. The greatest loss in life is what dies in us while we live (Norman Cousins)."

So, "a godsend," Ken from Orillia. At a later bookstore reading at Kingston's Novel Idea, a young man waited patiently for others to have their books signed before coming up himself. He appeared to be on a journey like Adam's. He was Rod, that next caller. Rod shared a letter he received that day from the Government of Ontario confirming his legal name change.

"Claire, remember that brilliant *West Wing* episode where our favourite American president, Josiah 'Jed' Bartlett (Martin Sheen), kneecapped a Christian radio personality on the slippery slope of selectively quoting the

Bible. She had corrected the president that it was the Bible, not her, that condemned homosexuality as an abomination."

"I loved his schooling of her," Claire added. "Should the president put to death his chief of staff, Leo, who worked on the sabbath? (Exod.35: 2) Should the Washington football club wear gloves to touch a football because Leviticus taught that touching the skin of a dead pig makes us unclean (Lev. 11:7-8)?"

"Right, Claire. And he cited other Old Testament passages permitting selling daughters into slavery (Exod. 21:7), forbidding trimming of hair (Lev. 19:27), or contact with women while menstruating (Lev. 15. 19-31)."

Far from ridiculing the Bible, Bartlett exposed the dangers when fundamentalists carefully selected passages to support a specious morality or subjugation of women. Any biblical text cried out for context, cultural, and linguistic analysis. My studies had taught the different literature in the inspired Word of God—poems, allegories and even satire. Jesus' liberation, openness, and non-judgment were the interpretation of even the Bible itself. The gospel's imperative to love, care for, and be identified with their sufferings is unmistakably clear. Father Richard Rohr, a Franciscan scholar, acknowledged he did not have all the answers to these gender identity and sexual orientation questions. He wondered if Christians were open to revisiting those Old Testament texts that Jesus liberated.[91] The Muslim caller certainly had. So had I.

---

91 Kaufman, Brian William. "Lessons from Fr. Richard Rohr on Sexual and Gender Diversity," *New Ways Ministry*, Dec. 14, 2019, https://www.newwaysministry. org/2019/12/14/lessons-from-fr-richard-rohr-on-sexual-and-gender-diversity.

CHAPTER 43

Fifty Bucks

Rita Celli, that host of *Ontario Today*, told this "Fifty Bucks" story when she acted as MC for my book launch at the Canadian Museum of Nature in Ottawa. A payback of sorts for a sweet, long forgotten, pay-it-forward act. First, Celli had to retell it to me a few years earlier when we had met for a catch-up coffee on the Sparks Street Mall.

"You remember what you did?" she asked, sipping her espresso.

I begged forgiveness, mentioning my mashed memory.

"Was it good or bad?"

"Very good."

Celli had attended Marymount College when I was associate pastor at St. Andrew's. In youth ministry, I connected the dots from boredom-inducing ancient scriptures or Rome's distant teachings to teens music, sports, dating, etc. I had met Celli and many teens through a popular Youth Encounter movement, a teen version of adult Cursillo faith retreats. Encounter offered gatherings from Friday to Sunday night as a priest with a team of adult and teen leaders camped out in a high school gym or parish hall with forty to fifty youth. They had sleeping bags but there was little sleep; the youth preferred long, soul-searching, late-night chats, all done in a soft sell of God, church, and family anchored on food, fellowship, music, and witness. Prominent among the speakers were youths recovering from addictions or other troubles. In hindsight, Encounter mixed grace and maybe a tinge of "cult" that hopefully spared their drinking the Kool-Aid. The intentions were good. Adults who had attended them as youth have shared with me their fond memories.

Sudbury Youth Encounter 1985

Celli remembered the fifty dollars more than the retreat. In Grade 11, she desperately wanted to go to Ottawa for a Model Parliament. She heard a loud no from her parents. Enough parents were strict with their kids, stricter with a girl who was whip-smart and poised for travel. With no money, it was a no until a young priest gave her fifty dollars. She could not wait to tell her parents that she had found the money to go.

Yes, Father Rick.

When Celli and I caught up for that coffee, she finished this story. The Model Parliament was life-changing, seeds planted, an inkling that she was meant for a life bigger than Sudbury, a new interest in Ottawa's public stage, politics, and current affairs. Somehow, her broadcasting career had its seeds in that Model Parliament experience.

What fifty bucks could do!

"Did you have fun?" I asked.

Celli smiled.

"Did your father ever forgive me?"

Celli laughed.

At the book launch, after Celli introduced me with this story, I looked at her and said:

"I gave you fifty bucks? I don't remember having fifty bucks to give to anybody!"

The next day, I was on *Ontario Today*. It was all good—her questions, probing the faith and parenting ride, through the calls that included Ken's damnation. When the program ended, Celli thanked me for appearing and handed me a card. I put it in my attaché case, but she asked me to open it. You know what was there.

Fifty bucks. Her own grateful payback for the long-ago gift.

"I'm not giving this back," I smiled.

"Of course not."

"What about the interest you owe me?"

We laughed some more. Paying it forward. Telling it back.

I left wondering what good these fifty dollars might do. I had my answer three months later when Jeff Connor, Jude's husband, and my friend, died after a courageous, long twenty-one-month battle with glioblastoma, the stage 4 brain cancer that took Gord Downie of the Tragically Hip. Connor, an engineering professor at Virginia Tech University, had struggled with bouts of depression; ironically, his death sentence invigorated him. He vowed to die well, which, for him, meant fully living with whatever time he had left. He lasted well beyond that cancer's deadly short life span. Connor overcame an introversion to embrace people, family, and life. He even completed and published a long-delayed book, *Engineering A Primer*, introducing to high school students his passion for a career that began at eight years old with a fascination for water, "Walking home from school in the rain, I remember squatting by the curb watching water flow to the drain. I have not stopped watching water flow."[92]

Connor had excelled as an early host volunteer trainer for service dogs who finished training with inmates in prison. Rehabilitation might come in a dog's licks or an inmate's new responsibilities. I donated fifty dollars to Saint Francis Service Dogs in Roanoke, Virginia.

I swear that fifty bucks has seen a better return than my mutual funds.

92 Jeffrey B. Connor, P.E., *Engineering, A Primer* (Jeffrey B. Connor, Hyde Park, VT, 2018.)

CHAPTER 44

The Ex

I have few regrets in my life. I tend to move forward, hopefully wiser, without too long of a look in the rear-view mirror. I do not regret much the failures that came with valuable lessons, like ending those seminary professor studies or leaving the priesthood to marry for love.

There are two life regrets that matter. Adam's premature death tops my list, a tragedy I could not manage nor control. Second to Adam's death is my marriage to Suzanne ending.

Before it became personal, I had already disliked the term "ex" when people referenced their divorced partners. Marriages were ending in my family and among friends and colleagues. Good people who were not able to remain together. Forty percent of marriages in Canada were ending in divorce. I wasn't keeping count but fifty-fifty appeared to be my own record for the weddings I had officiated at, despite pouring considerable time into marriage preparation. I had listened to good people with integrity unable to fulfill their lifelong commitment to their partner.

Those statistics were a small comfort for my personal news.

I disliked that "ex" word for erasing significant parts of one's life when facts, photo albums, stories, and memories testified otherwise. Of course, there was that other side to the ledger, some delighting in finally slapping the "ex" word on a partner.

Despite the good years, trips, the "all in" daily juggling, and struggles to love, it was clear Suzanne was not happy. No counselling, conversation, pleas, nor holidays could deliver the miracle I sought. Peeking in that rear mirror, I did wonder if a retreat for her, when I was in Guelph, might have brought her my own peace of mind for our vocation to marry. Indeed, I suspect Adam was always an integral part of our calling, his invitation to be his parents.

Our marriage ended in 2000. This broke my heart. I wore this sadness for a few years. I went to hell and back. Adam would teach us how to parent in separation, both of us still hands-on for the schools, sports, epilepsy, gender journey, and grieving ahead.

I respect Suzanne. She has a special place in my heart. She is Adam's mother. I am Adam's father. That bond is forever. For this faith memoir, I have nothing else to write. It would be only one side of the narrative. I have filed one hundred thousand words on this love and marriage in the *Book of Life*.

We both stayed on the parenting rollercoaster hurtling towards Adam's teens and his huge announcement on who he truly was. Past the *Harry Potter* years, through the monster trucks, my commuting Math homework with him, Rideau Canal skates, past watching Titanic a few hundred times, listening to questions, worries, wonders and all the stuff of parenting and family. I consoled myself, knowing I would be Adam's dad forever.

CHAPTER 45

Ex-Catholics

2020

I had spied a message from an Illinois woman on Twitter referring to her previous post on a "Corrupt Catholic Church." Apparently, enough Catholics pushed back because she was now asking her social media universe if she was the only ex-Catholic feeling this way. Within a few days, she had four thousand-plus comments.

"Claire, it was a glimpse into a fractured, polarized Catholic universe, what had happened in the two generations from me to you and now Cruz."

Indeed, many counted themselves as ex-Catholics. In Twitter's then two hundred eighty-character limit, they shared headlines for leaving. Clergy abuse was high in the mentions. Reading the long thread of comments felt like a day in the confessional, except now, most but not all confessed the sins of the Catholic Church and how folk had reacted. There were good memories too sprinkled among the criticism:

> "Catholic is the best religion because you sin Monday to Saturday, confess on Sunday, go home, and say a few silly prayers and go sin again."

> "The church is a cult."

> "Hell was a fiction invented to scare us into submission. How could an infinitely wise God put us in hell for a comment?"

"I can't be part of a religion that is fear-based and where women are second-class citizens."

"I remember the good Jesuits and wonderful nuns who taught values and social justice."

"There are undeniable problems, and yet, it was where I was unconditionally loved and supported as a young woman when I was alienated from my family. You can keep the good and leave behind the bad."

"Aspects I love that will always be part of me spiritually. Not all men of the cloth were bad, but not enough was done [or] fast enough for me to keep faith in it."

"I like Pope Francis."

"The hate on LGBTQ people."

"Single men in long dresses telling us how to behave."

"I am an Ex who went to Evangelicals and now question all."

"It was the joy of my youth, faults and all."

"The teaching, the management, like the big stores, sucks."

"Big fan of God. For the good it does though, it wrecks more havoc."

"All became corrupt for prioritizing themselves and surviving over core values, mission. Means to renewal lost in leaders but present in members who lack means to enact without starting over."

"Gay son not welcome."

"I was ostracized as a divorced woman."

"Precepts are good, help one another, be kind."

"Keep the good and let go of the rest."

"The church became calcified."

"I need my faith, my church."

Several called themselves recovering or retired Catholics. There were noted distinctions between God and churches, one's faith and one's religion. Some found fault with all religions.

"By high school, we were moaning and groaning having to go to church," Claire recalled. "Weekend jobs would be my excuse not to go. Dad and Mom gave up on making us go."

"You're not alone, Claire."

The Pew Research Centre tracked the steady decline of people identifying as Christian or any religion in Canada.

> A declining share of Canadians identify as Christians, while an increasing share say they have no religion, like trends in the United States and Western Europe. Our most recent survey in Canada, conducted in 2018, found that a slim majority of Canadian adults (55%) say they are Christian, including 29% who are Catholic and 18% who are Protestant. About three-in-ten Canadians say they are either atheist (8%), agnostic (5%) or 'nothing in particular' (16%). Canadian census data indicate that the share of Canadians in this 'religiously unaffiliated' category rose from 4% in 1971 to 24% in 2011, although it is lowest in Québec. In addition, a rising share of Canadians identify with other faiths, including Islam, Hinduism, Sikhism, Judaism and Buddhism, due in large part to immigration.[93]

A year later, Statistics Canada noted 68% of Canadians fifteen or older reported having a religious affiliation. It was the first time fewer than 70% of Canadians reported being religiously affiliated since tracking this began in 1985. Only 23% reported attending a church service at least once a month.[94]

Gallup reported in 2019 U.S. membership in houses of worship was below fifty percent for the first time in eighty-three years of polling. The oldest Americans are most likely to attend, with the religion recession increasing steadily from the oldest through Baby Boomers, 1946–64, Generation X,

93 Lipka, Michael. "5 facts about religion in Canada," *Pew Research Centre*, July 1, 2019, https://www.pewresearch.org/fact-tank/2019/07/01/5-facts-about-religion-in-canada.

94 Cornelisson, Louis. "Religiosity in Canada and its evolution from 1985 to 2019,", October 28, 2021, Statistics Canada, https://www150.statcan.gc.ca/n1/pub/75-006-x/2021001/article/00010-eng.ht

1965–1980, and more so through to the millennials, 1981–1996 and the current Generation Z.[95]

Indeed, the fastest growing religious preference is no religion. That group identifying as atheist, agnostic or nonreligious are called "nones"; four in ten millennials are forsaking organized religion.[96]

As a Canadian reading those Twitter comments, I was struck by how many Americans associated Catholics with former President Donald Trump supporters. Right-wing politicians retained support among a significant segment of right-wing Catholics. The recent U.S. Supreme Court appointment of Amy Coney Barrett, a devout Catholic and mother to seven kids, is a case in point.

"Amy Coney Barrett is associated with a Catholic right that wants to reduce faith to the realm, and selective one at that, of purely personal ethics, and leave the rest of human life—including health care—to the vicissitudes of the market and the glories of American exceptionalism, overseen by Republicans," wrote Bill Blaikie.[97]

This was anathema to the Catholic social teaching I had embraced. Lenten Development and Peace programs educated us on global injustices, moving responses from a charity model to doing justice. Popes who spoke out against abortion denounced capitalism's sins while extolling unions and environmental justice.

On this woman's Twitter, there was a clearly identifiable Catholic religious culture. They still identified themselves as Catholic because it was bred in

95 Jones, Jeffrey M. "U.S. Church Membership Falls Below Majority for First Time," *Gallup*, March 29, 2021, https://news.gallup.com/poll/341963/church-membership-falls-below-majority-first-time.aspx.

96 Goldberg, Emma. "The New Chief Chaplain at Harvard? An Atheist." *New York Times*, August 28, 2021, https://www.nytimes.com/2021/08/26/us/harvard-chaplain-greg-epstein.html.

97 Blaikie, Bill. "The problem with U.S. Supreme Court Justice Amy Coney Barrett is her right-wing brand of Catholicism," *Rabble*, Nov. 3, 2019, https://rabble.ca/columnists/2020/11/problem-us-supreme-court-justice-amy-coney-barrett-her-right-wing-brand.

the bone, ancestry, and childhood long ago. Cradle Catholics. They regarded themselves as "indelibly Catholic by culture, ancestry, ethnicity, or family tradition." [98]

Faith, religion, and spirituality are complicated. People tell the pollsters, "I am Catholic, but Catholicism is not my beliefs." Cultural Catholics might identify themselves as a follower of Christ, believer in the resurrection of Jesus, some practicing a social gospel, not "all in" on other beliefs. Say hello to a clan some label as cafeteria Catholics.

On Twitter, a Trump supporter said she was no longer talking to her adult children because of their politics. I threw caution to the wind to comment I was confident that Trump would not be at her death bed. If she wanted any loved ones there, she might want to rethink priorities. I would say the same to her children.

"Claire, the 'Ex-Catholic' posts underscored how embittered some people were about 'once upon a time' being Catholic."

Some women friends tell me that they fast from all organized religions, repudiating their experiences of a white, male, patriarchal, and hierarchical dominance. Some others stay to fight their fights and witness to reforms.

I was neither ex-Catholic nor a cultural Catholic. This was my reply to the woman's post.

"Good question, comments. I'm writing a faith memoir, a half-century 'crooked straight' journey to heaven's doors, eleven years as priest. More 'River of Life' now, Roamin' not Roman Catholic. Writing, I remember all of us, the ex, retired, recovering Roman Catholics, and those who figured out the wheat from the chaff."

Respecting different choices others made, I saw no point in personally throwing out the baby with the bathwater. There were the Jesus stories, prayers, beliefs, worthy life, death, and meaning questions to still ponder.

98 Mullen, Lincoln. "Catholics who aren't Catholics," *The Atlantic*, Sept. 8, 2015, https://www.theatlantic.com/politics/archive/2015/09/catholics-who-arent-catholic/404113.

CHAPTER 46

Black Lives Matter

Like many Catholic homes, the Prashaws had a copy of Warner E. Sallman's *Head of Christ* devotional painting hung in our house. Jesus was this handsome, blue-eyed man with dark blond hair falling to his shoulders, a Saviour benignly blessing us. Billions of Sallman's prints were distributed worldwide from 1940 through the years of our childhood and early adulthood. It became the icon for Christianity.

"The painting was beside the wall phone near the kitchen," Pati reminded me. "I'd look at Jesus for hours while talking to my friends."

We grew up thinking Jesus was white, Christian, a king, a friend of traditional family values, and an enemy of sinners.

"Cruz, remember when your mom and your friend Aliya (Dalfen) took you on that epic road trip across North America? In Chicago, at the Institute of Art, they tell me you were spellbound with another painting of Jesus on the cross."

"He was six years old yet so engaged by the art," Claire said. "He sat for a long time looking at this painting of Jesus on the cross (by Francisco de Zurbaran)."

"I didn't know why they did that to him," Cruz said.

"He was upset, and sad," Claire added. "When I told him why they had crucified him, Cruz wanted to know why they had bullied Jesus because of what he had said. Cruz used the word, bully."

"It was not nice what they did to Jesus," Cruz said.

De Zurbaran had painted his graphic, captivating death scene for Jesus and, like Sallman, portrayed Jesus as a white man.

"There's the Black Christ of Esquipulas that I saw in Guatemala near Honduras, one of the Cristo Negros of Central America," Claire said. "The Black Madonna too."

"Cruz, Jesus' name then in Palestine was Yeshua," I said. "He was part of a first-century Jewish family living in the Middle East that had a mix of skin colours. I'm guessing he had brown skin, dark hair, and darker eyes. He probably looked a lot like you; gorgeous olive skin and that beautiful long curly hair that you love, that everyone loves about you."

I worry for my bi-racial Cruz with the pervasive racism, individual and systemic, its clear discrimination manifested in so many ways. Carding of people stopped in cars. Police shootings. Claire worries as a mother, her boy on the cusp of teenage years. She remembered their times of innocence.

"When Cruz was about three, he was in this wagon with his two buddies, Theo and Henry, who are white," Claire said. "I took a picture of them. Later, when Theo drew that picture of them in the wagon, he drew Cruz with brown skin and curly hair. I asked Theo what the difference was between Cruz and them? Theo said Cruz has curly hair. We have straight hair."

If only we could pay attention to curly hair and not skin colour.

Why do people change?

Cruz is asking questions these days in the wake of George Floyd's murder and Black Lives Matter.

"Cruz, what did Floyd say when the officer pressed his knee on his neck for nine minutes?"

"I can't breathe!'."

He knew Floyd's story, the conviction of the officer. He follows the news about racism in Toronto.

"Cruz, you know the N-word?"

"Yes. It's wrong. It's bad to say."

"I bet you would be shocked if you ever heard me use it? I bet you would let me know how wrong it is to say it."

"I would, Uncle Rick. It's so wrong. You wouldn't say it."

Well, once my favourite uncle said the phrase. I was still a university student when, after hitch-hiking Europe, I went to Florida to visit Uncle Bill and Aunt Dorothy. Yes, Uncle Bill—*Playboys*, cottages, and Manhattans. In Florida, I heard him say the N-word. It made me sick, worse, because I loved him and knew he was a good man. When I told him how I felt, he said that I didn't live in the United States and in the south. I couldn't possibly know what he knew. It was like he patted me on the head. It bothered me for a long time.

In writing this memoir, I circled back to Bill who had died in 2005. I wondered if his views ever changed. We all make mistakes. There are opportunities to grow. I asked for an update on Bill from both my sister, Jude, who had lived in Virginia near Bill and Dorothy, and from Susan Adams, a special friend.

"I did challenge Uncle Bill with using the N-word," Jude told me. "And I challenged him with using a slur expression for the Japanese. He was in his mid-eighties when we had that talk. Growing up in northern New York, he heard the N-word. And he was on a destroyer that was torpedoed by the Japanese and he saw dead soldiers. He stopped using both of those words. I don't remember all the details. He never argued with me or thought I was nuts."

Susan agreed. "I don't ever recall hearing Bill use that word, and he had plenty of opportunities because, when he and I were together, I was working in the projects where at least half the population was Black. My boss was Black, and lived around the corner from us, and he and she were good friends! Bill was a gentleman at his core."

"Cruz, religion can be such a force for good yet for evil as well," I said. "I wonder if our religious pictures and icons had shown the true brown face of Jesus, would some Christians not have been slave owners? There were Christian abolitionists like William Wilberforce in England while many

Christians owned slaves, worshipping a Jesus they knew as white, patriotic, colonizing, church and State all one."

The sin of racism cries out for denunciation whether in our country or in religions.

Bill was not the only one changing. Others are finding the courage to speak out. Leaders of The Jesuit Conference of Canada and the United States are pledging $100 million in reparation to the descendants of slaves their religious order owned and sold in a century of "our shameful history of Jesuit slaveholding."[99]

I revisited lessons my parents had taught us, i.e., all people possessing the same dignity, differences being more fascinating than threatening, that vulnerable individuals with difficult lives were every bit as good as we were. Sadly, the prevailing "us-and-them" universes can choose chokeholds instead, meaning some cannot breathe, and others cannot be who they are and love who they love.

I had not appreciated near enough this gold nugget in my parents' example until I witnessed how many react negatively to people different from themselves. In the extreme, we block people in social media (sometimes, blocking is necessary for safety and sanity). Some forbid conversation on politics or religion at family festive gatherings. We erupt at others with drive-by shouting. We are engulfed in vaccination wars. One American teen on Twitter proclaimed Jesus was never vaccinated.

"Oh my God, where do we start?" Claire sighed.

"I suspect Jesus' Jewish mother inoculated him with all kinds of herbs, soups, and medicines. The teen may not have known nor cared that Jesus was neither American nor white."

In United States President Joe Biden's inaugural address, he called out the "uncivil war" that is the real enemy in our midst. The culture and political

---

99 Bryant, Miranda. "Catholic order pledges $100m in reparations to descendants of enslaved people," *The Guardian*, March 16, 2021, https://www.theguardian.com/world/2021/mar/16/jesuit-conference-canada-us-catholic-reparations-descendants-enslaved-people.

wars segregate us, even though in truth most of us start the day on the same ground—a visit to the bathroom, breakfast, worries for loved ones, and work.

"Cruz, that's how I see Black Lives Matter. Until Black lives really matter, all lives won't matter, can't matter. Jesus told a story of leaving the ninety-nine sheep to help the one sheep in trouble. We need to fix what's wrong and truly mean it when we say, all lives matter."

"We have a hardware store in the neighbourhood where the owner put up an 'All Lives Matter' message," Claire said. "He received some complaints. He genuinely did not understand what the problem was. He believed everyone was equal. Every life matters. That is what he was trying to say. When people explained how his message didn't really support Black people, he apologized and changed the sign to Black Lives Matter. It's still up over his store."

CHAPTER 47

Working on Parliament Hill—
God Bless America?

2003–2018

[Warning: This chapter contains information on residential schools that some readers may find distressing.]

During my first eight years at CCJC, I had been active nights and weekends in the Glengarry-Prescott-Russell NDP Riding Association east of Ottawa. Talk about a political wilderness. Every party has those third or fourth-place ridings in different regions. Nonetheless, we had keen activists flying the party's flag, lively debates as intense as Parliament, and the fun of mounting decent campaigns surfing the federal elections. My primary task as riding president was to strike a search committee to identify the next sacrificial lamb that would lose massively to the juggernaut of then Liberal MP Don Boudria. My real incentive was ducking being that candidate myself. I succeeded in 1993, 1997, and 2000, hitting a home run in 1997's candidate, Rev. Fred Cappucino, a minister and founder of Child Haven International that helped needy kids. Cappucino agreed to run on the condition that he would not criticize his friend, Boudria. My surrogate fun was to write media releases on Cappucino "steaming," "frothing," and "pouring cold water" on weak government social policy announcements. There were several!

However, a move to Kanata in the west end of Ottawa set me up for a real-life *Best Laid Plans* political campaign. Enthusiasm for the new NDP leader Jack Layton betrayed me. Activists wanted me to run in the 2004 federal election in the Carleton-Mississippi Mills riding that included mostly suburban voters and a dozen rural communities. In Terry Fallis' *Best Laid Plans* novel, the Scot, Angus McLintock, was another Rick sacrificial lamb chosen for a hopeless cause when, lo and behold, a political scandal and karma hurdled him to an astonishing, upset victory.[100]

That ending would be pure fiction for me.

On leave from CCJC, I did run, relishing the dozen debates, media interviews, conversations with voters, articulating a social democrat approach to federal and global policies for the economy, environment, and social inclusion for all. As in ministry, I told back to people their own stories that I had heard while canvassing— bills to pay, few childcare options, hardships facing small business owners, and farmers losing the family farm. In the same block, citizens slammed their door in my face while their neighbour chased me down the street to hear my views on the Middle East. Voters! Politics! When a rural debate in a packed community hall ended, I ran to the back doors to greet everyone as I had after a church service. One farmer slapped me on the back to pronounce me the debate's winner. It was evident though that he was sticking with his Conservative party.

With clergy abuse stories prevalent in the media, it was suggested I use vaguer "ministry" references for my bio. I insisted on priest. I had nothing to hide. Indeed, two voters asked why I left the priesthood.

"Love," I answered. That was no scandal.

I had wanted a better result than my third place, and the 6,758 votes that left me far behind the new Conservative MP, Gordon O'Connor. A week before the election, a Liberal friend had whispered their polling had the local NDP at seventeen percent. We couldn't afford any polling; we were jealous of opponents' radio ad buys and billboards. Seventeen percent was unprecedented support for the NDP there. However, strategic voting messages—vote Liberal to stop Conservative Stephen Harper—helped elect a minority Paul Martin government, delaying a Harper victory another two years. The riding association still earned its $1,000 campaign rebate for the

---

100 Terry Fallis, *Best Laid Plans* (Penguin Random House Canada, 2008.)

first time, delighting the merry band of tireless volunteers. I had my Layton leader-candidate photo as a keepsake and a renewed faith in democracy.

I should have known it would not be a McLintock ending. My housekeeper who liked my views confessed she could not vote for the NDP because "her father would turn in his grave." She laughed when I told her that, from even the little I knew of her past, her father had probably turned in his grave several times already. Voting for me might have him right side up!

Tony Martin, Sault Ste. Marie Soup Kitchen, MPP 1990–2003, MP 2004–2011.

That election, Tony Martin became MP for Sault Ste. Marie. He hired Janine Bertolo and invited me to join his team on Parliament Hill. Dare I leave the NGO universe to dirty my hands in politics, eyes wide open to its compromises, the crevices with power and money? Politics had been in my blood since I had staged high school political conventions and planted orange colours on our family's front lawn. That partisan sport with the daily sparring, campaigns, and Canadian team colours—red, blue, orange, and green—could be fun, up to a point.

"Like your video games, Cruz!"

However, what mattered far more for me was the politics of changing the world, stewardship for the earth, and doing justice for all. I loved NDP pioneer Tommy Douglas' *Mouseland* animated video,[101] illustrating mice who made up most of the population, yet who consistently elected governments comprised of cats. The cats the mice elected might vary but it didn't

---

101 The Story of Mouseland, as told by Tommy Douglas, Douglas Caldwell Foundation, https://en.dcf.ca/mouseland.

matter—white, black, or spotted—the cats passed laws that benefitted the fat cats rather than the mice majority.

"The story turns for Douglas when a little mouse comes along with a bold idea, that instead of electing a government of cats, they should choose their leaders from amongst themselves. Of course, that little mouse was branded a dangerous subversive and was locked up, but as Douglas says, 'you can lock up a mouse or a man, but you can't lock up an idea'."[102]

Yes, I was a social democrat, a lefty for all seasons, not merely for election campaigns. I have two Bernie Sanders t-shirts. On that writing trip to Mexico, I jettisoned a planned barhopping pilgrimage to the Austin City Limits and Friday Night Lights scenes in favour of a Sanders campaign rally.

Yes, I believed the government has a role in regulating business, promoting a social safety net, and infrastructure.

"My God, the pandemic screams for leadership by governments," Claire said. "We needed life rafts for long-term care, paid sick leave, benefits, shots in our arms."

When I was seventeen, I had this great urge to run away to join Bobby Kennedy's campaign for president. He, with Martin Luther King Jr., spoke in a way that made me believe we could change the world and that anything was possible. I watched in shock on television Sirhan Sirhan shoot Kennedy in the kitchen galley the night of his victorious California primary. As Trudeaumania swept Canada the same year, it was noteworthy that I was not swooning. I admired Trudeau's intellect, work on our Canadian Constitution, and embedding tolerance in moral matters. I wanted more. I became aware of the injustice of unbridled capitalism, the stacked deck of an economy that needed reshuffling, the seductive shortcomings of a trickle-down economy producing wealth for a caste of rich businessmen precisely because most others were struggling, oppressed, and especially docile.[103] I did

102 Aivalis, Christo. "Jason Kenney calls it Socialist propaganda, but Mouseland has abiding relevance in Canadian politics," *Canadian Dimension*, Oct. 9, 2018, https://canadian-dimension.com/articles/view/mouseland-has-abiding-relevance-in-canadian-politics.

103 Ball, Jennifer and Tepperman, Lorne. *The Stacked Deck: An Introduction to Social Inequality*, Second Edition (Toronto: Oxford University Press Canada, 2021.)

not believe that others had to fail in order for me to succeed. I did not believe that we were all at the same start lines in life. Hard work, as okay as that is, did not guarantee fairness for all. It's an old story that's not easy to change. Enough mice in favour of tax cuts and private enterprise fancy themselves as cats one day.

My politics and my faith were aligned. Martin's too. He was a practicing Catholic and MP steeped in the social teaching of the church. Martin spoke how near impossible it was for him to take off his faith cloak in politics, nor easily check his political cloak at church doors. Of course, in a hyper-partisan political setting, that tempted fate. At the mere mention of faith or religion, most in the NDP, pundits, and the media figured it was exclusively the secular left against the religious right. Preston Manning's Reform Party and Harper's Reform-Conservative caucus certainly set up that misleading, narrow frame. Harper successfully courted support from the pews almost exclusively on personal morality issues. Interestingly, it gave the religious right some influence in right-wing parties without often securing the legislation those voters demanded.

South of the border, since President Ronald Reagan in 1980, "God Bless America" was in vogue. During President George W. Bush's years, the slogan came back into play as the standard way to finish political speeches, particularly after 9/11. Lost in the phrase was any genuine invocation for God to help America. God had been co-opted on America's side.

"Abraham Lincoln had it right," wrote *Sojourners'* Jim Wallis, a prolific Evangelical writer who challenged the religious conservatives' monopoly on God-politics talk.

> Our task should not be to invoke religion and the name of God by claiming God's blessing and endorsement for all our national policies and practices—saying, in effect, that God is on our side. Rather, as Lincoln put it, worry earnestly whether we are on God's side.
>
> Those are the two ways that religion has been brought into public life in American history. The first way—God on our side—leads inevitably to triumphalism, self-righteousness, bad theology and, often, dangerous foreign policy. The second way, asking if we are on God's side, leads to much healthier things, namely penitence, and

even repentance, humility, reflection, and accountability. We need much more of all those because they are often the missing values of politics.[104]

I am reading *Journeys to the Heart of Catholicism*, where Ted Schmidt comments on the disgrace of Catholics confusing the flag with the cross, an idolatry known in other denominations and among many Evangelicals.

"The market Catholics (America's largest faith group) who have risen out of immigrant groups and taken their places as worshipping acolytes in powerful American corporations. These predators have relentlessly promoted globalization and reaped the rewards. Economist Robert Reich explains that economic globalization has managed to separate the interests of the wealthy classes from a sense of national interest, and thus a sense of obligation to the poor in whom Jesus primarily locates himself. In this they have never been challenged by the inward-looking bishops."[105]

Contrary to popular belief, Canada never had the American separation of church and state that is embedded in their Constitution. Here, it's been more of a blurry enforcement of freedom of religion from governments and, more recently, in court and human rights commission decisions, freedom from religion in the public square.

The God I knew and worshipped was non-partisan but deeply political. This God was not Conservative, Liberal, NDP, Green, Democrat nor Republican, Canadian nor American. Still, this God hears the "cry of the poor" (Ps. 69:33) and demands "let justice flow like water" (Amos 5:24). Gustavo Gutiérrez, the Dominican priest theologian, had said, "The central preoccupation of his life and work has been to answer one question, 'how do we tell the poor that God loves them'?" He said it is important to place the kingdom of God

---

104 Wallis, Jim. "God's Politics, A Better Option," *Sojourners*, Washington, Feb. 2005, https://sojo.net/magazine/february-2005/gods-politics-better-option.

105 Ibid., Ted Schmidt, *Journeys to the Heart of Catholicism*, 17.

within human history.[106] There were people of faith engaged in the public square, working for the common good.

One such politician then was the late MP Paul Dewar (Ottawa Centre), who grew up in a staunch Catholic family and later joined a United Church faith community with his wife, Julie Sneyd.

"You cannot be a person of faith without being political. Faith and politics are congruent, and we have no option but to be political if we are going to live the gospel," Dewar said. "We have to constantly question what the Christian message is, and we can never stop trying to change the way things are in society." Dewar added that, for him, the word "political" included electoral politics but also transcends it. "Our response to faith must be lived out in community," he insisted. "Faith is something that we must do and not only think about."[107]

I listened to a podcast where Rev. Serene Jones, a Disciples of Christ pastor and first female president of the prestigious Union Theological Seminary, echoed Dewar and Martin's beliefs.[108] "Good theology absolutely must be public theology, what is theology, if it's not talking about our collective lives, and the meaning and purpose of our lives, and how we're supposed to live together, and who God is, in ways that are part of our conversation together?"

"Claire, I noticed Ontario Premier Doug Ford importing this blessing phrase, ending his pandemic statements with 'God Bless the People of Ontario'."

"God help us all!" Claire said, lifting her Manhattan drink.

Lost in the polarized secular left-religious right paradigm was the NDP's own history and several current NDP MPs with faith backgrounds. There had been Douglas for starters. Before Pope John Paul II banned priests from political life, I had followed the MP careers of Nova Scotia's Father Andy

106 Gruending, Dennis. "Paul Dewar's Motto was 'Faith is Political'," *Rabble*, Feb. 21, 2019 (repost of Pulpit and Politics Blog, 2009), https://rabble.ca/blogs/bloggers/pulpit-and-politics/2019/02/paul-dewars-motto-was-faith-political.

107 Ibid., Gruending.

108 Rev. Serene Jones, "Grace in a Fractured World," *On Being*, podcast, with Krista Tippett, April 1, 2021, https://onbeing.org/programs/serene-jones-grace-in-a-fractured-world.

Hogan, who had been schooled in Moses Coady's co-operative movement, and later, Saskatchewan's Father Bob Ogle. Member of Parliament Bill Blaikie was a United Church minister. Layton and MP Bill Siksay spoke about their United Church and social gospel influences. Martin could talk faith politics with two fellow Catholic MPs, Charlie Angus and Joe Comartin. In his early punk rock musician days, Angus and his girlfriend (now wife) Brit, had opened a home for ex-prisoners, refugees, and immigrants. Posting pictures of the home on Facebook, Angus said, "We had read the autobiography of Dorothy Day and decided that opening a Catholic Worker House to live with the homeless seemed like the most natural thing in the world." Martin tried his best to reinvigorate an NDP Faith and Social Justice Commission that struggled for standing within the party.

Blaikie knew the Bible had more commentary on peace, helping the poor, and a just economy than on individual morality issues. As my first year with Martin ended, Blaikie delivered this statement on religion in the House of Commons.

> **Hon. Bill Blaikie (Elmwood—Transcona, NDP):** Mr. Speaker, in a time when religion is predominantly characterized in the media as a conservative force, there is a need to diversify the face of religion in the political realm and to emphasize that there are faith-informed progressive perspectives on issues which too often are dealt with as if there is only a debate between faith and non-faith.
>
> In fact, what is often happening is a debate between Canadians of the same faith and/or a debate between conservative faith communities and a secular liberalism that owes its values in large part to our common religious heritage.
>
> People of the same faith arrive at different conclusions about difficult issues and consequently join or support different political parties. This is as it should be.
>
> Religious speech should not be restricted to a few issues, or even worse, seen as inadmissible in debate. Questions of peace and war, the economy and the environment are also moral issues that can be informed by faith.

The task is to discern the appropriate ways of such speaking in a pluralistic world. Dismissing views purely because they are religious throws out the wheat with the chaff. Secular fundamentalism is not the answer either. Thanks be to God, Mr. Speaker.[109]

I welcomed Blaikie's acknowledgement of faith-informed progressive perspectives and how one might speak in a pluralistic world. However, his second point was crucial too. I lamented the "dialogue of the deaf" prevalent in politics and religion between opposing progressive and conservative factions. We on the left could demonize the other side, too, and discount those views that were anchored on values they believed in. We didn't share those values nor always the same interpretation of the scripture passage. Nevertheless, demonizing opponents put all of us on a slippery slope that undermined civil discourse. Unquestionably, this denigration of opponents contributes to the alarming number of alienated folks who feel discounted and sidelined by mainstream politics. The disenfranchised become vulnerable to dangerous agitators we see inciting violent protests. What happened on the U.S. Capitol on January 6, 2021, is evidence of what President Biden called his country's "uncivil war."

People of faith should participate in public discourse to counter prevailing beliefs undermining the dignity of every single person. In that *On Being* podcast, Rev. Jones had commented on politics meshed into life. "The thing I'd say about this political moment—and it's a deeply theological claim—is, I honestly think at the heart of our nation's turmoil is the fact that people honestly do not believe that we are all equal and loved equally and equally valued. They just don't believe that."[110]

In 2005, Martin, Angus, and Comartin faced down church sanctions for their support for the Civil Marriage Act that legalized same-sex marriage. They were criticized from the pulpit in their own parishes. Some priests denied them Holy Communion or ministry, which they had performed for years. A bishop threatened to defeat Angus in the next election. Again, as

109 Bill Blaikie, Open Parliament, June 28, 2005, https://openparliament.ca/debates/2005/6/28/bill-blaikie-1.

110 Ibid., Tippett, *On Being* podcast.

with abortion, the Eucharist was caught up and being weaponized as a tool in political warfare.

The Communion wafer wars for Catholic politicians catapulted me back to priesthood days and lessons on a Big God and grace. As for the voters, the three Catholic amigos—Angus, Comartin, and Martin—were re-elected handily in 2006.

I worked with Martin on this letter to the *Catholic Register* to explain his support for same-sex marriage.

> In reporting my position within the NDP caucus on same-sex marriage, your reporter wrote that my support was a matter of deciding that minority rights ultimately trump my personal religious beliefs.
>
> This is misleading. As a lifelong, church-going Catholic, I try hard to make sure that nothing trumps my personal, religious beliefs.
>
> Indeed, the recognition of minority rights is part of those religious belief. In our broader society while and teaching our own beliefs in our church. It is incumbent on us to protect the rights of all minorities.
>
> My personal religious beliefs dictated that I inform my conscience, give proper weight to my church's teaching and work to safeguard the principle of religious freedom to protect religious officials from being compelled by the state to perform same-sex marriage. I have done all that.
>
> I am celebrating the twenty-second anniversary of my marriage this year. As a married Catholic, I have to say that gay and lesbian couples I have known have never once threatened my marriage.
>
> I believe that access to civil marriage for gay and lesbian couples will add to the stability of Canadian families and Canadian society. This is a world that needs more people who are willing to make loving, lifelong commitments to each other and are willing to take full responsibility for their relationships.

Martin received a large volume of mail against his position, along with some support from Catholics. He had welcomed the Catholic bishops to the debate. Martin was never pro-abortion, but he respected the choices women made for themselves. Like Sister Joan Chittister's words on my CCJC desk, he believed fewer women might choose abortion if a baby had a fighting chance in life with housing, education, childcare, decent work, and more.

In the next campaign in Sault Ste. Marie Algoma, Martin, former MPP Bud Wildman, and I were out in a rural district canvassing when a farmer on a John Deere tractor raced up full throttle to only a few feet away from us to splatter mud, profanity, and damnation on the Catholic MP candidate. I was distracted, counting the impressive blasphemy and swearing from this God-fearing man. Wildman joked the NDP was not forcing him to marry a guy. That did not go over well. We retreated to our car and headed back to the city.

It is a tall order to infuse the temporal order with faith values without imposing one's religion and beliefs. I find it worth the struggle.

It was all uphill, on the margins, worthy good works, nevertheless. Martin launched national poverty elimination and universal childcare campaigns. They became important markers for future government legislation. I grinned when one legal scholar who helps MPs draft their bills inquired whether Martin had really intended to eliminate poverty or, did he not more likely mean to reduce poverty in Canada.

"Eliminate," I replied. I knew Tony's ideals. I made sure to include faith communities in outreach then and later for a national dementia strategy initiative sponsored by Nickel Belt MP Claude Gravelle.[111]

Martin attended Parliament Hill faith breakfasts. He was in the minority there, seats filled by conservative Catholic and Evangelical MPs. There was a group of Conservative Catholic MPs hosting a Mass with a kindred priest as the celebrant.

Three specific dates stand out in my years on Parliament Hill.

---

111 Gravelle's legislation preceded MP Lisa Raitt's bill in the next Parliament and the 2017 "A Dementia Strategy for Canada: Together We Aspire," *Canada News Wire*, The Government of Canada Releases Canada's First Dementia Strategy, June 19, 2019.

On June 11, 2008, on behalf of the Government of Canada and all Canadians, Prime Minister Harper stood in the House of Commons to acknowledge the inter-generational damage caused to former students at residential schools, their families, and communities. He asked for forgiveness from the Indigenous Peoples of this country for failing them so profoundly. The apology underlined Canadians' resolve to learn and never repeat this tragedy. The day was historic, humbling, and spellbinding.

The first words of the monumental Truth and Reconciliation Commission of Canada report lay bare the harsh reality of those schools.

> Canada's residential school system for Aboriginal children was an education system in name only for much of its existence. These residential schools were created for the purpose of separating Aboriginal children from their families, in order to minimize and weaken family ties and cultural linkages, and to indoctrinate children into a new culture—the culture of the legally dominant Euro-Christian Canadian society, led by Canada's first prime minister, Sir John A. Macdonald. The schools were in existence for well over one hundred years, and many successive generations of children from the same communities and families endured the experience of them. That experience was hidden for most of Canada's history, until Survivors of the system were finally able to find the strength, courage, and support to bring their experiences to light in several thousand court cases that ultimately led to the largest class-action lawsuit in Canada's history. [112]

Any money in settlements was a small part of addressing the harm those schools did then and now, given the thousands of deaths as well as the spirit and soul holes in the survivors, passed on to successive generations. Martin had said we could never truly move forward as a country until we dealt with our history with Indigenous Peoples. Even with the formal apology and partial government and church settlements for claims from former students, there is still a massive "moving forward" yet to happen. Indigenous writers

---

112 Honoring the Truth, Reconciling for the Future, Truth and Reconciliation Commission Final Report, (www.trc.ca, 2015.)

like Tanya Talaga and Jesse Wente warn against bogus reconciliation talk that looks progressive and appealing in election slogans. They knew the history of two sides coming together, missing the one side.[113]

"Claire, my Catholic friends were disheartened by the Catholic Church's slow, legal response to another scandal that cried out for justice."

The Canadian Conference of Catholic Bishops had explained that, legally, they were not the spokesperson nor the authority for the Roman Catholic Church in Canada. Several Catholic entities—most of the religious orders and dioceses who understood themselves to have central or partial liability—banded together and secured legal counsel to assist them with their risks through collective negotiations. (It turned out to be fifty-two entities, although the Jesuits negotiated separately and early.) Risk was the operative word. These entities feared losing the funds they had left to support older members. From media accounts, they were slow to produce archives and records as demanded until some good old-fashioned public browbeating from TRC Commissioners spurred significant efforts at the last minute.

The settlement with the churches was a smaller part of the multi-billion settlement claims that Canada paid. The Catholic entities negotiated financial obligations that were set at seventy-nine million dollars, a total not even remotely reached when only four million of a twenty-five million fundraising goal was raised in a lacklustre campaign. The bishop's lawyers went to court to successfully argue that they had fulfilled the "best efforts" clause inserted in the settlement.

"It's scandalous, really shameful," said Saskatoon priest and Order of Canada recipient, André Poilièvre. "It was a loophole. It might be legal, but it's not ethical."[114] Five Saskatchewan bishops have since committed to renew the fundraising campaign in their province.

113 Wente, Jesse. "Reconciliation is dead, and it never was really alive': Jesse Wente *CBC News*, Feb 25, 2020, https://www.cbc.ca/news/canada/toronto/jesse-wente-metro-morning-blockades-indigenous-1.5475492.

114 Warick, Jason. "Priest slams 'pitiful' lack of Catholic fundraising for residential school survivors," *CBC News*, July 10, 2021, https://www.cbc.ca/news/canada/saskatoon/priest-slams-lack-of-catholic-fundraising-for-residential-school-survivors-1.6096717.

There is still so much "Breaking News" on this story. I will comment only on the matter of apologies from the Canadian bishops and the pope.

In late September 2021, reversing the church's long pattern of defensive, legal manoeuvres, The Canadian Conference of Catholic Bishops finally expressed their profound remorse and unequivocal apology to Indigenous Peoples in Canada for the suffering endured at residential schools. The bishops pledged thirty million dollars to survivors. Reaction was mixed, some Indigenous leaders welcoming the late apology while other leaders were skeptical on whether, this time, the money and deeds would follow the new words.

"Many Catholic religious communities and dioceses participated in this system, which led to the suppression of Indigenous languages, culture and spirituality, failing to respect the rich history, traditions and wisdom of Indigenous peoples," the bishops wrote.

"We acknowledge the grave abuses that were committed by some members of our Catholic community; physical, psychological, emotional, spiritual, cultural and sexual."[115]

Other churches involved in residential schools had formally apologized. As this book went to print, the Vatican announced Pope Francis will visit Canada at a date to be determined to help in the pastoral process of reconciliation with Indigenous Peoples here. A papal apology is likely. The news of his visit came after a long overdue invitation from the Canadian bishops' conference. There had been incomplete or distant, indirect "apologies"—first. Pope Benedict XVI's statement of regret and Pope Francis apology from South America for church injustices throughout the Americas. The visit should fulfill the TRC report's Call to Action number fifty-eight.

"Roman Catholics in Canada and across the globe look to the Pope as their spiritual and moral leader," the TRC report stated. "Therefore, it has been disappointing to survivors and others that the Pope has not yet made a clear and emphatic public apology in Canada for the abuses perpetrated in Catholic-run residential schools throughout the country. Survivors said I did

---

115 Zimonjic, Peter, "Indigenous organizations conflicted about Catholic bishops' apology", *CBC News*, Sept. 24, 2021, https://www.cbc.ca/news/politics/ cccb-issue-apology-role-residential-schools-1.6188998

not hear the Pope say to me, 'I am sorry.' Those words are very important to me . . . but he didn't say that to the First Nations people."[116]

History long ago by "not us, not now," is indeed Canada's living history today. It was inspiring to hear Cadmus Delorme, the forward-thinking young chief of the Cowessess First Nation where seven hundred fifty-one remains were confirmed, speak positively of forging communities and economies that are fair and inclusive to his people.

Those years with the NDP team felt more like hanging out with a family than with work colleagues. We shared a mission, ridiculously long hours, and then Brixton Pub beers served up by our "NDP bartender" Julie McCarthy.

A second memorable date, sadly, was when I wept driving to work on August 22, 2011, hearing *CBC News* confirm the death of Layton after an unspecified cancer returned. Only three months earlier, "le bon Jack" had propelled the NDP to an unprecedented second-place finish with thirty-one percent of the vote and one hundred three seats, becoming the official opposition for the first time. We had lost a father and a brother. It was untimely and unfair, a tragedy robbing the country of better times ahead.

I vividly remember the morning of October 14, 2014, when a lone gunman killed Corporal Nathan Cirillo at the War Monument before breaching Centre Block in Parliament where a security officer killed him. On the seven-year anniversary, a colleague who was on a conference call that morning jarred my memory. "I'll never forget your voice changing from curious about what silly thing was causing the yellow-bar notice on your screen to fear to, 'I have to go, there's a shooting,'." Staff on my floor huddled behind locked doors in Angus' office until security gave us the all-clear signal hours later. For weeks afterwards, I passed the War Memorial. More tears, and a prayer for a fallen soldier.

The thirteen years working for three MPs was rewarding. I met good people, both MPs and staff, working in different parties, a fact lost in a growing disdain for all politics. The best days were helping ordinary folks. I enjoyed

116 CBC News, "Pope expresses 'sorrow' for abuse at residential schools," April 29, 2009, https://www.cbc.ca/news/world/pope-expresses-sorrow-for-abuse-at-residential-schools-1.778019.

moving bureaucracies when we might assist a veteran with access to denied benefits, or when I drove across the bridge to Gatineau to pick up an emergency passport for an anxious constituent. I shied away from the standard replies to the avalanche of correspondence, answering in a way I expected if I wrote the letter myself.

Politics was still a blood sport, "us and them," winners and losers, the tiniest of slivers across party lines.

Rick's 2004 candidate campaign photo with NDP leader Jack Layton.

A few friendships of MPs in different parties hinted at the greater good that might be accomplished by more collaboration. In exit interviews, former MPs rhymed off reforms needed in politics. The hyper-partisan toxic environment and the whipped votes topped their complaints. I would add the problems arising from too many disinformed voters, party activists unwilling to criticize or pressure their own party, the automatic, unquestioned vote support for one's party (my housekeeper), the lack of voter engagement between elections; taken together, they undermine the enormous, potential good of politics. "The good in being good," to quote Dorothy Day.[117] There were several disappointments, none so important as the Liberal majority government reneging on its campaign promise to replace the first past the post electoral system with a form of proportional representation, i.e., fair voting, making every vote count so that people are represented even when their party candidate lost. That's a game-changer in Canadian politics, in birthing and demanding more consensual, different forms of party co-operation. All parties in all regions would get seats in proportion to their share of the vote. There would be no political wilderness for party supporters. More than ninety democratic countries use some form of a multi-member, fair voting system.[118] Those who have been in power, who want to keep unilateral power, will oppose that fundamental change. It was not surprising to read political operatives defend the breaking of that promise for fair voting, claiming there was no agreement on which proportional representation system to adopt in Canada. In fact, the Liberal promise had been to change the way we vote, period. They created a committee to explore options. It appeared orchestrated to fail. The government could have picked one fair voting option for Canada to experience for a few elections.

In 2014, waiting for a bus for work, I felt dizzy, feeling some tingling and weakness in my arm and head. A neurologist diagnosed a transient ischemic attack (TIA). The twelve-hour days were taking its toll, aggravated, no doubt, for three years when I would race home to Kanata to change into my usher uniform for *Ottawa Senators* hockey games. The boy in me still marvelled at being paid to watch my sports teams.

By late 2015 after an election, I was ready to retire, to write for myself instead of for other bosses. Adam's death in early 2016 took me down the rabbit hole of grief and then to a first book I had never imagined writing. The pile of unpaid bills forced me back on the Hill for one final year in 2018 with MP Rachel Blaney. When I did leave for good, I handed in my security pass and told the Parliamentary precinct officer that, if I ever showed up again to work, to "shoot me."

I still see friends at Brixton's. Disappointments and all, I loved working on Parliament Hill.

---

117 Dorothy Day, https://www.catholicworker.org.

118 Fair Voting Canada, www.fairvote.ca.

CHAPTER 48

Grief Chasing Gratitude

2016–2021

I hiked with my dead son on December 25, 2020, my black lab, Dallas, Adam's dog really, happily tagging along. It's a new, pleasant, and weird Christmas tradition, five years and counting since that tragic weekend in 2016.

Life's plan.

"Cruz, that worst call of my life."

Adam, then, recovering from his second brain operation two months earlier, had received a good prognosis. He was ready to return to his assistant chef job at Café Nature in the Canadian Museum of Nature. He was enjoying a hot tub with friends on the penthouse floor of his Elgin St. apartment building. The friends left to retrieve articles in Adam's apartment. When they returned, they found him face down in the hot tub. Paramedics resuscitated Adam. He was on life support as I raced home on a literal "red-eye" flight.

Family and friends spent a final weekend vigil hoping in vain for a miracle.

This Christmas morning, Adam, Dallas, and I headed out past Manotick to an old, abandoned railway bed transformed into a trail.

Living with the dead. Talking to the dead.

There was no one to hear me chat away with my boy. No one to call 911 to detain this solo, crazy man talking to the wind. Anyway, it's too late for 911.

I wear my son's ashes around my neck. Unimaginable.

"Dust to dust, ashes to ashes . . ." was a verse I, as Father Rick, had proclaimed at hundreds of funerals. The burial service's prayer, "in sure and certain hope of the resurrection to eternal life," appeared far less sure or certain leaning into my wailing walls. The neck jewelry urn is a black steel cylinder that resembles a bullet, the bullet Adam took, we all took that day. I chose the shape consciously. Sentimental hearts or doves did not capture the story.

Adam's ashes symbolize a loss while hinting at new life. Rubbing the cylinder, I smile. Its steel hardness steeling me for what lies ahead. Adam's courage had him bounce back after every seizure and those two brain surgeries to relieve the grip epilepsy held. He inevitably would head back to a sunny place to live. He was now my compass to do likewise.

I talked to Adam while sitting on his memorial park bench in St. Luke's Park across from his favourite Elgin St. Diner.

"Sit down. Relax. Enjoy," invites the plaque. I sit. I rub Adam's urn necklace wishing he would appear.

Come out, come out, wherever you are!

Adam obliges me occasionally, although, as in life, now his ghosts can act elusive, uncontainable. He is in charge, not I. When Atherton Drenth, the energy intuitive, had released my blocked energy in one appointment, she chuckled, reporting a drive-by visit from my son. She passed on his messages.

"You were shocked by my death, Dad? Let me tell you how shocked I was…. I love you…. I am busy, meetings with other trans kids, visiting family and friends, surfing and stuff."

I didn't pretend to understand it all, except the messages were so Adam. He had choreographed crucial decisions on *Soar, Adam, Soar.* For example, its exquisite cover. He had posted a phone picture on Instagram minutes before his drowning, shirt off, a shaft of sunlight cascading on his head through the penthouse pool sunroof. His angels watching him. A year after he died, Adam whispered from the other side that his final, crappy pixel phone photo would be the book's cover.

Don't worry, Dad!

Sorry kid. I am a parent. I worried. On another night, while fiddling with the urn, I heard my boy urge me not to paraphrase his Facebook posts in the book.

"Use my words, Dad!" He muscled in as the co-author.

Adam's mischievous, enduring presence was noticed throughout the revealing of John Dickhout as his heart recipient. Again, at night in bed, Adam whispered, "Heart recipient," to shake my grief-addled brain to check out the new Facebook friend I had accepted a few days earlier. John's golden attitude teamed up with Adam to initiate introductions. John would later tell us that his own anonymous letter to his donor underwent several drafts as he was asked to delete personal information. Meanwhile, our reply sailed past the censors with a few clues intact—Adam's epilepsy, hockey goalie, and a Celebration of Life. Was Trillium Gift of Life Network staff on a coffee break when Adam blew our letter across to the approval pile? Those clues led John online to discover Adam's obituary, then to early exchanges of anonymous messages, and to him identifying himself. Finally, we had that incredible meeting in the Dickhouts' home where, with his wife Lynn's stethoscope, I heard the beating of my son's racing heart, John's heart.

Adam and I had frequently texted when he lived in Ottawa. Now, occasionally, from wherever, I get a clear text from him that moves down the top-centre part of my head. He is in good humour, in a good place, I sense. Better than where I find myself some days.

I want more. I want Adam in the flesh. My grief chases gratitude though to new, unthinkable chapters as a transgender human rights and organ donor advocate, an author, and storyteller breathing life into Adam and my corpses.

It's not all up, up, and away. I clutch the urn on dark nights of the soul. That's the reality check on the permanent mourning facing the bereaved. Forget what people say, best intentions and all. There is no getting over it. Mourning has no clock nor calendar. We are lifers.

Did you know there is no word in the English language to define a parent who loses a child? We know whom orphans miss and whom a widow mourns. There are no words to describe a parent who mourns a child.

"Claire and Cruz, there are no words!"

In parish work, I had facilitated a Death and Dying ministry. Training began by listening to tapes outlining Elizabeth Kubler Ross's five stages of grieving, followed by participants sharing their own experiences with loss, all to shape future ministry. Kubler-Ross identified five stages then: denial, anger, bargaining, depression, and acceptance. She has since identified more stages or emotions. She never intended them as any logical, consecutive stages forward. Life, people, and especially our feelings are never so neat. Broken hearts, the valleys, loneliness, jumbled and jarring reminders that Adam is dead, gone, all debilitating alongside dawns breaking, whiffs of renewal and hope.

Grief chasing gratitude. This is all sacred ground. I feel no urge to fix it.

As a priest, I had spoken to people in mourning about time helping to turn down the volume of the grieving, moving the hurt to corners in the room. There is truth in that. Nonetheless, the mourning is forever because the love is forever. It feels like a muddy goo to wallow in and, at times, to get stuck in, too. It can be exhausting. I managed somehow to write Adam's and my first memoir in the depths of grieving. It was a lifeline that almost killed me.

As I signed books, there were moments I swear I was back in ministry.

"My son died about twenty years ago, your son's age, after a gunshot wound," a woman whispered. "He had the most beautiful blue eyes."

I blinked, imagining those beautiful eyes.

"My son was stillborn," another woman confessed, leaning over the signing table. "People don't understand my sadness."

Five years and counting. There is his presence and his absence. I remember Adam intentionally, less he is forgotten. I concoct complicated bank and business passwords that reflect Adam's story. I avoid anything experts label as harmful denial as leaving a bedroom intact, keeping his clothes closet full, or setting a placemat for him at my dining table. Who knows? In truth, a bit of denial is not all bad, as it sailed me through a few days for sure. I am Gertie Beaton's son though. I gave Adam's Carey Price Habs jersey to Dickhout. Good grief! John is a Habs fan, like Adam!

There is welcomed respite from the grieving, new life and energy, surprises beyond the stopgap, useful remedies of keeping busy and moving forward. It works for a while.

Freedom is what we do with what is done to us.

Jean-Paul Sartre's words work my bones. Past the fury and unanswered questions, an invitation beckoned. My father had lived Sartre's wisdom. Dad found his freedom past his being scared as an orphan and a soldier. His blood flowed through me to Adam, who likewise could wink back at woe. I admired both Dad and Adam for choosing life, for not being afraid. I try this. I hope others can as well. This is not a "take two aspirins, choose life" prescription. Life can be menacingly tough.

Bittersweet, not bitter nor cynical. I ran from despair. Doors to gratitude opened.

In 2019, I followed the story of J-35, that magnificent mama orca whale off the west coast of British Colombia who was spotted carrying her dead baby calf, bobbing it to the surface on her nose or on a fin. *CBC News* reported J-35 pushed her dead calf in a funeral-like procession through 1,600 kilometres of the Pacific Ocean for seventeen days of mourning. My God! I loved J-35 as a sister. I was with her every metre she swam. She knew what having your heart ripped out feels like. Now, I tell stories, bobbing Adam to the surface in those eighty-foot waves after the shipwreck that weekend.

Scars leading to love, circling the mourning.

Choose life, Dad!

Other remedies massaged my grieving. Music, baths, wine, solitude, lighting a candle, re-visiting Adam's insane Facebook posts, Zoom calls this 2020, chasing after nephews and nieces and their own young children, meeting Adam's friends at the memorial bench. And yes, those long Christmas morning walks bending Adam's ear, along with the organ donor, transgender advocacy, and telling the stories. My sister Jude's painting of Adam's final minutes in the water heals me. The painting hangs in my bedroom. Adam's eyes follow me around the room. Dallas rests best beneath the painting. I smile when people ask me about Adam. Boy, do people grieving want to talk about our loved ones.

I treasure awkward friends showing up, lost for words. "Just Show Up" is author Yvonne Heath's gorgeous advice on befriending we who mourn.[119]

Rick listening to John Dickhout's new heart, Adam's heart

Cleared months after his recovery from the heart transplant, Dickhout with his wife, Lynn, flew to Ottawa to meet more of our family, Adam's friends, and his caregivers at The Ottawa Hospital. We went to Adam's Café Nature workplace. In the parking lot, John asked me where Adam had lived. I winced because it was where he also died. I had shunned looking at the building. I turned and pointed to the high-rise on Elgin Street. John put his hand on my shoulder. Baby steps forward in this new life. When I get anxious about John's health, forgetting momentarily how young his heart is, John smiles and calls me, "Donor Dad."

The Dickhouts' visit unstuck grief that had paralyzed me. That first Christmas after his transplant, John had posted this message:

---

119 Yvonne Heath, *Real Life Podcast*, Rogers TV, Orillia.

December 25, 2016

A Tale of Two Christmases

It is the best of days. It is the worst of days. Through the year, for each door unexpectedly and joyously opened, another was suddenly shut. While one family rejoices at previously undreamable dreams, another sadly reflects over so many dreams gone undreamt. Many families find their festivities filled with celebration and joy, while others join hands around dinner tables forevermore missing a chair.

For some of us, the greatest gift received this Christmas came at a countless cost to so many. As our hearts swell with love, gratitude, and joy, they ache with sorrow at our donor families' losses. Christmas is bittersweet . . . It is the best of days. It is the worst of days.

With peace, love, and gratitude,

John d, Adam's heart recipient . . .

Dickhout and I taped a four-episode *Gifts of Life* podcast to tell the entire heart transplant story from donor and recipient perspectives.[120] As he did in his childhood bedroom, Adam asks me to tell this story again and again. Dickhout auditioned and was chosen as a narrator for the audiobook.[121] The miracles continue.

Through pain and trauma, incredible love surfaced. I sensed a future calling, a purpose again, something positive from Adam and our tragedy. Death and resurrection. My faith and beliefs influenced this path. So did Adam, parents, family, friends, and my crazy self. I let joy back in my life. I had a choice to embrace gratefully, even though it was not the first choice I wanted.

---

120 Gifts of Life podcast, www.giftsoflife.ca, a project supported by the Canada Council of the Arts, produced by Evan Forbes, with Joe Cappadocia, Lianne Castelino, John Dickhout, Rick Prashaw.

121 Rick Prashaw with John Dickhout, narrator, Soar, Adam, Soar, Tantor Audio, 2021.

CHAPTER 49

Judgment Day

Whenever

Father Peter Moher and I have joked about how Judgment Day plays out for us. Peter even told our parable once to his Holy Redeemer Sudbury congregation.

Friends for more than thirty years, we land at heaven's doors together. The other Peter, Saint Peter, comes out to greets us. Saint Peter gives us the once-over look, shakes his head a few times, checks the *Book of Life*, looks up still frowning, and then quickly looks left, then right. As no one is watching, he says:

"Get in, get in. Quick," waving us inside with a sweep of his arms before slamming the doors shut.

A pass into Paradise, likely devaluing the property with our admission, well, my admisson! In truth, I suspect Father Moher will walk in on his own merit, notwithstanding his blessing Lake Michigan and devilish puns. My *Book of Life* ledger, with the *Playboy* magazine, strap, and "priesthood, marriage and divorce," might require a good lawyer and plea bargaining.

"I'm with him," I assure Saint Peter.

At Father Peter's retirement party in Sudbury, I decided our parable needed a proper, further exegesis. First, I confessed to his friends, was it not delusional, on my part, thinking I was getting into heaven at all unless on my good friend's coattails? He has been faithful in forty years of ministry. Peter surely earned a pass into Paradise, too, as he remained a steadfast friend of mine, ignoring some advice to shun me.

Something else now struck me. In either of us ever retelling this Judgment Day scene, we had missed the important detail of arriving outside heaven's doors together. Obviously, we had died together. This was worth mining on a Sudbury Saturday night. I told those there our deaths had likely happened after a car accident with Peter driving, I in exasperation seizing the wheel to commandeer his vehicle. The laughter in the room hinted others might have been passengers with Peter.

Peter is a six on the Enneagram, a test that identifies different personality types and how we see the world differently. Sixes are a Godsend for churches. They are loyal, disposed to adhere to laws, rules, and super faithful to superiors. And speed limits. Peter religiously drives at the speed the sign tells him to, no matter that everyone else is passing him. When I, frustrated, advised him that drivers had met up and decided it was safe to drive fifteen to twenty kilometres above the speed limit, and that police would let us drive at that speed, he replied that, then, "they" should change the speed limit signs. No offer to pay a speeding ticket could move this immutable force or shorten our trips if he were behind the wheel. I am a seven on the Enneagram. At this point in my story, if you know that type, you are not surprised. We inhale life. We want to be buried at Disneyland. Sevens should check speed limits!

"I must be a seven, Uncle Rick," laughed Claire.

On that fatal day, I seized the wheel from Peter. We met Saint Peter. We slipped into heaven.

I have often said that, come Judgment Day, I am heading straight to the inevitable long line up to finally get satisfying answers to my faith questions, better ones than I heard here on Earth.

Or would I?

Hosanna, Rick, YOU ARE IN! I am good with those who imagine heaven as their best times on Earth, for me, never-ending golf, pickleball, and Blue Jays games, Claire's Manhattans poured at a heavenly Havana bar stool as I write my next novel.

"Where do I sign up, Uncle Rick?"

Suddenly, though, Adam snatched me out of that line for faith questions. There he was, in all his glory, surrounded by every dog who had lived in our families. THIS IS PARADISE!

"Claire and Cruz, I forgot all my questions."

Bright, bright.

White, white

Beautiful light

Jackrabbit jumps the meadow.

Celestial dogwalker, this son of mine. Kelly, Piper, Murphy, Molly, Josée at his feet.

What, no feet?

No footprints

Adam?

ADAM!!!!!!!

Eat the moss, Dad. Better than the club sandwich.

My Adam and Rebecca pull me into this "like two spirits" dance.

Furious, feverish, still fast lane.

What happened to slowing down?

Whirl, you dervish.

Dance, dance, dance, Dad.

Dance to this never-ending love

It's all we got.

It's all we need.

But my faith questions, son?

Later, Dad, the classes reveal all.

Classes?

The party beckons.

Your mom, dad, Danny awaits!

And the music plays.

And the feast begins.

And the Gods laugh.

CHAPTER 50

Still Standing, and Roamin' Catholic

Matt Dineen is my pandemic superhero, a high school teacher, risking, like many teachers, his health and safety. It's his passion, his vocation. Through COVID-19, we all know a Batman or Superman.

To be honest, the pandemic simply solidified Dineen's superhero status.

In 2012, Dineen had panicked when he started noticing bizarre behaviour from his wife, Lisa. They had attended the same high school, Lisa, a year ahead of him. They later became sweethearts and married in 1998.

It was now January 2013. Lisa was forty-three and Matt forty-two with three children, Justin, twelve, Rebecca, ten, and Peter, eight. Lisa's personality was drastically changing. She slept way more, secretly spent money, talked to inanimate objects, and uncharacteristically forgot safety measures for their children. This was not the Lisa Matt knew. A lack of empathy and a general malaise became defining character traits. It would take one doctor's appointment, and one visit to a specialist before Lisa was diagnosed that January with Frontotemporal dementia, a ravaging illness that typically afflicts those between the ages of forty-five and sixty-four. Frontotemporal dementia is the most common form of dementia for those under sixty.

In two months, Lisa would be in a secure long-term care home. Matt's love now meant daily visits to Lisa. Matt knew she would have done the same for him. He endured regular COVID-19 testing and was fully vaccinated as her primary caregiver. With restrictions, they could walk, dance, and sing in the back garden at Lisa's new residence.

I had met Dineen in 2013, working for Claude Gravelle on his national dementia strategy legislation. Gravelle lost his mother to dementia. We had met dozens of allies and especially families and exhausted caregivers snared by this dreadful disease. When Dineen left the office, I turned to a parliamentary intern to confirm what I had heard.

"Is he talking about his wife or his mother?"

Indeed, it was his wife, the love of his life. Matt is a devout Catholic with a traditional spirituality I knew long ago. He remains faithful. It's not perfect, nor a "happily ever after" story. It is a faithfulness to her, the mother of their children and the "plan" we never imagined happening when we pledged forever as lovers.

Freedom is what we do with what is done to us.

Faithful to a calling, to God, the gods, and to ourselves. To love to the end, diminished and all.

I need these reminders when life's plan has me whining. Enough times, Dineen and I, now good friends, chose wine and beer instead with a heaping side order of sports, stories, and humour. He belongs to the Dineen NHL clan of players and coaches. Dineen has since become a dementia advocate in Canada, including educating faith communities and places of worship on how they might become more dementia-friendly and communities of care.[122]

Am I still Catholic?

Rosemary Klein, a friend, playfully suggested I nail the stories I've told here to the wooden front doors of The Pro-Cathedral in North Bay. I never counted them but there may even be one hundred stories, close to Martin Luther's Ninety-Five Theses that he purportedly hammered in the Castle Church in Wittenberg, Germany, five hundred years ago. Luther, another devout Catholic, was disgusted with the sale of indulgences as a pass to Paradise. Apparently, he wanted his church reformed, not replaced. The Reformation

---

122 Chorney-Booth, Elizabeth. "Keeping the Faith," *Dementia Connections Magazine*, July 1, 2020, https://dementiaconnections.ca/2020-7-1-keeping-the-faith.

happened instead, a Holy Roman Catholic Church splintering in many directions. I am no Luther. God forbid, the world does not need another religion. I pray rather that the clergy and believers wherever be light for the world, salt for the earth. May religious Crusades end once and for all. Is it not building a better world if we hold to our beliefs without thinking everyone else is wrong and compelled to damn them to hell?

There is sweet solace in telling my "wonderful and dangerous" faith stories, those adjectives spoken by the Indigenous novelist Thomas King in his Massey Lecture series as he laid his own stories down to his audience.[123] What will people do after hearing our stories?

It was hard at times in the storytelling to silence the preacher in me, to let the stories speak for themselves. I get excited about good news. As a boy in North Bay, I would watch a good movie or television show alone in the recreation room and race upstairs to invite my family to watch. They teased me about being scared. I may have been, but the real story here is that I felt compelled to share the good news I was watching. I could not contain myself. It is no surprise that journalism and priesthood came calling.

"Claire and Cruz, these stories are for you, for now and for later, for this generation and more to come. It would be amazing for a Prashaw or a Beaton seven generations from now to know their ancestors better."

I am grateful for this crooked, straight faith journey, for being Rick, Father Rick, and father to Adam, for the resilient Prashaws, the "go with the flow" Beatons.

There is deep gratitude for The Pro, St. Andrew's, Rome, and Taizé. I count my blessings from Chicago, Peru, Guelph, the Boat People, Hidden Talents, Antonio and Carlos, the clowns, Uncle Bill, Matt Dineen, the freedom in faith, the wisdom from the sacred texts and yes, the newspapers too. I've changed. I ceased calling Holy Mother Church "our only Mother." Many mothers have nurtured me: Gertie Beaton, above all; my sisters, Margie, Jude and Pati; Edwina Gateley; Ellen MacKinnon; Joan Chittister; Helen Prejean; Bonnie Chesser; Lorraine Berzins; Mary Beaucage; and more. There are good

---

123 Thomas King, Massey Lectures, *The Truth About Stories: A Native Narrative*, *CBC*, 2003.

priests, religious sisters, and ordinary saints in our midst, some I am blessed to count as friends.

I am a believer. My baptism has been a blessing, its call to service, daring to believe this audacious claim that we are made in the image and likeness of God, that a divine spark lingers within each of us. Different faith traditions have similar creation and redemption stories. Mystery, miracles, and mercy have been welcomed companions for the journey.

My faith was now definitely more Roamin' than Roman Catholic, a God bigger than any catechism taught me. Be who we are. Love who we love. A believer, still standing, astonished by it all.

Not everything from my childhood nor adolescent faith journey I found childish. I continue to cheer, curse, and pray for the popes. I try to separate the wheat from the chaff, for all the bad, not to throw out the good, to quote religion scholar Elaine Pagels.[124] I suspect I would like Judas, as I do Peter. I am kin to the grumbling people who tagged along with Moses. It's complicated.

I have named the bad I observed in religion. I get why people have walked away, why some must walk away. Like Pagels, I hope those who did leave the Catholic Church or other religions find new landing places to nourish their hopes—people, new rituals, places to eat, sing, dance, and mourn. It may happen at a church, synagogue, mosque, or temple. It may well be somewhere else, among the pine trees, on the water, at the kitchen tables, and wherever people gather.

Writing this book did surprise me. Yes, I was drawn to other people's suffering and to the complicated places we live. However, I was intrigued by how the boys at the Spanish school outfoxed the Jesuits, the brilliance and success of many Indigenous folk in their journey of healing, how Edwina Gateley's "experience of God" kept her in the Roman Catholic fold, and the hundreds of spiritual front-line workers dying from COVID-19 doing their

---

124 Gjelten, Tom. "Through Personal Testament, 'Why Religion?' Explores
      Belief in the 21st Century, review of Why Religion, Elaine Pagels,
      NPR, Nov. 7, 2018, https://www.npr.org/2018/11/07/664683874/
      through-personal-testament-why-religion-explores-belief-in-the-21st-century.

good works anointing the sick and dying. People daring to find that tiny mandorla sliver of opposite worlds overlapping, where we work to heal the divides and discover a safer place for conversation and growth.

We move forward. The pandemic reminds us of the beauty and the beast in us all, gazing in our mirrors, nodding to Aleksandr Solzhenitsyn and Robert Johnson. The pandemic exposed humans being predictably human, the hoarding, queue jumping, the Hall of Shame corporations ripping off pandemic benefits, a few politicians or hospital executives travelling while telling us to stay home. And it has shone a light on the enduring magnificence of the human spirit, the singing on those balconies, the drive-by birthday parades, and a thousand acts of kindness by neighbours and friends. My own suffering curled up to the acute suffering I observed in friends who became COVID-19 long-haulers,[125] as well as to family and friends who postponed their weddings and mourned the passing of loved ones without a proper celebration and community of hugs.

The boy in me still stirs; that teen who listened to Bobby Kennedy and Martin Luther King Jr. convince me we can change the world. Our challenges are enormous, seizing power from the powerful in everyday, simple ways. I believe survival and salvation depend on us re-learning life lessons, specifically on community and on embracing diversity as the gift it is and not the threat some fear. Teaching how we might again be civil in our discourse with one another and understand those rights that we demand for ourselves come with duties to others.

This is where I head.

"Claire and Cruz, there is so much more to say but have I said too much? You honour me with your listening."

"Your lips to God's ears, Uncle Rick."

"God bless us all. Let me make the Manhattans."

---

125 Payne, Elizabeth. "'There are days when I worry this is never going to go away': Living with Covid-19 for the long-haul", *Ottawa Citizen*, July 20, 2020, https://ottawaciti-zen.com/news/local-news/there-are-days-when-i-worry-this-is-never-going-to-go-away-living-with-covid-19-for-the-long-haul.

Indeed, I still believe. My Beaton-Prashaw stubborn idealism is bruised but intact. Surrender is not an option. I go to the light. I am excited for what lies ahead.

ACKNOWLEDGEMENTS

Are we there yet?

How many trips have we said those words, tired or excited, missing the beauty in the journey itself? The stories I have told to get us here capture a faith journey that is still happening. I am grateful for that. I acknowledge a forever gratitude for Adam, for my parents, their goodness, faith, and terrific sense of adventure, for my spectacular brothers and sisters, Marty, Margie, Jude, Jon, and Pati. Their partners are precious family too—Maggie, Jerry, Jeff, and Nancy. Every day, I delight in my nephews and nieces and their family stories that help keep me young and excited. It's been extraordinarily good fortune to count myself both a Prashaw and a Beaton. I am grateful for wise friends, companions, and colleagues. Life's circle has you all present now. Writing this memoir brought me back to many yesterdays, and, hopefully, forward together to more tomorrows.

I am indebted to special friends like Peter Moher, Greg Humbert, and Tony Martin for their encouragement, assistance, fact checks, and friendship. Readers of specific chapters were real gifts, lending their expertise and memories, people like Peter and Greg, Claire Prashaw, Sam Restivo, Maryann Fraboni, Lorraine Berzins, Jamie Scott, Kevin O'Connor, Joe Fazzari, and Matt Dineen. The mistakes still here are mine. I steel myself for family corrections coming when we gather again around the fire.

Thank you, Jude Prashaw, for helping to design the cover, and for the countless love notes back and forth as we battled weary author chores to finish our respective writing projects.

This was a challenging book to write for both anticipated and yet surprising reasons. The pandemic lockdown forced me online for research while relying virtually on heroic archivists, librarians, and other individuals. I am indebted to Ted Hargreaves and Suzette Fabris with the Diocese of Sault Ste. Marie, Karen Steel at The Pro-Cathedral of the Assumption, Michelle Black at The North Bay Library. My memory especially needed prodding, and so I am grateful to my Facebook family, to the "Bit of the Bay" Facebook Group (Jeff Fournier), the "I Grew Up in Sudbury" Facebook page, to several former parishioners, to Mary Anne Garvey, Sharon Oliver, and Frank O'Connor. There are more to thank. I will find you, for a drink and a story. I thank my photograph hunters—Greg, Peter, Dan McIntyre, Bonnie Chesser, Paul Dunn, Lisa Humphrey Emons, Al Orlando, Sharon MacLellan, Bridget Bertrand and Tom Cashen.

I thank Friesen Press staff, including my editor, E. Brettner, publishing specialist Lee-Ann Jaworski, its design team, all their expertise and wizardry.

I close with special thanks to God, the gods, and my Spirit guides, who generously shared their wisdom for living and telling my story. Last, and certainly not least, thank you, readers, for the honour of sharing my story with you. May we never stop telling our stories.

IMAGE CREDITS

Pro-Cathedral exterior: Pro-Cathedral of the Assumption archives

Rick, Claire, and Adam: Scott Saunders, Peaceful Ram Photography

Bishop Alexander Carter: Diocese of Sault Ste. Marie Archives

Father Brian McKee: Greg Humbert, Diocese of Sault Ste. Marie Archives

Pro-Cathedral interior, Pro-Cathedral of the Assumption archives

Father Don MacLellan: Sharon MacLellan

Challenge The Wiz, 1981: Anne Tremblay-Pedersen, Polar Studios North Bay.

Hidden Talents: Anne Tremblay-Pedersen, Polar Studios North Bay.

Sudbury Youth Encounter: courtesy of Bridget and Tom Cashen

St. Andrew's Church Fr. Rick photos: Dan Beaucage, wedding of Leo and Nicole Duford

Adam Prashaw: Sandra Corbeil

John Dickhout and Rick Prashaw: Lynn Dickhout

ABOUT THE AUTHOR

Rick Prashaw is a former journalist, Roman Catholic priest, social justice advocate, and staff to Members of Parliament. Since 2014, he has been an advocate for both transgender human rights and organ donor registration. He currently resides in Ottawa, Ontario, with his Labrador dog, Dallas.

Father Rick, Roamin' Catholic is his second memoir. His first, Soar, Adam, Soar, is based on the life of his inspiring son, Adam, who tragically died in 2016.

Printed in Canada